THIS AIN'T NO DISCO

The Story of CBGB

This Ain't No Disco: The Story of CBGB © 1988 by Roman Kozak
First edition published in 1988 by Faber and Faber
Second edition published 2024 by agreement with the Roman Kozak estate.

Cover and inside photographs by Ebet Roberts
Cover and interior designed by Kristina Juzaitis / February First Design

ISBN 979-8-9898283-3-3
Library of Congress Control Number: 2024943381

Published by Trouser Press Books
Brooklyn, New York

First paperback printing September 2024 [B2]
Printed by Bookmobile Craft Digital in Minneapolis, MN

www.trouserpressbooks.com
facebook.com/trouserpressbooks
E-mail: books@trouserpress.com
www.trouserpress.com

THIS AIN'T NO DISCO
The Story of CBGB

by Roman Kozak

Photographs by Ebet Roberts

Foreword by Chris Frantz

Afterword by Ira Robbins

TROUSER PRESS
BOOKS

ACKNOWLEDGMENTS

First thanks have to go to Hilly Kristal, without whose help and cooperation this book would never have been written or, for that matter, without whom there would never have been a CBGB. Thanks also to Karen Kristal, Lisa Kristal and Dana Kristal, as well as all the musicians, staffers, technicians, journalists, music executives and others who have taken the time to share their memories and observations of CBGB. I must also thank Carol, who first brought me to CBGB; Lisa, the lawyer, who made sure we won't get into any silly trouble with this book; Neil Cooper, who got me started on this project; and Connie Barrett, who spent many hours with noisy tapes and a typewriter transcribing interviews.

And a special thanks to Richard Hirsh, who discovered this manuscript after I thought it a lost cause; to Vicki Rosenberg, who helped shepherd it through; and to my editor, Betsy Uhrig, who I know has spent many hours making this a much better book than I could ever have done by myself. And I cannot forget all those at Faber and Faber who have contributed to making this book.

And thank you, too, to my family and friends who always believed I had a book in me, even if it is about a joint like CBGB.

Roman Kozak [1987]

Trouser Press Books would like to thank Helena Kozak for making this reissue possible.

To Merv

FOREWORD

BY CHRIS FRANTZ

It's been 50 years since I first walked into CBGB. In early October of 1974, a good friend of mine who lived across the Bowery on Bond Street said, "I know you're interested in music. There's something happening over there at that place called CBGB. You should check it out." So, that night I did. There was nothing happening at all, but I heard the sound of a pool game going on in the back. One of the players was wearing a silver sharkskin suit, black shirt and purple tie with big silver late-period Elvis Presley-style sunglasses. I asked him if there would be any music that night. He said in a strong Spanish accent, "Not tonight, but come back on the weekend and the Ramones will be here." I thought to myself, "Oh, wow. A Spanish band!"

I did come back to see the Ramones, who were not the least bit Spanish, and the following weekend I returned to see Television. Not long after that, I saw Patti Smith perform with Lenny Kaye and Richard Sohl. The next weekend, I saw an early version of Blondie and, Wow! It was clear to me that something really exciting was going to happen at CBGB. I wanted in.

On March 18, 2002, Talking Heads and the Ramones were inducted into the Rock and Roll Hall of Fame in our first year of eligibility. Both bands famously began their careers at CBGB. Talking Heads invited Hilly Kristal to join us onstage as we accepted our award. We wanted to show our gratitude to him for providing us with a stage where we could hone our craft and establish ourselves as a band. CBGB was like an incubator where young bands could develop their own unique style without any interference from the mainstream music business. CBGB was a place that not only allowed but encouraged self-expression, and the bands who played there had a lot of ideas to express. We thought that CBGB would be for us like the Cavern Club in Liverpool had been for the Beatles, and we weren't wrong about that. Despite its seedy Bowery address, the club became internationally known as a cool place to hang out and rub shoulders with young musicians, writers, painters and filmmakers. These were artists who were ready to get it on and, with time, they created cultural landmarks.

Thirty-six years or so have passed since Roman Kozak wrote *This Ain't No Disco: The Story of CBGB*. That funky little underground rock club on the Bowery is no more. After years of legal issues with the landlord who owned the building (which included the desperately sad flophouse upstairs called the Palace Hotel), Hilly Kristal's club was finally evicted.

Joey Ramone died of cancer in April of 2001. He was only 49 years old, but he certainly left his mark. East 2nd Street and the Bowery has been renamed Joey Ramone Place in his honor. In fact, all the original Ramones — as well as their amazing graphic and lighting designer, Arturo Vega — died too young.

The last show at CBGB was on October 15, 2006. The Patti Smith Group performed the final set. Blondie headlined the night before. Neither band had performed at CBGB since the '70s. Tina Weymouth and I were in the audience those nights, silently wishing that our band could have performed to show our gratitude to Hilly, his family and his team.

By August of 2007, Hilly had died of cancer, no doubt accelerated by all his trials and tribulations trying to keep the club alive.

There was talk that Hilly dreamed of opening a CBGB club in Las Vegas, but that never happened. After Hilly died, some venture capitalists bought the CBGB trademark.

The neighborhood has changed so much since 1974 when our band lived three blocks away from CBGB in a raw loft at 195 Chrystie Street. I guess it's safer now. There are expensive restaurants, chic hotels and the address that was CBGB's, 315 Bowery, is now a stylish clothing boutique. On the corner of Houston Street where bums used to congregate and wipe your car's windshield with a greasy rag there is now a giant Whole Foods.

Most of us who lived on the Bowery and in the East Village have moved away, but Richard Hell still inhabits the same apartment he's lived in since 1974. He says he'll never move. After all, his apartment is in the same building that Allen Ginsberg once lived in.

The unique ambience of CBGB looks best in black and white. People who were smart took photos of the bands and the scene. Now they are available in beautifully published editions featuring Godlis, Bob Gruen, Ebet Roberts, Chris Stein, Bobby Grossman, Roberta Bayley and Julia Gorton. Collect them all!

A feature film was made about CBGB. It's great to see Hilly portrayed by a famous British actor, but don't look to the movie for historical accuracy. Still, this Disneyfied version of the club is sweetly entertaining for those youngsters who were never actually there.

In the fall of 1988, Tom Tom Club made our first public performance at CBGB. We had the idea to play a residency. I spoke with Hilly about it, and he loved the idea. We would play five nights a week for three weeks. Fifteen nights! Each night featured a couple of different opening acts, and every night was packed and sweltering. We projected images created by our friend and cover artist James Rizzi onto the walls of the club. We ended each week with a surprise guest. At the end of the first week, our guest was the amazing savage, Dee Dee Ramone. Our second week's surprise guest was the fabulously charismatic Debbie Harry. At

3

the end of our third and final week, our surprise guest was Lou Reed. The applause and love these three got from the crowd was magical. I think this residency was the longest run any band ever played at CBGB. I will never forget the pleasure it gave us.

When the club was gutted after the final shows, Hilly saved as much of the interior as possible. When visitors to CBGB recall their experiences at the club, they inevitably mention the bathrooms. They were shockingly filthy, but thanks to Hilly and his friends, those famous toilets and the awning over the front door now reside at the Rock and Roll Hall of Fame in Cleveland!

Since Roman wrote this book, so many of the characters who performed and frequented the club have departed this world, including Roman himself. On the other hand, so many of us are alive and well and still making music and art. Surely, one day another music venue somewhere will blossom and encourage inspired musicians to create important music and a scene of their own, like we all did at CBGB.

So, enjoy this definitive history of the club and the people who made it happen. CBGB was an extraordinary place in an unforgettable time. That's not merely nostalgia on my part. It's historical fact. The bands that played there have enriched our culture forever.

Chris Frantz
July 2024

ORIGINAL INTRODUCTION

Everybody who has gone to CBGB on a regular basis has his or her own special memories of the club. So do I. The first night I went there was in the fall of 1976. I had just moved to New York from Rome, almost literally falling into the middle of the major league music business when I got a job as a reporter covering rock and roll for *Billboard* magazine, the music industry's largest trade paper.

Even before coming to New York I was a fan of the Velvet Underground, and later Lou Reed, the Stooges, Iggy Pop, the MC5 and the New York Dolls. In Italy I was familiar with Patti Smith, while Roxy Music was more popular there than they ever were in the U.S. But CBGB and the New York underground music scene were completely alien to me.

Working for *Billboard*, at least initially, was no introduction either. A trade magazine reflects the business it covers. At the time, the music industry in general was not very interested in this rough new "punk rock" and neither was *Billboard*. Besides, working for *Billboard* left little time in a daily schedule — where evenings usually began with a cocktail party, followed by up to three shows a night — to learn about anything other than the acts the industry wanted me to see. So, who knew about CBGB?

Then one night I was brought there by a young woman of the evening with whom I shared a love of rock and roll. The band playing at CBGB that night was the Miamis, who appeared a lot more interesting and vital than most bands I was hearing. They were doing a song called "We Need a Stronger Navy." This was something I was used to hearing from the embassy and military guys in Rome, but rock bands were supposed to be singing about peace, love and understanding and getting stoned. I had never heard a pro-military rock song before. But the crowd at CBGB seemed to take it in stride. Obviously, there was a new scene here.

I cannot say that from then on I haunted the place nightly, but I was interested and I did come back regularly. For what it's worth, the first front-page story I wrote for *Billboard* was "What Is Punk Rock?" There was something definitely happening that even *Billboard* couldn't ignore. CBGB became part of my beat, my own humble attempt to let the music business, and through it the rest of the world, know that there really was something worthwhile coming up from the Bowery. I was there when the Damned became the first English punk band to play in the U.S. I panned their show because the Dead Boys blew them off the stage.

A week later I interviewed the Dead Boys. I was sick that day, and they were scared — it may have been their first interview ever — and the story got cut down to four paragraphs. Later I was one of the first to review the Plasmatics (I loved them). I wrote stories about the ill-fated CBGB Theater, the benefit for Johnny Blitz, the theft of the sound system, *TV CBGB*, hardcore matinees, whatever was going on there.

When Johnny Blitz of the Dead Boys got stabbed, Stiv Bators called me the next day, not to give me some sort of a scoop, but just to talk to somebody. I felt honored. If you loved the music, the CBGB scene was close enough to get personally involved. When I needed a favor for a band I was advising, or a venue for them to have a record industry showcase, a call to owner Hilly Kristal was all that was needed. Within a week the showcase happened, no special return favors asked or expected. I found Hilly to be an honorable man, one who really does want to help new acts.

So, when the opportunity came to write this book, I was more than happy to do it. CBGB has been a part of my history for a few years now, and it is still a fascinating place. Drop by some Sunday afternoon for a hardcore matinee or visit the new Record Canteen. Or be there any night: the next Talking Heads or Blondie or the Police may be up onstage. Who knows? Some of the best rock and roll music in the world has been played in that dark little bar on the Bowery. And we have been richer for it.

Roman Kozak
August 1987

CAST OF CHARACTERS (1987)

Literally hundreds of thousands of people have passed through the doors of CBGB, some more prominent in its history, some less so. With such a huge cast of characters we thought it useful to provide this little introduction to some people you will be coming across and their various affiliations.

Sandy Alexander: President of the New York chapter of the Hell's Angels. *See Hell's Angels.*

Connie Barrett: Security person and assistant at CBGB who began managing bands. Heavily involved in hardcore rock.

Stiv Bators: Lead singer for the Dead Boys and later Lords of the New Church. Played often at CBGB. *See Dead Boys.*

Roberta Bayley: Photographer, door person at CBGB. Became publisher's assistant at *Spin* magazine.

Luther Beckett: Administrative person at CBGB mostly involved with more offbeat hardcore bands.

Snooky and Tish Bellomo: Singers for Blondie and later the Sic F*cks. Own the Manic Panic clothing store in New York City's East Village.

Alan Betrock: Music journalist. Wrote often about CBGB.

Johnny Blitz: Drummer for the Dead Boys. A major benefit was held for him after he was stabbed. *See Dead Boys.*

Blondie: A major band that started at CBGB.

Clem Burke: Blondie's drummer. Also played with the Ramones and Eurythmics.

David Byrne: Founder, singer, guitarist, composer for Talking Heads. Also, filmmaker, artist, actor.

John Cale: Member of the Velvet Underground, he later embarked on a solo career.

Jim Carroll: Singer/songwriter, poet, author.

Robert Christgau: Influential music editor at the *Village Voice*. Dean of rock critics?

Cheetah Chrome: Guitarist for the Dead Boys. *See Dead Boys.*

Carol Costa: Booked bands into CBGB. Also, singer, fashion designer.

Wayne (Jayne) County: Colorful punk pioneer. Had an unhappy night at CBGB.

Peter Crowley: Ran Max's Kansas City during club rivalry with CBGB.

Dead Boys: Probably the most energetic band to come out of CBGB. Managed by Hilly Kristal.

Deerfrance: Former bartender and doorperson at CBGB. Now a musician who works with John Cale.

Barbara DeMartis: Worked at CBGB and with the Shirts. *See Shirts.*

Dictators: Early New York punk band. *See Handsome Dick Manitoba.*

Willy DeVille: Fronted Mink DeVille during CBGB heyday. Song stylist of note.

THIS AIN'T NO DISCO

Dennis and Norman Dunn: Dennis did the lights, Norman the sound system at CBGB. Dennis has gone into computers, while Norman produces hardcore bands.

Eric Emerson: Early new wave scenemaker, leader of the Magic Tramps. Died before CBGB got fully going.

Merv Ferguson: Manager, number-two man, advisor to CBGB staffers. Died in 1982.

Danny Fields: Veteran rock and roll journalist, he helped discover and managed the Ramones.

Steve Forbert: Folk-influenced singer/songwriter, he would spend many nights on the CBGB stage.

Chris Frantz: Drummer in Talking Heads. Married to Tina Weymouth.

Elda Gentile (Stiletto): Singer for the Stilettos, later to become Blondie without her. *See Stilettos.*

Jimmy Gestapo: Lead singer for Murphy's Law, among the more successful hardcore bands. *See Murphy's Law.*

Gildersleeves: Rock club on the Bowery near CBGB.

Annie Golden: Lead singer for the Shirts, principal in the film *Hair*. Has an ongoing career on TV and stage. *See Shirts.*

Robert Gordon: Lead singer for Tuff Darts before embarking on a rockabilly solo career. *See Tuff Darts.*

Connie Hall: Books many hardcore bands and does promotion for CBGB Records.

Debbie Harry: Lead singer for Blondie, has a successful ongoing solo career. *See Blondie.*

Richard Hell: Bass player for Television. Later formed the Voidoids and the Heartbreakers. Pioneer of punk look and style. Many years later married Patty Smyth of Scandal.

Hell's Angels: Friends of Hilly Kristal and of CBGB.

Hilly's on the Bowery: Bar Hilly Kristal owned before CBGB.

Hurrah: First New York rock disco, it became an alternative to CBGB.

David Johansen: Lead singer for the New York Dolls. Wears a tux when performing as Buster Poindexter. *See New York Dolls.*

Jonathan: Hilly's dog. CBGB mascot.

Lenny Kaye: Patti Smith's guitarist. Compiler of *Nuggets* LPs. Suzanne Vega's producer. *See Patti Smith.*

Hilly, Karen, Lisa, Dana Kristal: Father, mother, daughter, son. CBGB principals.

Richard Lloyd: Guitarist for Television, the seminal CBGB band. Pursuing solo career. *See Television.*

Handsome Dick Manitoba: Lead singer for the Dictators, he had a slight problem with Wayne County.

Charlie Martin: Did booking and sound at CBGB. Moved on to the Ritz. *See Ritz.*

Max's Kansas City: Famous New York rock trend club. For a while it was in bitter competition with CBGB.

Legs McNeil: Helped start *Punk* magazine, which depicted a somewhat stylized version of the punk scene.

Mercer Arts Center: Forerunner of CBGB. Its walls collapsed.

Miamis: One of the original CBGB bands. Considered by many to be the best unsigned band to play there.

Mink DeVille: Willy DeVille's original band. Its soul/blues style was a little different from most CBGB bands, but it was among the first to get signed.

Murphy's Law: Considered among the best of the new CBGB hardcore bands, they recently toured with the Beastie Boys.

Maureen Nelly: Bartender at CBGB.

New York Dolls: Influenced a generation or two of young rockers, many of whom found their way to CBGB.

Richard Nusser: Writer for the *Village Voice* in the early '70s, he later worked at *Billboard*.

Cosmo Ohms: Lighting technician at CBGB. Became an executive for a tour production company.

Terry Ork: Managed Television, actively promoted very early CBGB rock scene.

Palace Hotel: Next door to and above CBGB. It's a flophouse.

Palladium: In the late '70s and early '80s it was the best place to see mainstream rock acts. Turned into a disco.

Louise Parnassa: Hilly Kristal's assistant at CBGB. She likes classical music best of all.

Plasmatics: Theatrical punk rock band. Blew up cars onstage after outgrowing CBGB.

Iggy Pop: An early influence on the whole CBGB scene. Still very much out there.

Private Stock Records: First record label to sign Blondie.

Dee Dee Ramone: One of the founding members of the Ramones, he is currently pursuing a second career as a rap singer.

Joey Ramone: Lead singer for the Ramones. An inspiration to many an upstart rock and roll musician.

Ramones: Started at CBGB, hung out there. Defined its style.

Genya Ravan: Produced first Dead Boys album. Alleged instigator of notorious CBGB event.

Lou Reed: Singer, songwriter for Velvet Underground (before pursuing solo career). Had there been no Velvet Underground a couple of years earlier, would there have been a CBGB?

Ritz: New York City rock palace.

Ira Robbins: *Trouser Press* editor and writer. Produced a new wave source and guidebook.

Lisa Robinson: She hangs out with and writes about the superstars now, but in 1974 she was one of the first Ramones fans.

John Rockwell: Influential classical music critic now, he's logged a few nights at CBGB as well.

Runaways: A Los Angeles female punk band, it gave us Joan Jett and Lita Ford and probably inspired the Go-Go's and the Bangles.

Shirts: A band from Brooklyn, they were an early CBGB favorite; managed by Hilly Kristal.

Bill Shumaker: Helped run the club and helped start the new CBGB Record Canteen.

Sic F*cks: Outrageous and funny band. A personal CBGB favorite.

Sire Records: First record label to actively pursue CBGB bands. Signed Talking Heads, Ramones, Dead Boys. *See Seymour Stein.*

Jim Sliman: Los Angeles-based publicist, he was a CBGB bartender and road manager of the Dead Boys.

Patti Smith: Poet and singer. Her appearances at CBGB first put the club on the media map.

Soho Weekly News: Now-defunct news and culture weekly, it extensively covered CBGB.

Chris Stein: Co-founder of Blondie with Debbie Harry, this guitarist/songwriter is still very much part of her life and solo career. *See Blondie.*

Seymour Stein: Head of Sire Records. He found Madonna.

Stilettos: Became Blondie before Blondie became famous.

Richard Stotts: Original lead guitarist of the Plasmatics. He gave the rock and roll world the mohawk haircut.

Suicide: Two-man techno-pop band. The keyboard player made a lot of noise and singer Alan Vega yelled a lot and abused the audience. A pioneer band.

Rod Swenson: Plasmatics and Wendy O. Williams manager.

Talking Heads: Started at CBGB. As big as they want to be.

Television: The first real CBGB rock band. Never achieved the fame it deserved.

Marty Thau: Rock manager/executive since the New York Dolls and before; he knows the scene.

Roy Trakin: Most recently a senior editor of a music trade paper, he had a compelling early style and insight.

Trouser Press: Now defunct, it was a favorite new wave glossy magazine. *See Ira Robbins.*

Tuff Darts: One of the early CBGB bands. Their manager helped finance the *Live at CBGB* album.

Alan Vega: Alan is now pursuing a solo career. A man with "the soul of a poet" and the heart of a rebel. *See Suicide.*

Velvet Underground: *See Lou Reed.* Get their records.

Tom Verlaine: He and Richard Lloyd convinced Hilly Kristal to book their band, Television. *See Television.*

Village Voice: The bible of the downtown New York cultural world.

Joel Webber: Frustrated early trying to get new wave records on the radio, he has since achieved professional success organizing the New Music Seminar. Recently director of A&R at Island Records.

Tina Weymouth: Bass player for Talking Heads, she showed she could do it as well as any guy.

Wendy O. Williams: Amazonian solo artist and lead singer for the Plasmatics.

James Wolcott: Writing for the *Village Voice*, he was one of the first to recognize that there was something going on at CBGB.

CHAPTER ONE

"I opened CBGB because I thought country music was going to become the big thing. And it did, though not here."

—HILLY KRISTAL

It was the fall of 1973, and neighbors in New York City's upwardly mobile West Village were not amused. It wasn't so bad that a burly ex-U.S. Marine sergeant had a honky-tonk bar among the brownstones on West 13th Street where one night he brought in live animals — a pig, a sheep and chickens. And not many actually noticed when the pig escaped, though "it's pretty hard to catch a pig, even if it's not greased," comments Hilly Kristal, owner of Hilly's, the offending bistro. Hilly's hayrides around Greenwich Village weren't so bad either. But that country music blaring all hours of the night was a bit too much.

Hilly's had to go. Community democracy swung into action. Petitions were signed, calls were made, complaints were registered. Hilly's closed. "They just didn't want music in the area," explains Hilly. "After me, they closed down the Bells of Hell and Reno Sweeney, which was a very elegant place. But towards the end, when I knew I had to leave, I had a party for the Hell's Angels. Sandy Alexander, the president of the

New York chapter, asked me to host an anniversary party for them. I was happy to do him a favor, and if the neighbors didn't like it, so what? They didn't do me any favors. There were about 150 Angels at the party from all over the country. We had a lot of fun. There was no trouble, but you can be sure the neighbors walked on the other side of the street that night."

Hilly had already found another neighborhood more receptive to his ideas. Back in 1969 he had gotten together $20,000 (too much, he says) and bought a derelict bar on the Bowery, right next door to the Palace Hotel, one of the city's more notorious flophouses. During the last year, while he was struggling to keep Hilly's alive on 13th Street, he had shut down his downscale Hilly's on the Bowery. But in December 1973, after he and his former wife and current business associate Karen renegotiated the lease, they opened CBGB-OMFUG in the same location as Hilly's on the Bowery. The initials stood for "country, bluegrass, blues and other music for uplifting gourmandizers." Surely in this neighborhood nobody would complain about country music.

The Bowery, where Hilly was embarking on his new enterprise, was a dangerous place. One of the oldest thoroughfares in New York City, the original mail route to Boston in colonial times and home of some of the new world's first millionaires, the Bowery had fallen on rough times since the Revolutionary War, when occupying British troops were billeted along what was then called Bowry Lane. An entertainment district of saloons, whorehouses, cockfighting and ratfighting pits, girlie shows and pawnshops sprang up to service and entertain these troops. Though the Redcoats left when independence came, there were sailors, native New Yorkers and immigrants who happily took their place for the next hundred years. Running from Manhattan's Chinatown and downtown business district to the tenement Lower East Side, the Bowery became the center of New York lowlife entertainment. Like Times Square now, it was the brightly lit place to go for illicit pleasures. For rich and poor alike, the area was sin city.

And, as with Times Square, the avenue began to decay. By the turn of the century, New York City guidebooks were warning tourists to venture there only at their own risk. The concubines, carousers and the local colorful "Bowery Boys" of the earlier century — the latter sometimes volunteer firemen, sometimes street gangs, sometimes both — were pushed out by the drunken, the sick, the homeless, the despairing. It's the street that gave the world the term "Bowery bum," and the bums are still there, living on that same street. The bar Hilly took over was one of the dives that served this unhappy clientele and had done so literally for generations.

Recalls Hilly, "When I first opened it as Hilly's on the Bowery I ran it for a while as a derelict bar, and bums would be lining up at eight in the morning, when I opened the doors. Then they would come in and fall on their faces even before they had their first drink. You had the hawks and doves really, the jack rollers and the real alcoholic older men, though some were younger. I think a lot of these people had depression and nervous breakdowns and had to escape. Here they were safe; nobody knew where they were. But you started getting these guys who would mug them all the time. I remember I was working at the bar, and I heard this choking sound coming out of the men's room. I had to take two guys off this one poor guy. They had him backwards on the toilet, and they were stripping him down, taking all his money. I got one by one collar and the other by the other and dragged them off."

The Bowery south of Houston Street is now mostly full of restaurant supply stores, while north of Houston, where CBGB is, became a bit safer after the club opened and became popular, thanks in part to CBGB itself. It was one of the few places in the Western world where the influx of punks and hard rockers actually upgraded a neighborhood. In 1973, "There was Phebe's [a restaurant] up the street and the Tin Palace [a jazz club] and both were packed with theater people, but nobody would take a few steps to come down to 315 Bowery, which is where we were," says Karen Kristal. "And because nobody would walk those two extra blocks, anybody who did was disliked. Anybody who passed 315 Bowery after ten o'clock in the evening risked getting a knife in the back. Somebody I knew was knifed in the ribs."

But back in 1969, Hilly saw the area as a growing artists' colony, just off the East Village, the more artistic part of the Lower East Side, where '60s-era hippies and artists lived uneasily next to old Jewish and Ukrainian immigrants. Such artists as Roy Lichtenstein already had lofts in the area. There was no reason for the Bowery and the Lower East Side not to become new centers of artistic activity. Unfortunately for Hilly, the New York art scene moved to Soho, where abandoned factories and warehouses offered more and cheaper loft space than the crowded East Side. It has been only fairly recently, with Soho getting out of the financial reach of up-and-coming artists, that there has been some movement back. But there were always hungry musicians in the area.

The success of CBGB and the opening of Gildersleeves, another rock club up the street, did bring a lot more traffic into the area. For one thing, CBGB always let its patrons go out in the street and then re-enter later. Sometimes there were (and are) more customers out on the sidewalk than inside the club. The police don't mind. At least everybody from CB's is more or less vertical. "The cops were especially good when we had big shows and the kids would be in front of the club for hours. They would be there at one o'clock in the afternoon lining up. Some of the bums were cool, and the kids loved them," says Bill Shumaker, former CBGB night manager. "But others were real hit artists. And when the cops heard that — we would call them — they were really cool. They would casually come over and tell the guy to get his blank-blank out of there."

"From time to time I talked to the police, and they have told me that CBGB has done more than anyone or anything else to clean up the area and bring safety," says Karen Kristal.

Nevertheless, there was and still is the Palace Hotel, which occupies most of the building where CBGB is located, taking up the upper three floors. "The back part of CBGB is not part of the Palace, but that is where the air conditioning units are on the roof. They would get clogged every so often and I would have to go through the Palace," recalls Shumaker. "One floor is just bunks, straight down. Another floor, where I would walk through, has little cubicles with just beds in them. Some people would put wire up so nobody could break in, molest them or steal whatever meager belongings they have. The smell you would curse. And sometimes they got violent. They would throw bottles and spit. That's why you see the screening around the awning. Old punks never die, they just move upstairs."

It has been suggested that it would do some of the punk poseurs some good to actually spend a little time in the Palace, and virtually all encounter it in some way both outside and inside the club. "The first time we played CBGB's, just as we got out of the car, a bum staggered up to us, and *urrgh*, threw up right in front of us," was the way Lita Ford of the Runaways was greeted.

Willy DeVille, one of CBGB's pioneer artists, had a different but equally unpleasant encounter: "One time I'm on stage happily doing my bit, when all of a sudden a mixture of piss and wine starts dripping down on the mike. We used to have a terrible ground, people would get blown 30 feet at CBGB. Sparks start flying from the mike, and this piss and goddamn sweet Thunderbird wine is coming down, hitting the mike, splattering on my lips, burning me with sparks," he says.

"The CBGB experience was by the time you finished your second show, the sun was just coming out. You were coming out of there hauling out your equipment, and the Bowery inhabitants and some of the audience were lying outside on the sidewalk. It sharpened up your emotional skills," says Rod Swenson, manager of Wendy O. Williams and the Plasmatics. "One night recently I just came out of the club when I saw this guy lying on the street," says one former employee of the club. "He was quite dead. There were cops and people there and one of the cops looked at the other, and said, 'Well, John, what do you think? Looks like a suicide to me. Jumped out of the window.' Then somebody said, 'Excuse me, officer, but there is a knife sticking out of his groin.' One of the cops pulled out the knife, wiped it off, put it in his pocket and said, 'Suicide. He fell on his knife.' You see a lot of body bags go by there."

It's American big city mean streets, but there is also a school of thought that the funky atmosphere in the neighborhood has added to CBGB's ambience and may have contributed to its longevity. In its time, CBGB has had its share of bums polishing the windshields of limousines parked outside, but even in its heyday it never was a mecca for the trendy beautiful people. Celebrities would show up, and still do, but it was never a place for aspiring fashion models to be seen in. Other places opened up for them. At CBGB you really had to have a commitment to the music. Ira Robbins, editor and publisher of *Trouser Press* magazine and editor of its record guides, explains: "The thing about CBGB in its earliest days is that it was not perceived as a scene place to be. People went to see the shows. Max's Kansas City was the hang-out place. The back room at Max's was where you could see David Bowie or Lou Reed. CB's was much more proletarian. It was much more of a concert thing. That had to do with the atmosphere, and all that."

Adding to CBGB's ambience, atmosphere and security has been the New York chapter of the Hell's Angels, headquartered nearby. There were fights once in a while, but generally relations between the club and the Angels have been very good. "The Hell's Angels didn't bring drugs into the place. They respected it and tried not to do anything that would hurt us," says Karen Kristal. "They have been among our best customers. They used to come to the club before it was CBGB, but they seemed by mutual agreement not to come in large numbers. One or two would come in with dates, order a drink, but never get drunk. We respect them as Hell's Angels and they in turn respect us. And it has always been that way. I wish we would have as little trouble with everybody else as we did with the Hell's Angels."

Occasionally they even help out. "A couple of them came for the Spinal Tap show and I was very pleased to see them," says Connie Barrett, who worked in administration and security at the club before embarking on a new career managing hardcore bands. "The people I had working with me knew nothing about crowd control. But one look from the Angels and it was amazing. All they had to do was look. They never said a word. If I moved in a direction, three of them would stare, and boy… When Joan Jett was playing here, the Angels were called at the same time as the police because there was almost a riot in front of the door. They both arrived at the same time, and I never saw two groups happier to see each other. They cleared the doors quickly."

Basically, it's a matter of personal relations between Hilly and New

York chapter president Sandy Alexander. "Sandy and I worked together," explains Hilly. "We tried to do a couple of things together to have concerts to raise money to bring back the POWs from Vietnam. But the Angels don't hang out at the club. They come in once in a while. Then they don't come in for a while. I've seen less and less of them in the last few years. But I tell you, if I had any real trouble, I wouldn't hesitate to call them, if there was any emergency."

Not that the Angels never had any of their own kind of fun. Barbara DeMartis, former road manager of the Shirts, tells this story: "Annie Golden [of the Shirts, one of the original CBGB bands] was going out with one of the guys from the Tuff Darts [another early CBGB band]. She was in the audience watching them play, and she was practically anorexic that summer, she was so thin, and wearing next to nothing, when the Angels said, 'Let's see if we can guess her weight.' And they picked her up, one by one, I don't know, by the neck or by the shoulders or under the arms. It was a frightening experience. One of the guys had a hook for a hand, and he just had to look at you or touch you with the hook, and my God."

Yet, for all that (or maybe even because of it), CBGB never needed any real bouncers working for the club. There have never been any serious fights or injuries there, though transgender rocker Wayne County did break the collarbone of the Dictators' Handsome Dick Manitoba one time. And there have been occasional thrown fists and bottles and other incidents, sometimes among club regulars, sometimes with visitors.

"I had two physical confrontations over there," recalls Robert Christgau, longtime music editor and critic for the *Village Voice*. "One was at [rock writer] Lester [Bangs'] wake and one at a Replacements gig. At Lester's wake, Marty Thau wanted to play the entire Richard Hell album. There were lots of guest DJs — my sister Georgia, who was a good friend of Lester; [writer] John Morthland, who was Lester's best friend; and Bob Quine, who was his other best friend. And none of them would play it. Not even Robert Quine, who played on the record. Because that was not the idea, the idea was not to hype some album that Lester actually never heard. But Marty was Marty, a very insistent person who doesn't give up. Quine ultimately just shrugged his shoulders and Georgia sat in. He just walked out; he couldn't take it. But I felt that I had to go in there. I was organizing the affair and I ended up knocking a cigarette out of Marty Thau's mouth. I think it is to his credit that he didn't then slug me. But I was really pissed at him.

"At the Replacements gig some kid burned me with one of the candles that were on the table. I have no idea why. He was an English guy — very, very drunk. My wife, who had never been in a fight before in her life, pushed him and he fell down the stairs. He landed in a rubber heap, got up and started kicking everybody in sight. He was completely stewed. I don't think he knew who I was. I was just sitting next to him, and he didn't like my looks."

"We've had more broken glasses in this place," says Hilly. "The Dead Boys used to throw them. Cheetah Chrome was the beer mug thrower, that's why we got plastic mugs. But we used to have a lot of broken bottles. People used to break things when nobody was looking, but the Dead Boys would do it in front of anybody. No fights, just breaking things."

Hilly threw a big party to open his new place. A few celebrities showed up, it was a nice bash, and everybody went home. There was not much reason to return. Says Karen Kristal: "Then Hilly offered a suggestion. He said he would put in live country music and poetry readings. So, he put in the music and had the poets without any admission charge. But I would go over to the customers and ask what they were going to have, and the standard answer would be, 'Nothing. I came to listen.'" The basic economic principle of any bar with live entertainment is that the venue makes its profit from drinks while the performers get paid from admission at the door. Better-known entertainers demand guarantees, but these, too, are based on estimates as to how many bodies the star will draw through the door. An "I-just-came-to-watch" clientele only takes up space as far as the club owner's bottom line is concerned.

In keeping with his country motif, Hilly tried something new: country at sunrise. Hilly says, "Originally at CBGB we tried to promote it as a morning country nightclub. I thought it was a horrible idea, but I had a public relations man at the time who wanted to do it. So, we invited all the local television programs to see us having country music in the morning while we served big country breakfasts. It started at six or seven in the morning with live country music and the news crews initially all came in. We kept it going for about a month, but I got very tired since we were also open at night. It didn't prove a thing. Country music was a good idea; it just didn't work out. There were just not enough groups to be able to do country consistently. So gradually we started putting in different things."

Recalls Karen: "Hilly said, 'I have an idea. I'll put in rock music.' So, he brought in rock musicians, most of whom couldn't even read a note of music. And Hilly, of course, a musician himself, wanted to pay them. I said there was no way we can afford to pay musicians from the bar. This bar is desperate for money. And unknown musicians are desperate to be heard. So, we were doing them just as much of a favor as they were doing the place."

"Everybody booked into CBGB gets paid," says Carol Costa, who did bookings at CBGB in the early '80s and now has her own band. She explains the payment system as it has evolved at CBGB: "There is always a percentage of the net door. There is a deduction that CB's takes for the PA, a percentage that Hilly takes, but bands always get paid unless I am doing them a favor. If I have four bands here one night, and one band needs a favor, somebody is coming to see them, and I throw them on early, then there is no percentage to be paid. But they know the circumstances. Otherwise, it's always a percentage, sometimes it's a large percentage and sometimes it's a small percentage. It depends on who they are and what they've done. I try to be fair in the percentages; I try to give a band what they deserve. If a band deserves 80 percent, they'll get 80 percent. If they deserve 10 percent, that's what they get. It also depends if a band has a lot of freebies coming in, if there are 50 or 70 people coming in free."

"There were all sorts of various rumors and everybody had their theories about the accounting system," says Cosmo Ohms, who helped build the sound and light system at CBGB and is now general manager of a sound reinforcement company. "If you want to rock on the Bowery there are certain things that you have to go along with, that you don't question. I think the Ramones called it the Hilly tax. But I also have to say that, of all the promoters, Hilly was the fairest, especially compared to some other clubs where performers had shotguns pulled on them during negotiations."

Elda Gentile, a.k.a. Elda Stiletto, whose band the Stilettos was the precursor of Blondie, says: "As for bands making money, if you are a musician, you know that when you are coming to New York you are not going to make money in this club. You are coming to be seen by people who might be able to help you get into the recording business. You want to play gigs where you get paid? Go to Long Island."

"It's not that some people didn't make money here as they got better known," explains Hilly. "When we could charge $4 at the door on Friday and Saturday nights they could make $1,000. By 1977, we could gross $10,000 on a four-day weekend, of which the bands would get $9,000."

Karen Kristal likes the ballet and opera. She never pretended to have any knowledge of the New York rock scene. But she was absolutely right: CBGB would be doing aspiring New York rock musicians a big favor by letting them play, simply because there was hardly any place for them to play, especially since the Mercer Arts Center had collapsed.

There were other venues for the mainstream rock acts, backed by record company tour support money. Those were the days of the emerging rock superstars: bands like Led Zeppelin, the Who or the Rolling Stones could play Madison Square Garden, while Santana, Hot Tuna and a host of other bands, even with the Fillmore closed, could play the Academy of Music, which later became the Palladium.

But in the early '70s there was also a New York-centered underground scene that had grown out of the Velvet Underground and Andy Warhol's Exploding Plastic Inevitable in the mid-'60s. By the beginning of the '70s, the Velvets were no more and Lou Reed was in semi-retirement, but there were still the New York Dolls, suburban bad boy poseurs, macho but in drag, funky but chic. And there were others, centered around the Mercer Arts Center.

"There were about ten groups that played the Mercer Arts Center regularly: the New York Dolls, who were the biggest, Teenage Lust, Wayne County, the Miamis, maybe Television," says Marty Thau, then the manager of the New York Dolls.

Richard Nusser, a writer for the *Village Voice* in the early '70s, remembers the scene this way: "Two things happened. First of all, the whole rock and roll scene, the superstar scene in '72 or '73, really started to take off. All these kids who had been teenagers in the '60s were now old enough to drink and go out, and they were the youngest generation that was still heavily influenced by the thinking of the '60s hippie-derived music scene. But there was also a very New York street rock and roll scene, with groups like the Dolls and the Harlots of 42nd Street, and that was really the scene. Then, all of a sudden, there were all these clone bands of the Dolls. There was also a homogenization and cross-cultural influences that were coming to bear on the music. A reggae influence was being filtered into New York by the Jamaican immigrants; there was the Long Island suburban hard-rocking crowd coming in trying to do their Stones impersonations-cum-Elvis-cum-Dolls and David Bowie clones. But it was still a sort of select audience. It certainly didn't approach the numbers of some of these big mega-sellers who came out.

"[Even in the '60s] there weren't that many places to go [to see underground music]. There was Max's Kansas City. At various times in the '60s there was Ondine's, where the Doors made their first appearance. It was a little dive underneath the 59th Street Bridge. Steve Paul had his Scene. And that was about it. There was also the Electric Circus, and a couple of other places, but no more than six places and not more than three that were really hip and worthwhile and the proprietors were part of the scene themselves. That would be Max's, the Scene and to a lesser extent the Electric Circus, because the Electric Circus, when Warhol started the Exploding Plastic Inevitable there, became a venue for a lot of the bands from San Francisco, so it was the forerunner of the Fillmore.

"Then, in '72, the Mercer Arts Center came into being. It was the back end of the old Broadway Central Hotel where Trotsky once sat in the restaurant, an old elegant hotel on the fringe of the Village, over a hundred years old and seedy. But there was an artists' bar and a complex of rooms and ballrooms off the bar. During the intermissions in the various rooms people would mill around and the rock and roll people would mingle with the video people who would mingle with business people. There was a great overspill there.

"I produced some stuff there. I think I gave Suicide their first gig ever. They kept everybody waiting for 45 minutes, which was apparently part of their torture aspect. They were the forerunners of performance pieces where Alan Vega, the singer, a sweet-looking guy with the soul of a poet, would confront the audience and spit on them."

Elda Gentile [Stiletto] adds, "There was nothing like the Mercer Arts Center. Once the Dolls got going, forget it, you couldn't move. Eric Emerson and his band the Magic Tramps were playing when the Mercer Arts Center fell down. [One of the seminal figures in new wave, singer/model Emerson died before CBGB really got started.] They were rehearsing. Then, all of a sudden, the wall behind them fell out and they're standing there, and there was nothing but debris. They could see across Broadway. They ran for their lives."

Comments Marty Thau: "If CBGB hadn't happened, probably some other place would have happened, because the groups had to play. They are very inventive and diligent in their pursuit to find places to play when they have the need, like they found the Mercer Arts Center, but it's my opinion that the Mercer Arts Center really set up the opportunity for CBGB's when it collapsed."

That was because there weren't too many other options. There was a small place on West 23rd Street called Mothers and a place called the Coventry on Queens Boulevard in Queens. Club 82 [a basement bar on East 4th Street] was doing some shows. And there was Max's Kansas City.

Richard Nusser recalls: "Max's started a cabaret with Eric Emerson. I was instrumental in this, encouraging it in the *Voice* and just being on the scene. Eric Emerson and some of the Warhol superstars used to give impromptu performances in the back room. Owner Mickey Ruskin wasn't doing that much business at the upstairs dining room so, after a while, people used to go up there to linger, and it became sort of a different kind of scene. They started putting their little parties up there and entertainments. Mickey put a jukebox upstairs and that started people dancing. Then Eric and some of the others would get up and do impromptu cabaret skits, poetry reading, that sort of stuff. Around '72, this cabaret scene blossomed. Guys were coming up and setting up. Alice Cooper appeared there without even a drum riser; he did it right on the cabaret floor. The Dolls played there occasionally. The Velvets did their stand there [in 1970] which, of course, became that *Live at Max's Kansas City* album.

"Everybody was dying to play Max's, to play the limited number of venues in New York. When the Mercer Arts Center collapsed, that really caused the scene to scatter and proliferate because bands were so starved for venues. I went to see many acts, from jazz to rock, in lofts which in the daytime were factories or warehouses. I went to one where I saw Wayne County, and I had to get off the elevator at a floor that was full of drills and lathe presses and then go down to the end where there was a big space they had broom cleaned. That's where they set up the drums. It made it real underground.

"I did an article on that entitled 'Shaving Cream and a Hairy Climax' and it was about psycho-sexual rock and roll, which was right up my alley. It was the strangest thing. I got off the elevator, and there was this real diverse New York, a wonderfully rich cross section of New York types. There were about 150 people there, but it was a full-scale production. Right beyond the drill presses was sort of a makeshift stage with all these speakers and amps. And sitting in the middle of it was a girl, a sweet, innocent, gorgeous-looking girl; she had her hair pulled back in a neat, almost grandmotherly bun, and she was only about 19. She was playing an acoustic rhythm guitar and wearing a brown granny dress and sensible shoes. She could have been the granddaughter of Elizabeth Cotten, who wrote 'Freight Train.'

"It was kind of an incongruous thing, sitting among those amps waiting for Wayne County to come on in this garish outfit with a headpiece made out of cut-up ties and laundry machine labels from soap boxes and a blond wig. She [Wayne became Jayne in 1979] was supposed to be a nightmare vision of a suburban housewife. She came out and sang all kinds of psycho-dramatic songs, screwing his mother and killing his father. That was the big rage then, you could really get explicitly Jungian with the lyrics.

"He had this wonderful backup group. The guitarist and rhythm players looked like the Everly Brothers dressed as gnomes, on a combination of speed and acid, a little Southern Comfort, and maybe a couple of other drugs as well. They played in these horrible guitar keys. The bass player was this handsome guy, classically trained, who looked exactly like, and had the manners of, Tyrone Power. He wore his own outfit, which was red and white with this white lace surplice over a red turtleneck sweater. The surplice was like an altar boy's, so he looked like this gorgeous High Church Episcopalian acolyte. I forget who was on drums. And then there was Wayne County. The climax of this thing was that Wayne straps on a rubber vagina which he bought at a 42nd Street porno shop and goes to work with Via Valentina, who was one of the last Warhol superstars. Via was this half-pint Italian girl with a nice set of knockers that she was not afraid to display. And Wayne sort of jerks off a shaving cream can onto her chest. He is wearing a swastika hanging off his girdle which is worn outside his other clothing. It was a complete farce, and it followed in the tradition of the original Theater of the Ridiculous and was all part and parcel with the Living Theater at the time. But the loft scene also was the forerunner, the precursor of Hilly's place on account of the ambience, that beer-drinking, sawdust on the floor, gutsy, grungy thing. It was the perfect spawning ground for punk."

And Hilly's on the Bowery was willing to take a chance once in a while on an unusual band. "We played there in late 1972, when it was still called Hilly's," says Jim Wynbrandt, later with the Miamis. "We had a band called Queen Elizabeth where Wayne County would have a strap-on vagina and he would fuck himself using a dildo. It was a pretty wild act, needless to say, and our first performance was at New York University in the fall of 1972. The president of the university happened to be strolling by and he was accosted by a gay activist who thought the act was demeaning to gays. He had the power shut off. That was our first date.

"We were disappointed, but that was tempered by the fact that we had another gig lined up at Hilly's, which was then frequented by Hell's Angels. On the bill with us, and it wasn't really a bill because everything was so informal, was another band that didn't have enough equipment to play. I remember the show because there were three Hell's Angels in the audience, and Wayne, who was dressed in drag, sat on their laps. But it turned out okay, though there may have been a long dry spell after us for our kind of bands, though there were other acts playing there, like jazz or country."

Hilly was ready for Television.

CHAPTER TWO

"Think what a coat of paint could do for this place."
—HILLY KRISTAL

Though Hilly was ready to play rock in principle, it took the band Television to make him take the big step. Remembers Richard Lloyd, guitarist for Television: "We were rehearsing in Chinatown and we were there for years and years. Terry Ork was our patron because he did some artwork for Andy Warhol and he made some money from that and he had this enormous loft. We were playing here and there and advertising and getting quotes, and we realized that we needed a place to call our home, a place to play once a week.

"One day Tom [Verlaine] came and he said, 'I saw this fucking hick, like up on a stepladder — he's opening a bar, calling it CB or something, GB. Do you want to go up there and we'll talk the guy into letting us play?' I said, 'Yeah, of course.' So, after rehearsal, we walked up and Hilly was outside standing on a stepladder, putting up the awning. We called him down and he came in with us. I bought a drink and I think Tommy had one of his rare white russians. We said, 'What are you calling the place? Are you going to have live music?' And he said, 'Yes, I'm calling it country, bluegrass and blues and other music for "undernourished" gourmandizers.' That's what OMFUG is. Anyway, he asked, 'Do you play country?' We said, 'Yeah, we play country.' He said, 'Do you play blues and bluegrass?' We said, 'We play blues, bluegrass, anything you want, we'll play it.' And he said, 'Alright,' and penciled us in for the Sunday.

"Then we had four or five days to get this together, so we went around to people like Nicholas Ray, who was the director of *Rebel Without a Cause,* and he said, 'You are four cats with a passion,' and we went to Danny Fields, who was the editor of *16,* and he said something like 'These guys make me cry, they are tough as nails.' We got together all these quotes and put a little ad in the *Village Voice* and we started playing at CBGB. By god, we drew enough people, and Terry Ork bought enough drinks by himself to set the place up. Hilly was making money."

"It was Terry Ork who kept pushing me to have Television on," adds Hilly. "He would also come up with other bands like the Ramones and the Stilettos. He would have them open for Television. They were all very crude at first and not really very good. They didn't play their instruments that well. There really wasn't much of a scene either. Terry Ork would put up handbills, and we would charge a dollar admission. But there weren't many people in 1974 and 1975. It wasn't until 1976 that the club really began to take off. But back then, with Television there was virtually no response, though Terry worked very hard at promoting them, getting the *Soho News* involved as well as the people he knew from the Andy Warhol and theatrical crowds. He really pulled it together. I knew folk and jazz, but rock was really foreign to me. I just knew a little bit here and there."

"If there was no Terry Ork, there would have been no CBGB, there would have been no punk, no new wave, no Richard Hell, no Sex Pistols, no Television, no Patti Smith — well, maybe Patti Smith," says Lloyd about the man who, ironically, did not consider music his first love. That was film, to which he has since returned. Now Ork says he is bitter about the whole scene. Lloyd explains, "He was a great patron of the arts but wasn't up to managing a successful entity like a band.

Besides, he was always so much into movies. When we finally signed for management, it was a political move. We needed it. We tried to keep him on, but it didn't work out, so we had to let him go. He was bitter from that day on."

But back in the early days Ork was the real sparkplug of the scene. Continues Lloyd: "[In the beginning] no record company would take a chance on us, and when Patti Smith put out her own record and it did well, Terry subsidized our first single, 'Little Johnny Jewel,' on Ork Records, which sold 20,000 copies by post. We literally wrapped those records ourselves. It was an amazing propaganda thing, Ork Records."

"Terry didn't do the booking so much as he instituted the Sunday night rock concerts. I would do the bookings and he would suggest certain acts and he was usually right," says Hilly. "He persuaded me every which way. He did those Sunday things for a period of about six months, until the fall of 1974. He brought in a lot of theater and poetry people from this area, since he lived around here and knew them all. It wasn't really so much his bookings, but because he knew so many things about theater, films and art, and he knew all those people. He also had the energy and was very excited about the whole thing. He excited me about it. I do think it is true, the whole scene wouldn't have happened without him.

"By the fall of 1974, CBGB became a mixture of country, jazz, blue-grass, folk, poetry and rock and roll. It wasn't all that successful, but we started to establish ourselves as a place for new rock. At first, a lot of the bands came from the glitter era with the old-fashioned stance, and you weren't sure if they were male or female. Maybe they weren't that sure either, but that's how it was. But, gradually, especially with Television, the dress became torn T-shirts, if only because CBGB became a practice place, though they were practicing in front of people. They were actually developing and creating as they played. And I think the dress even typified how they were progressing musically. It's as if they rolled out of bed, came in and played. That's how their music was, except the better ones started to develop and the other ones didn't. But there was not that much excitement. The Ramones and Television were beginning to stir some up, but no other groups really. The Mumps, maybe, but not that much."

Meanwhile, the clientele at CBGB was beginning to look a little different. "It was so funny," laughs Elda Gentile. "When you walked through the door you would have to go through this little crowd. They were not really bad bums, not like the ones down on the ground in the street, but Hilly did have his regulars, these old guys sitting there at the end of the bar, and you'd go, 'Oh, my god.' And then you'd see all these other people further down, who were young people. They had nothing to do with the Bowery at all. And then, once in a while, the Hell's Angels used to come flying in and out, but they were always peaceful down there."

"Starting in December of 1974 it was pretty much rock all the time," Hilly says, picking up the story. The club still wasn't making money, but when the rock bands played, they would bring in other bands and friends, usually equally poor. Maybe it was that poverty, maybe the club's ambience had a lot to do with it as well, but the then-fashionable Ziggy Stardust/Gary Glitter — even New York Dolls — androgynous makeup look never made it big at CBGB. It was not a place for platform boots.

Says Hilly: "Admission was one or two dollars, with the bands getting a percentage of the door. The audience pretty much came as they were. The glitter look turned into the street kids look. That was before the punk look. Maybe they took the torn T-shirt look from us in London and added razor blades and funny colored things in their hair, but I must say the torn T-shirts started here. Richard Hell and the Ramones were the most torn."

Hilly continues: "When the rock started I didn't think of them as punks. I didn't know the word back then. Punk was this stuff you found in the bushes and you lit it up. That was all I knew about punk. All I heard was these guys and girls, mostly guys then, who needed a place to do their own music. And I thought it was very crude music. It was not that it was strange, but it was hard to take. It was very loud and abrasive. It was not what I liked in music. But what I liked was that these people were really into it. They were very sincere, and they really believed in themselves. They had a real desire to express themselves.

"In fact, when I think of that as the beginning of new wave and why it was new wave, it is because they were not musicians. They were kids who used music — even if they couldn't play their instruments — to express themselves. The fundamental thing was a form of expression. And that's why it started getting into a different area from what was happening in other places. It was creative. They were making their own melodies, and it was very inspirational to have it here, though it was very hard to take, to listen to. But I loved what they were doing because they had lights in their eyes. Tom Verlaine really did. He loved to perform.

"The truth of the matter of CBGB is that it was an accident. If it wasn't CBGB it would have been another place. It might have taken another year or maybe not. But these bands had nowhere to play. These kids were there and as they came in I saw it and I liked it. Maybe somebody else wouldn't have liked it. I don't know. The point is what kind of people were there. They weren't punks. Regular people came from all over the country. We all called it street music. Why? Because nobody did the glitter stance. That's where the T-shirts came in. They had torn T-shirts, and they came the way they were. They came in looking like they practiced. I wish it were that way now. Because there were so few places and because there were a lot of people coming just for the club, a band could do four to six shows each weekend. Imagine musicians who could play Thursday, Friday and Saturday, and do two shows a night and how they could grow. And then they could play six weeks later and they could grow again. It is wonderful to be able to do six sets in one place. But now I can't do it. And that's a problem I feel.

"It wasn't too long after the rock started [that] we were booking some 20 bands a week. There was my place and Max's and always a place here or there, and that was all there was. Think of my problems in getting all the bands in. And they were all vying. They all tried; some badgered me. And when they did, I told them to go fuck off. I didn't use those words before; I had never used vulgar language. But I learned from them. I really learned through the years. I would get exasperated. I liked to have some of them in a lot, but how much can you take? Some of them are whiners and they all have ways of saying, 'We have to come in' or 'We are great' or 'You are not treating us fairly.' And you have all that. Everybody is right in a way. At least a little bit. Because we all take advantage of each other and we don't always treat each other right. We just try to do the best we can.

"The club didn't really begin to make money until 1976. To help support the club, I had started a moving business right after I came here. In the early spring of 1974 I just got a truck, a 12-foot beer truck, and I started moving chairs, whatever I could get to make some money. A few months later I had to get another truck.

"I slept in the club for maybe two years. I had my cot there, actually my big king-sized bed. I lived there until I found another apartment nearby at Second Street. It was tough."

Throughout 1974 Television played at CBGB virtually every Sunday night. There were other rock bands playing there, but nobody was stirring much interest. However, Television, and specifically Tom Verlaine, did attract one admirer who did as much as anybody to bring recognition to the club: Patti Smith.

"The first I remember hearing about CBGB was in the back room at Max's Kansas City," says Lenny Kaye, rock archivist and guitarist for the Patti Smith Group (who is a successful record producer now). "I believe it was Richard Lloyd who came up to me and told me about his band, or maybe Tommy Ramone. One of those guys asked me to come see them at CBGB. The actual first time I remember going there was Easter of 1974, right after the *Ladies and Gentlemen: The Rolling Stones* movie premiere. I went there with Patti Smith to see Television because we got friendly with the guys in Television. They would come to some of our early shows at a place like Metro at West Fourth Street when we were opening up for folksingers. It was very nice at CBGB. It wasn't too crowded. There were about 20 people there. We would go there every Sunday night and shoot the breeze."

"Patti had this crush on Tom Verlaine, so they were an item. That was cool. It got us exposure," explains Richard Lloyd. It did the same for CBGB.

Thanks to Terry Ork's invaluable input and connections and Hilly Kristal's aggressive booking policy, shortly after Television began to play regularly at CBGB, four other bands walked through the door and got up onstage. The Ramones, Blondie, Talking Heads and Mink DeVille were among the first bands to play CBGB. There were other bands playing there as well, and certainly other bands followed them into the club, but if it weren't for those four bands, Television and Patti Smith, ten years later CBGB would not even have been a footnote in the history of rock. These bands were virtual unknowns when they first played at the club, and they developed their talents there. By the time they left, they had created a whole new music scene centered around the scruffy little club on the Bowery.

The Ramones, who became the first of the regular CBGB bands to be signed by a major record label, were formed in the summer of 1974 by four young middle-class men who grew up in the Forest Hills section of Queens. Each one adopted the surname Ramone: Joey Ramone, Johnny Ramone, Dee Dee Ramone and Tommy Ramone. The name was taken from Paul McCartney, who Dee Dee remembers called himself Paul Ramone when the Beatles played briefly as the Silver Beatles in Hamburg. Dressed in torn jeans, T-shirts and black leather jackets, the Ramones played hard and furious rock and roll like nobody before them. It was very basic two- or three-chord stuff, but condensed and speeded up. The Ramones sounded only like the Ramones.

Among the band's influences were the MC5, the Stooges, the Beach Boys and even the Bay City Rollers, but it was a local band that provided the real inspiration. Says Dee Dee Ramone: "What really kicked it off was seeing the New York Dolls in clubs around Manhattan. It was so inspiring to see a bunch of young people playing rock and roll that we wanted to do it, too. It took off from there. The first club we played was CBGB. Chris Stein and Deborah Harry were our friends and they got us the job there, opening up for them in 1974."

Jim Wynbrandt of the Miamis says, "The Ramones have a lot to do with the success of the place. They take a lot of jibes about their music being so simple, but I don't think there were many other bands that practiced harder or more consistently than they did. They just did it over and over again until they got everything just right. They would do the whole set just over and over again."

Dee Dee Ramone: "People thought we were all organized, because how can you do stuff like that? But we would stop and argue with each other and that was for real. Sometimes I would count 1-2-3-4 and everybody would start playing a different song. Then we would stop and argue about which one was supposed to come first."

"The first time we saw the Ramones they were great. In the middle of the set, they would stop and throw instruments," recall Snooky and Tish Bellomo, formerly of the Stilettos, Blondie and the Sic F*cks. They own the Manic Panic punk clothing store near CBGB, there since 1977, and they still do occasional shows, either as backup singers or solo. "The Ramones were so funny and so good. We were their biggest fans. They would do 17-minute sets, but 17 minutes is long enough for anything — eating, sex, anything."

"When the Ramones started playing, I hated them," is another view, expressed by critic Ira Robbins. "I was violently taken aback by them because it seemed so wrong. They were breaking all the rules in a way that was not at all amusing. One time, Johnny had to tune Dee Dee's bass for him onstage during a song. It wasn't until about the time they got signed that they sunk in. Then I was blown away. I remember having a huge fight about the relative merits and demerits of the Ramones, discussing philosophical views of rock music. It was really stupid."

"I didn't appreciate the Ramones so much because they were very, very loud," says Hilly. "The only thing that kept it good was that they did their 40-second songs with so much energy and created such a scene with the crowd when they played that they could do their set in 17 minutes and that was it. It was enough. Everybody was satisfied with these sets. And some people were in ecstasy over them. They later went to England and started the whole thing going. All the other groups saw them and realized they could do it, too."

"Our sets progressed from 10 minutes to 12 minutes. We did all the songs we knew," explains Joey Ramone. "A lot of songs were very short and fast, so they just flew by. And then sometimes if a song didn't sound right, we'd have to stop and start again or argue with each other or something like that. I don't remember exactly how we found CBGB; it may have been through the *Village Voice*.

"After the first time we played, Hilly said to me, 'Nobody is going to like you guys, but I'll have you back.' I remember the sawdust floor, and I remember having to sidestep the [dog] shit, like stepping over mines or something. We liked the place. It had a nice atmosphere, good acoustics and it was very comfortable. And when we started playing there Television was there, Patti Smith was there as a poet, I think, with Lenny Kaye and Blondie, who at the time were the Stilettos. And we tried encouraging other bands because we felt we could create a scene or a movement of some sort.

"We would play there and hang out there. It had a nice watering-hole type of atmosphere. Also, in the early days, a lot of people didn't know about it, so it was basically musicians and art-type people. Our first audience was the bartender and the dog, and then our first fans were the Warhol-type crowd, like the gay crowd. There was a guy named Gorilla Rose and Tomata du Plenty, they were in the Cockettes [who later became the Screamers and the Tomato Band]. They were friends of Arturo, our soundman.

"Then Johnny [Ramone], who was a big fan of the Stooges and MC5, found out about Danny Fields and that Danny had kind of discovered them. Danny was really excited about us, said that we were really different and unique. He told [rock columnist] Lisa Robinson about us and she came down to see us. She was probably the first major press type to see us, and she was really excited about us. She brought a whole bunch of people. Then we started getting a scene and all that stuff."

Danny Fields remembers it slightly differently: "I had been at CBGB before to see Patti Smith, who was an old friend, and Television, whom I adored. At the time I was covering the scene with a weekly gossip column for the *Soho News*. I first saw the Ramones thanks to a tip from Lisa Robinson. They had been after me to see them, and they were after her to see them, too. We used to divide up the people who nudged us a great deal and I would go to one place and she would go to another. She said I would absolutely love the Ramones. So, I went to see them on her say-so. And I loved them then.

"I managed the Ramones almost from the first night that I saw them. It was in the fall of 1974. After the show, I stayed and asked them what I could do for them. And not much later after that I called Tommy Ramone and told him I wanted to be their manager. I borrowed money from my mother to buy them drums, so she's really responsible. I want her to get credit for starting the punk movement."

When the first bands started to play at CBGB it was a dark and seedy place that had been a derelict bar since the turn of the century. There was not much renovation done when Hilly brought in live entertainment: he built a rudimentary stage which was later moved and enlarged. There have been many changes in the club since it opened, but the place still looks basically the same.

CBGB stands in the middle of a humble block on an exceedingly humble street. It's another gray storefront, with graffiti-smeared metal gates over the windows forever keeping out the sun (if not potential burglars). No glitz or glitter here. A once-white canvas awning, the second in ten years and already showing rips and gaps, crowns a wooden door that is pockmarked by generations of stapled notices proclaiming the coming of this or that hopeful band. Enterprising acts still announce their imminent presence inside with their homemade flyers outside, their signs outlasting their stay in the club until somebody else's affiche replaces theirs.

When the staples and tattered paper form their own barrier against further door advertising, someone from the club — if not Hilly himself — goes out with a knife or small screwdriver and de-staples the door. It is a job that has been done 50 times in the history of the club, says Hilly, who sometimes complains about the mass of tiny detail involved in running even a relatively small music venue.

At first, CBGB itself would put out signs in front as to who was playing that night, but after a while that was left to the bands. In the very beginning Hilly also left it to the bands to collect their own admission at the door. That didn't last long.

Every venue has a box office somewhere between the street and the entertainment, but rarely is that the actual business office. At CBGB it is. What changes it from an office in the daytime, where Hilly runs his managerial business as well as the club, to a box office at night is an oblong unpainted wooden box placed atop one of two gray metal desks. A hand-lettered piece of paper taped to the box proclaims the price of the evening's admission: $3.00 for audition nights, usually $6.00, and up to $8.00 (but very rarely more) for top weekend headliners. Before there were desks, the wooden box was put on a table and daytime business was conducted from behind the bar.

The office is to the right as you enter the club. It is furnished in CBGB's version of the usual complement of office paraphernalia: telephones, chairs, file cabinets, some anonymous boxes, a dusty old bed covered with yellowing magazines and newspapers and a television set. (Some nights it gets a little lonely for the doorman.) On the wall are posters, mostly from shows in 1979 and 1980, when Hilly had them commissioned on a regular basis. A couple predate CBGB, brought over from the previous Hilly's. Overhead is a clothesline with CBGB T-shirts hanging from wooden pins and a giant orange beach umbrella advertising Kronenberg beer.

"The umbrella was around here, and I wanted to get rid of it, so I put it up [over the desk]. I feel it makes things kind of homey," explains Hilly. "I also thought of putting sand on the floor and making it look more like the beach. At one time I wanted to put a swimming pool in the club. But I couldn't get the basement. We used to have a Christmas tree here that I made up with broom sticks and any pieces of wood I could find. I made what I felt was a CBGB Christmas tree. I'll put it up again [come] Christmas."

That's on the right side. On the left is a tool shed. Some staffers refer to it as the "office," but it never was that. For a while the space was used as a cloak room, which appears to be its logical function, except when that was tried too many things were stolen. And the CBGB crowd is not particularly partial to checking their denims and leathers. So, the space became a general storage area, where Hilly keeps the hammers, screwdrivers and wrenches he needs for small maintenance at the club. It is also where boxes of unsold *Live at CBGB* albums are stored.

Once admission is paid and a hand is stamped, entry is made into the club itself. CBGB is not very big: it can hold about 350 people. It is shaped like a boxcar, but almost three times as wide and three times as long. The stage is about three-quarters of the way to the back with a narrow passageway on the side allowing access to the artist "dressing rooms," the former kitchen and the stairs down to the bathrooms. During crowded shows over the years this floor arrangement has caused its share of bladder problems, often alleviated by CBGB's policy of allowing patrons to go out on the street and then come back. You can get away with stuff like that on the Bowery.

Since 1974, in addition to the stage being moved and the bathrooms being relocated to the basement, the kitchen has been abolished, a set of side doors were built and then walled over, a pool table was put in, taken out and then put in again, graffiti has been covered by more graffiti, platforms have been constructed and seating arrangements have been changed. Yet the club remains basically the same. "It has a nice seedy, lived-in look," says Hilly.

Even in its heyday, CBGB was never a big-budget operation. Improvements were made as they were needed. One of the first things that visitors notice about CBGB is the gamut of neon beer signs over the passageway between the bar and the elevated pool table/seating area. A few of the signs predate Hilly's on the Bowery. A couple of old Ballantine Ale three-ring signs (purity, flavor, body) may belong in a museum — they literally drip congealed dust. But most are newer. They only look old. That's because Hilly ages them with dark spray paint.

Hilly has built a wooden roof over the turn-of-the-century bar that runs about two-thirds the length of the club. There is a reason for it. The old bar is in three sections, and it is crooked. Hilly built the roof to make it look straighter. Beer cases and a few boxes of master tapes are stacked against the back of one section of the bar. That's to hide the broken mirror behind them, smashed one night by a flying beer mug hurled by Cheetah Chrome of the Dead Boys.

The original stage at CBGB was built by Hilly himself from the remnants of an old wooden service bar that was already in the place. It was about twelve feet square, flush against the left wall, with the bathrooms behind it. Across from the bathrooms was the original pool table. The kitchen was in back of that.

"Hilly originally was planning to have it like a drive-in movie, with the stage set up facing the back where you would walk in around it," explains Richard Lloyd. "I told him the acoustics would be terrible and it wouldn't work. We convinced him to put the stage in a responsible place and he built this three-tiered wooden stage that when you stood on it would squeak."

"It was nice when we had the smaller stage," says Hilly. "When the club was crowded people were able to crowd around the stage. And it was big enough. The Shirts were able to get six or seven people on there. We had maybe two or three lights. It was very minimal. The stage shook a little bit, but it was resilient. It was very strong wood." Others remember it a bit differently. Says Cosmo Ohms: "If you were ever on that stage, you might know that if you put too much pressure in one area it may be your last stand. All of a sudden, you could be relegated to a midget. Some bands were smart enough to bring a slab of wood with them to cover that area of the stage. Chris Frantz of Talking Heads would always bring wood with him. But some other drummers, they would get into a heavy riff, just get all excited, start putting that right foot to the bass drum … and they would go through the floor. It didn't happen every night, but often enough that you knew the smart bands by their attempts to cover it. And then as the scene and the bands started to grow, that stage became too small, and another stage had to be built."

A new stage, 17 feet long at its widest point and 17 feet deep, was built in the fall of 1976, and equipped a few months later with one of the best club sound systems anywhere. The bathrooms were moved downstairs. Though this created more space, the club was also getting more crowded, and no dressing rooms were ever built for the musicians.

Though there are two small cubicles behind the stage where performers can hang out between sets, they were never furnished with proper mirrors or doors that actually lock. Hilly didn't think that was necessary for his type of acts: "I managed a club, the Village Vanguard, for a while, and there is no dressing room there. There was this little thing that some of the women used, but it was tiny. And there is so little space here. And nobody had to dress up. This is not a place where you had to dress up to go on stage. There are places to rest and hang out, so there is no need for it, and there was very little space for it. I had planned to get the basement for it, but I never could."

Lack of space is one reason for the many cases of beer stacked around the club. "It's a real problem with any place that has beer, because you have to keep cases," says Hilly. "You may have 50 cases of empties and 50 cases of full and you always have to rotate them. You have to keep so much in stock that there are just beer cases all over the place. We used to sell draft beer, but it is so difficult to keep, especially if you have women working here. The barrels are just so difficult to move. The best thing is if you have a place in the basement, a big walk-in beer box, with one keg being used and a full one next to it. And quite frankly, in this country, unless it's an Irish bar, or a bar where people know you get good draft beer, most people don't want it, especially in a club. They suspect there may be something wrong with it. Draft beer has a better, fresher flavor, and it goes down faster. But here they prefer drinking out of a bottle. I think it's also easier to carry around a bottle."

"It's the type of place, the type of bar, where your mouth rejects saying anything but 'Give me a beer,'" says poet/singer Jim Carroll. "You can't order anything else, I don't think. I don't usually drink beer, but I can't ask for anything else, like, 'Give me a margarita' or even 'Give me a shot of vodka.' It's just a beer type of place. Maybe it's some country-and-western ghost or something."

Bill Shumaker recalls: "One of the greatest lines I ever heard at CBGB was when Patti Smith was playing. My wife and I were sitting in front, like security, so nobody could touch Patti. One of the guys behind my wife turned to somebody and asked, 'Have you ever had any food here?'

And the other guy turned around and said, 'Food? I'd be scared to order a mixed drink here. I only drink out of bottles.' But the funny thing about the food was, the chili was actually quite good."

Continues Shumaker, who also teaches hotel and restaurant management, "The hamburger meat came from a very good meat store. The menu was limited — chili and burgers. The chili was made ahead of time and the waitresses made the burgers. If it was really busy, then somebody else on the staff would jump in and help. But I will say that a whole generation of rock bands would have died without it. The food never made any money, which is why they stopped it, but name any band that was around, the Shirts or the Ramones or the Dead Boys, and they lived on the chili and the burgers."

"We were very poor when we played there," recalls Dee Dee Ramone. "But all the girls started giving us the eye when we started working there. One of them was this girl, a rock waitress, who worked there. Joey came up to me after a show, and said, 'Listen, eh, she's not the most glamorous thing in the world, but don't get excited, I'll tell you what my plan is. She works here and she can get free hamburgers, steal them out of the kitchen.' So, we used to wait for her to get off work every night and every night when she would leave CBGB she was stuffed with hamburger patties. She would come across the street and we would cook them."

"No matter what anybody says, the hamburgers were good, and Karen made some good chili," says Hilly. "The chili was an easy thing. We would make it in a huge pot and then refrigerate it. Chili, like soup, is better the second or third day. We used rice, ground sirloin and big kidney beans. We also had french fries for a while but I stopped them. It was a problem. With deep fat frying you have to have someone you know who is trustworthy to work the fryers."

Not everybody was so keen about the food at CBGB.

"I used to get a hamburger at CBGB until I found out better when I took a peek at the so-called kitchen, which is where the dog would be shitting," says music journalist Roy Trakin, currently associate editor of *HITS* magazine.

"Let me tell you about the hamburger stuff you got there," says Cosmo

Ohms, who began as a cook at CBGB. "You never knew who or what was in the meat. I used to go pick up 40-pound sacks of ground beef. I'm a vegetarian, which adds to the irony of the whole thing, 'cause I was making the famous chili, Hilly's Bowery stew. A secret family recipe. I never tasted it. I would get one of the guys on the staff, and ask, 'Is it ready? What do you think? Is this four-alarm or five-alarm?'

"I cooked all during the recording of the *Live at CBGB* album, and the advances for that were the hamburgers out of the sack. Oh, god, there was a rat there, a big rat. This rat was friendly. He used to come over. He had a pair of balls. The rat would walk right over your foot, think nothing of it, walk into the kitchen, say, 'Hey, how about a cheeseburger?' He'd walk off with a hunk of meat and find his way back down to the basement.

"The health department visited one afternoon and gave us until nine o'clock the next morning to get the place ready for inspection. So, all night, the staff and whatever band Hilly was managing at the time were on cleanup duty. We had the Cryers, the band that was on Mercury Records, cleaning the bathrooms. Everybody pitched in. We took the whole club apart, stitch by stitch, everywhere, except we forgot to move the cash register by the back of the bar. The inspector comes the next morning, he looks left and right, doing his inspection, and he moves the cash register. 'Hmm,' he says, 'this appears to be mouse excretion.' 'No way,' we say. 'How could they be living here, at a clean place like this?' He says, 'Whatever you choose to call it, get rid of it. I will be here later this afternoon and check it over. I don't want to see any mouse excretion here.' So, there were a couple of visitations from the health department. But part of the unwritten law was that if you didn't like it, you didn't have to play here."

"We still have [problems with] mice in the club," says Connie Barrett. "You can't put traps in the club because somebody will walk into them and crush his foot. We have an exterminator who comes in once a week. He's been coming here for years. I don't think what he sprays is dangerous, because as sure as hell it doesn't kill any mice. Hilly has hung all the potato chips on a clothesline behind the bar, but the barmaids don't like that at all, because two of them are convinced that they are very intelligent mice who, like everyone else here, have to adapt to CBGB. And the barmaids became convinced that these mice are going to learn how to walk on the rope and jump on them as they serve liquor. This was a big thing. But I have never seen any mice up there."

More than the rats and mice, CBGB in its early days was known for Jonathan, Hilly's Saluki dog. "He was our mascot," Hilly says. "We dedicated the CBGB album to him for fertilizing the stage. He just walked through the place like he owned it. He didn't care who was on stage. He would just get up there and curl himself up into a ball. With Salukis, you can't let them out. Once he went out the back door and they found him on the Brooklyn-Queens Expressway a half-hour later.

"They are very fast and love to run. During a performance by Patti Smith, he ran out the front door and got hit by a car. We took him to the animal hospital and he was alright. There is no significance to this except that everybody knew during the performance what had happened, and it was very traumatic for everybody because he was a very lovable dog, very beautiful and elegant."

"There would be dog shit everywhere. It was horrible, because it was up to us to clean up the shit," one ex-staffer remembers. "We'd come in at six p.m. and I'd start fixing up the bar. The waitresses would start to trickle in and sort of hopscotch down the little aisle between the shit. After a while we refused to clean it up because that's not why we were hired, and who wants to clean up dog shit anyway?"

There was also a cat. "His name was Fluffy," notes Connie Barrett. "Then Karen Kristal put in an alarm system where anything that moves in the club sets it off. The alarm was connected to Hilly's and Karen's apartments and to the police. One night the cat jumped and the thing went off. Everybody raced down there and there was the cat cleaning itself. So, the cat had to go.

"Fluffy was a trip. He was there for a long time. He loved the noise. He would sit on an amp and go to sleep during a performance. Cats have incredible hearing, so I don't know how he did it. But he loved the noise, loved the crowd. He was a real rock and roll animal."

As Tish and Snooky recall, "It was like a zoo in there." Bill Shumaker says, "I think some of the staffers had their arms covered with bites from the bugs from the dog shit, but that was the worst of it. It was part of the style; the animals and the dog shit were all part of the atmosphere at CBGB."

It's considerably better now, but in the early days the atmosphere at CBGB was pretty funky. There were the dog droppings, of course, but there were other problems as well. Fifty years of history as a Bowery derelict bar left its own fragrance. "It really stank here when it was Hilly's," admits Hilly. "No matter how I cleaned it up, it always stank."

A year's shutdown before the place reopened as CBGB helped, but then there were other problems. For years, there has been only one working toilet in the men's room because patrons would periodically blow them up with firecrackers and cherry bombs. After a while it just stopped being worth the effort to keep more than one toilet functional. And there were problems with sewage. Hilly says: "For two years, the toilets were stopped up no matter what we did and how many times we called the plumbers. Then we found out that in the back, where the water was coming in, there was a leak. No matter how much pressure we got there was not enough. So, we had to do a whole job in the back, clean up the thing and fix it."

There is another theory about the smells at CBGB. "Once you hit the place after six p.m. I think all these bugs and weird odors kind of wake up and come out of the wood. I think it's the bands, the vibrations of the bands that bring the odors out," says Willy DeVille. "I caught the crabs there four fucking times, swear to god. It was really too much. I thought I was losing my mind after the third time. I think they were trained there, they would jump at you off the fucking urinals."

CHAPTER THREE

"They called my father the king of punk rock."

—DANA KRISTAL

Television and the Ramones arrived at CBGB as already formed — if unknown — bands. Blondie, the third great CBGB band, was a real child of the club.

Before there was Blondie, there were the Stilettos. One of the group's singers was Debbie Harry; the guitarist was Chris Stein. Elda Stiletto tells the story: "My son's father was Eric Emerson. He was an Andy Warhol superstar. So, as a result of that, I had many days growing up in the back of Max's Kansas City and watching all the stars do their trips. At one point, I guess it was 1970, I started getting really frustrated because there was no music around. Then the New York Dolls appeared and the Mercer Arts Center and all that started to happen. I was very involved with them. After they got a record deal, I said, 'Gee, I should do this myself.'

"I had met Debbie Harry during the wild days of the Dolls. She had this little car and we used to go driving everywhere, partying. She was a hairdresser or a cosmetologist in New Jersey. I hadn't seen her for a while and then she showed up at Max's one night. At the time I was looking for two girls, thinking it would be really nice to have a new vamping thing, like the Ronettes or the Shangri-Las, but only for it to be more open, to have every girl have her own lead songs and have the other two back her up, so each one would have a chance to get out there and do her thing. So, I got Debbie and Rosie Ross, who was friends with Wayne County and Queen Elizabeth, who became the Miamis.

"It was me, Debbie and Rosie and we borrowed backup musicians from everybody. Chris Stein came in that package. He was playing with Eric at the time, and he was a real temperamental guitar player. But when he saw Debbie, that was it. He became the most cooperative guitar player I've ever seen on the face of the Earth. He fell head over heels in love with her and she was taken aback because her life was so detached from New York City at that time. She had some boyfriend in New Jersey and it hadn't worked out for a long time. It was just a real hassle. So, when she met Chris, they got along really well. They got together. It's the love story of the century.

"This was in 1972 and we didn't have any place to play because there just weren't any places to play. So, we broke up for a while, and then I decided I'll put the band back together. But we lost Rosie; she didn't want to work anymore. Chris and Debbie came back, and we got a girl named Amanda Jones, who was this dynamite sweet Black girl with an adorable face. We auditioned her, and Debbie said, 'Why not take her?' Then Terry Ork, who was involved with Television and Richard Hell, mentioned to me that there was a club downtown and Television was going to be playing there. He brought me down to see Hilly, and we decided to do these double bills, Television and the Stilettos. And as soon as we did that, CBGB was jumping."

Unfortunately for the Stilettos, in the summer of 1974, just as the CBGB scene was beginning, the band broke up, by all accounts for the usual personality and business reasons that destroy so many acts. Chris and Debbie left first, to be followed in their new venture by drummer Billy O'Connor and bassist Fred Smith. The new band played as Angel and then did two gigs as the Snake before becoming Blondie and the Banzai Babes, doing covers of such tunes as "Lady Marmalade." Snooky and Tish Bellomo sang backup for them.

"We were in a show across the street from CBGB, *The Palm Casino Review* at the Bouwerie Lane Theater, and we would run over to CBGB between performances to see bands like Leather Secrets and Eric Emerson. Eric Emerson asked us to do a spot with him, and that was our debut at CBGB," recalls Snooky. "We met Debbie and Chris then. The Stilettos were in the process of breaking up, and they asked us to join them. We were with Blondie about six months, playing at CBGB about ten times. I was going to school at the time and, between sets, I would be weaving a rug for a crafts class I had. I had a big loom and, between sets, I would be schlepping this rug. Sometimes I carried a typewriter in my bag. Hilly didn't know he was booking minors.

"At the time I think Debbie and Chris were not sure in what direction they wanted to take the band. We did a lot of gigs and were always successful. We had a drummer then, his name was Billy, and he would fall asleep before our performances and sometimes he would not wake up in time for the show. Jerry Nolan of the Dolls would sometimes sit in. We had other guest drummers as well. We started auditioning new drummers and we got Clem Burke. Shortly after that, we were out of the band.

"Clem had just joined Blondie and we did a couple of gigs with them. Debbie used to work at this bikini/leotard bar in the business district and we used to play there. I remember her being all upset and thinking that the band wasn't happening and thinking maybe something was going on between her and Chris, not that they were on the rocks, but that they were having difficulties. They were very confused and needed a change. It was either going to be us out or Clem out. She said to me that Clem wasn't working out. Then Tish asked if she could sing lead on something, and I think that was the last straw."

Clem Burke got off to a rocky start with Blondie. "I joined after passing an audition. Chris asked me if I could sing, and I said I sang like Iggy Pop. He said, 'Who's that?'" laughs Burke. "I was 18 years old, and I couldn't believe what was going on. I was just exposed to this whole CBGB thing with the Ramones and Television and I was enthralled by it. I would watch the Ramones and then beat up my friends because there would only be ten people in the audience. And I was just going crazy for the music.

"But my first gig with Blondie was the last one for Fred Smith and also the last one with Snooky and Tish," he continues, recalling Blondie's debut as Blondie at CBGB. It was a "jungle night" show with the three women dressed as jungle girls in leather skins and bits of fur. "It was a disaster. We had a three-night stand there with the Marbles. At the end of the first set, the three girls were in tears. Patti Smith, Tom Verlaine and [Brian] Eno were in the audience, and Fred Smith announced he was leaving the band to join Television. After that, Chris and Debbie wanted to wrap it all up for a while and I just stayed home. I don't think we went back to CBGB until the summer of 1975."

Tish continues the story. "I wanted to have a band meeting because everything was so weird. Debbie said to me, 'I guess there is no band.' Those were the last words I remember her saying until afterwards. Later we ran into Chris and he told us there would be a date. I said I thought there was no band. And he said, 'Oh, I don't know' and walked away. And that was it. Snooky and I felt a little bit hurt, but we've seen Debbie since then. She did a photo session wearing Manic Panic clothes. She's a good egg. But we don't travel in the same circles anymore."

Blondie reformed again a couple of months later, with Burke's friend Gary Valentine on bass and CBGB regular Jimmy Destri joining in later as the keyboard player. For about seven months Blondie played CBGB regularly, giving the band time to develop and grow. At first, Blondie was the perennial opener — for Television, the Ramones and other local lights — better known for their outlandish shows than for the quality of their music. They did not earn much critical acclaim, but they got better, so much so that they became the third CBGB band, after Patti Smith and the Ramones, to have a record deal.

"Concentration is the most important thing a performer must develop," Debbie Harry writes in the book *Making Tracks: The Rise of Blondie*

(Dell, 1982). "During one of the first gigs Blondie did at CBGB with me singing solo, I was so nervous I forgot the words to all the songs because I put myself in the place of the audience to see how I looked instead of intensifying further what I was there for... When I split from the Stilettos and decided I wanted to do less schtick and more music I dropped a lot of the more obvious theatrical things. But at this point we tried to think up as many tricks as we could. The sicker and funnier the better. Some of the props we developed were great, though. I had a black Morticia dress, a gold lamé dress, a couple of stupid wigs, a green day-glo cross, a wedding dress and a fishbowl with a goldfish in it. I was developing the Blondie character. She wasn't quite there yet but was on her way."

"We used to rehearse from six o'clock to twelve in the evening, and then go down to CBGB from twelve to four and then go home to sleep, get up at five and do the same thing again, and be at CBGB every night. And it was never boring," remembers Clem Burke.

Things were not always smooth from then on for Blondie at CBGB; at one point the band didn't play the club because Gary Valentine yelled at Hilly Kristal for booking four other bands on the same night with them. Hilly says that he never banned the group per se, though he does recall that some of the Blondies were more difficult to deal with than others, and he admits that his gruff manner may sometimes have been misinterpreted. But he says a mutual respect grew between the two camps, with Hilly even adding his strong back to the effort of moving a piano up several flights of stairs when Chris and Debbie moved to a loft a couple of blocks away on the Bowery.

"They had a big upright piano which they got to the stairs and couldn't get it up any further," says Hilly. "They called me. Though the story has become that they got on one end and I was on another, actually I knew how to do these things and I simply had us all do it step by step. One step at a time and we got it up the stairs with no hardship at all. They were amazed."

Many of the musicians who came to play at CBGB and the staffers who have worked with him have found Hilly Kristal to be a pretty amazing fellow. Obviously not everybody has liked him — a club owner considered a saint cannot last too long on the Bowery or anyplace else. And Hilly has had his share of detractors. But there are more admirers.

"Hilly was a pretty incongruous figure. Nobody knew anything about his personal life. He was this guy who lived in the back, who maybe had an M16 under the bar, but who, for some reason, let these maniacs run rampant around his bar. He would let them in for free, and when the music happened, he didn't particularly seem to enjoy it, but he had an open mind about it," says Clem Burke.

Jim Wynbrandt recalls: "For a long time the Miamis didn't go in there because of a story my brother [Tom] wrote. One night we asked Chris and Debbie, when Blondie was playing, if we could do a couple of songs. But when Hilly got wind of it, he refused. Hilly has this great reputation. It used to be a rumor that he had a loaded M16 back there. [Hilly vehemently denies that he ever in his life owned a gun.] He has this gruff exterior, and though he's very soft inside, he had this image that made people think you didn't mess around or you would get blown away. And then there were all those bikers there. He also used to sleep there. It was his home."

"In the early days there was a little area along the side back wall past the stage which was set up with a bunk bed," remembers Marty Thau. "And Hilly with his dogs and his cats and whatever would take a rest, a breather from time to time. The music would be blaring, the pool balls would be smashing, people would be running back and forth, and Hilly would be out for two hours. And then he'd wake up with the dawn. But I think he deserves a lot of credit for balancing all the different elements that he has been confronted with, from the musicians to the Hell's Angels to the Fire Department to the record industry to the hucksters that eventually swooped on him, and in light of his Second Avenue Theater venture that went wrong, he still managed to fight through."

Says Willy DeVille: "I got totally disgusted with him; it was just a club owner trying to get over by using the bands that he had to use and he was lucky. Talking to Hilly was like, Okay, I'm gonna be talking to this goddamn wall to try to get a date for the next two weeks. But somehow the guy kept turning the shit over, and it worked. It was kind of funny, because all these guys, they could stand on their heads trying to get their bands record deals, try to con people with all the political pull they had, and they couldn't get their bands a deal. But this guy, I mean he's a real outer space character, and he just fell into it.

"One good thing about the place was that Hilly let us play our own material. There was never anything said about trying to entertain the customers as far as what we were playing. He pretty much encouraged us to play our own stuff and kind of encouraged us in being individual in the band sound. Hilly did do that. I have to say that about him. He would always say to me, 'Well, I got a band coming' — he was always real proud of how far the bands were coming to play in his club — 'We got a band coming in from Cleveland and as far as Toronto, or Florida coming in.' I think Hilly wanted to be some sort of entrepreneur of the scene."

Richard Lloyd: "I do a great Hilly imitation: 'We don't need you. Don't play here. We don't need you. It's already booked. Yeah, call me next week. I'm an entrepreneur. So don't play. You play too loud anyway. Why don't you grow up.' But I love Hilly, I really do. He's like this Santa Claus for us. When he's not drinking cognac and Fresca, he's great."

"Hilly never put any bounds on what we did, not in the slightest bit whatsoever," says Rod Swenson, manager of the destructo band the Plasmatics. "Hilly is a person who it takes a while to know. You have to develop a trust, but I think if he gets to know you and trusts you, that's it. He feels that if you do not jeopardize his thing, that is, you don't burn down his club or maim somebody, that's it. And it was nice. Very tolerant."

Connie Barrett: "I remember the first time I saw Hilly. I couldn't believe he owned the place. I had heard so much about him. He was in his plaid work shirt and bib overalls, wandering up and down the way he does with his Fresca and cognac. That's what he used to drink. I don't know what he drinks now. Everybody used to talk about it. But Hilly has gone out of his way for his bands and has kept a few of them alive. He will bend over backwards for musicians. Sometimes he is not really understood. He can be very moody but, like every creative person, he's thinking. And he will work things out in front of you. You wonder why he is saying what he is saying, rapping out an idea for two hours, but that is the way he thinks. He is always talking about how to improve this, how to make that better. The man's mind does not stop going.

"Hilly likes to get new stuff in here even if he hates it. A lot of the people who work here also can't stand the bands he likes. 'Lets hope he doesn't manage them or else they'll be here five nights a month, and who can stand that shit.' But Hilly keeps trying. We had this ballet troupe come in, the Transformers, five girls who dance to Ramones tapes. Everything and anything gets put into here. We used to have a rock and roll comedian.

"You come to him with a booking idea, and he'll listen. And he's had a lot of people steal from him during the years. But he always gives them the benefit of the doubt. He has to absolutely catch somebody to fire them. Some things went on that were so ludicrous that everybody knew about them. But Hilly will not fire somebody until he's sure."

Says publicity agent Jane Friedman, former manager of Patti Smith: "If there is something that he could do for you and you're way on top, then Hilly will do it for you. If there is something he can do for you and you're way on the bottom, he'll do it with the same spirit, as if you're the most important person in the world for him. It makes no difference to him. That kind of friendship and loyalty are so rare in this business. So many people will do anything for you if you are going to be important to them and their future and their present. But Hilly isn't like that. I am sure he is like that to a certain extent, everybody is, but he doesn't do things because of what he can get out of it necessarily. He'll do things because he's friendly with you and cares about you. And I think you get rewarded for those kinds of things."

Cosmo Ohms knows Hilly as well as any former staffer. "Hilly was great when he used to settle an argument in the very beginning, before there was a stage manager or any sort of regimen set up. I remember going to do a show, and there were five bands. They would call up Hilly and say they wanted to play. Hilly would ask what time they wanted to go on. They would say nine p.m., and he would say okay to three different bands for nine p.m. So, every band comes in there. There are five bands, and equipment is stacked all the way through the club. And it's, 'Hey, man, I'm up at nine.' 'No, you're not, we're on at nine; I have people coming in from the city.' 'Fuck you, I have people coming from Columbia, and Hilly told me nine.'

"Then Hilly would saunter in at seven or eight and everybody would confront him. So Hilly would say, 'Look, I'm going home, show's over. All of you pack up your gear and put it in the truck. Nobody is going to play.' And suddenly things would magically get sorted out. Hilly has his own ways of subtle persuasion. On numerous occasions I saw people come in there just to dish a little bit of the old ca-ca, and Hilly would handle it personally: 'Are you threatening me? Are you threatening my bar? Nobody threatens me. C'mere, let me show you my sidewalk. Here, what's your name?'

"One time this guy comes down the street, this raving Indian. The Lower East Side, everybody knows, is cowboys and Indians, and this one guy comes running down the street and starts throwing things. Then he pushed a trash hopper right through the front door. He really wanted to get in. He had a band that he wanted to be seen and nobody really wanted to see him or hear his band. He looked pretty out of it, and this was his way of getting attention. He rolled the hopper right through the front door, yelling and screaming at Hilly. Well, Hilly just grabbed himself a sledgehammer and started walking toward the guy. He followed him around the block. This guy is throwing stones at Hilly, and Hilly's going, 'C'mere, c'mere, you have something to say to me? C'mere, I'll catch you — I'll kick your fucking ass.' And this is the way they're parading down the Bowery. There was Hilly, kind of looking like Thor coming off his mountain with a hammer ready to kill somebody. If he'd caught him I have no doubt Hilly would have given him a permanent reminder of the Bowery."

"I don't think Hilly really went out to screw people," says Bill Shumaker. "If he did, I wasn't aware of it. He has always just survived... He's learned the business. I think he has basically disliked the record business and the people in it, but he has seen how they work, and he has matured."

"I think that insofar as Hilly hasn't been a big-time success in show business the reason is that, in order to become such a big-time success, you have to be a killer. And he is just not. He doesn't have that instinct. He is just not that greedy, otherwise he wouldn't live the way he does. But he is a survivor. And we all owe him a lot," says Robert Christgau.

"I came from a farm in central Jersey," says Hilly about his early years. "We had a hundred acres and had corn, wheat, soybeans, asparagus and chickens. My early life was as a kid on the farm. It was in Hightstown, New Jersey, 41 miles from Philadelphia and 49 miles from New York. It was an interesting town from the point of view of the people who were there. It was the kind of place that was nice to live in in a rural way. But I was not a townie, I was on the farm. I came in on a school bus.

"I was in the high school orchestra, and I sang. Then we had a quartet. This is the kind of thing we did during the '40s. But I think I had a very good grounding in music, the arts and theater just because my parents had many friends from all over the world who would come down to the farm and loved coming there. And, in the old tradition, somebody spoke and I listened. I listened to a lot of things. I listened to conversations, and I learned a lot about life from a lot of different people. I prized that learning. I think that I've used it in listening to some very brilliant people. I also think life on the farm is very good for developing ears for sound, because people in the city don't realize that things are very quiet. There is a tremendous amount of quiet, and so things become very distinctive and you learn to hear. People in rural areas hear things differently. They hear more because they listen more. There are fewer things to hear. Your ears don't become jaded.

"And then when I studied the violin, I had a violin teacher who was a strict Dutchman. He was the headmaster for the Curtis Institute in Philadelphia. He was disliked by many because he had strong ideas. The first part of every lesson was that he would take out many violins and bows and he would ask me to tell about this tone and that tone and what was the difference. He felt that, in order to produce a beautiful tone, you had to hear a beautiful tone. And what he taught me above everything else was to listen and listen and say what you heard and know what you heard. To make something happen, you have to hear. And you have to understand what you are hearing. At the age of 12, 13, 14, when I studied, I was very impressed. He was one of these pink-faced, white-haired old men, with creases in his forehead. Stern, and yet he was a kindly man. I listened. I have been listening all my life.

"I ran away from home when I was 16 and went to Montreal and then Chicago, Arizona, Mexico and L.A. and then back," Hilly continues. "I joined the Marines in 1952 when I was drafted during the Korean War. I think it was a very good thing for me. I ended up a sergeant but that was not very meaningful. Depending on your specialty rating you either go up in rank very quickly or slowly. At that time I was put into a radio station. And I started broadcasting because I had a good voice, I knew things about music and I had written. So, they put me into a radio station called WCPR in Cherry Point, North Carolina. I broadcasted from there. It was a Marine Corps station, but we had talent from NBC and all over the place. So, I learned a lot about pop music over there. I bet I was more attuned to the beginning of rock and roll than anybody. We were getting things from Sun Records, and these kids, the 14-, 15- and 16-year-old girls, and Marines were dancing to rock and roll records made by local record companies who were also doing it. There were little groups in these little clubs and it was a whole different kind of thing.

"When I left the Marine Corps in 1954 I went back to New York, where I worked and studied theater. I was married at the time and we had a child. I was a singer. I finally got a very steady job at Radio City Music Hall singing in the chorus, getting solos, for about two and a half years after 1955. Then I went back there off and on for the next three years. I was a bass, and I sang pop and all sorts of people wanted to make me a star, but for some reason or other I never became a star. Paramount Pictures wanted me. I had all sorts of contracts. It was interesting, a lot of ups and downs. I sang different things, and I started writing my own music. Then I was offered a deal with Atlantic Records through Jerry Wexler.

"I sent him a demo, and he liked the stuff. But then he went on vacation, and Herb Abramson took over. He offered for me to sign with him. But nothing happened, nothing was ever released. So, I went through that whole thing and through many other opportunities.

"I did get records out on different labels. There was 'Jubilee' and something else. 'Man of the Sky.' But I never did anything with Atlantic. From singing I started into the folk thing. Then Max Gordon of the Village Vanguard lost his manager, and I applied for the job. So, I got into jazz. This is 1959, '60, '61. The first time I started there it was with Miles Davis. And then there was Cannonball Adderly and Carmen McCrae and the Modern Jazz Quartet and Oscar Peterson. After that there was Miles Davis again, and the Clancy Brothers and Tommy Makem, and it went on and on until Christmas when there was Lenny Bruce, and I heard Woody Allen and Stiller and Meara, so it was a cross between mostly jazz and new comedy. Before I knew jazz, but with this I really got into it. I could hear two or three sets a night by some of the greatest.

"I also sang folk and pop, and one thing led to another. I started producing shows and did many things inbetween. I did the *Ford Caravan of Music*, which was 300 college concerts. They needed someone to promote this stuff and do advance work on it. It was a test-marketing thing, so they called me. They knew I could do it, and I did it. I ended up producing the shows. I was getting all this talent and making all the arrangements with the colleges and the universities and working with the Ford Motor Company. It was a real learning process. I learned about being a big concert producer. Even though I was working for a company, I was the producer. I was putting it all together. It was a wonderful experience *and* I got paid for it. I think that was the first time I really heard a lot of country music, traveling all over the country. What was happening on more radio stations than anything else was country music. And I liked it. It was just enjoyable music to hear.

"The Beatles happened while we were doing this, but it was mostly folk and jazz. We had Nina Simone, Herbie Mann, Oscar Peterson, Roger Miller, George Shearing, things like that. When I was doing this, I got involved with someone who was a Roman Catholic priest. His name was Tom Plafka. And we started Hilly's on Ninth Street together. He later left the priesthood and got married.

"We did our thing at Hilly's, where we had Bette Midler and a whole lot of other people from Broadway. It was that kind of thing. The place is now Bondini's and holds about 150 people. Sometimes I employed three pianists at the same time. It was a good place, right near Sixth Avenue in a bustling area. A lot of my customers were artists and writers, a cross-section of the world. I enjoyed their company. We started to do well, and I came down into the Bowery because I saw all this stuff happening with all the artists moving and buying lofts there. I started this place called Hilly's on the Bowery, which was to lead to all kinds of things. I had that feeling for country. I heard country music creeping up into all the jukeboxes and all the in clubs and little bars. And I felt that it was starting to happen a little bit in the South and the Washington area. So, eventually, when I really wanted to get into it, I sold the place on Ninth Street and got a place in the West Village, on 13th Street, where I started to do country music, because I thought country music was going to be the biggest thing.

"When I started Hilly's on the Bowery, the Hell's Angels lived a few blocks away and they would come in. When I first met them I was on crutches after breaking my leg in a skiing accident. And we had a little discourse. They came in and were rowdy and had a good time. I think there were five or six guys, and I stood my ground not condemning them but respecting them. And they liked the way I did it, a guy on crutches and all that, but they liked how I did it. They started coming in and we built up a rapport. Somehow, when people started coming in they were very supportive of me."

Owner Hilly Kristal in front of CBGB-OMFUG, 315 Bowery.

Talking Heads performing on March 3, 1977.
(L-R) Jerry Harrison, Chris Frantz, David Byrne, Tina Weymouth.

The Dead Boys, April 24, 1977.

Richard Hell leading the Voidoids, April 1977.

The Ramones performing on March 31, 1977.
(L-R) Johnny, Tommy, Joey and Dee Dee.

Television, February 26, 1977. (L-R) Tom Verlaine and Richard Lloyd.

Debbie Harry of Blondie in 1978.

The Jam backstage on October 15, 1977. (L-R) Bruce Foxton, Rick Buckler, Paul Weller.

Annie Golden of the Shirts with manager and CBGB owner Hilly Kristal.

Sting performing with the Police, April 8, 1979.

Poly Styrene performing with X-Ray Spex, March 25, 1978.

Mink DeVille performing on May 12, 1977.

The audience at a show by the Shirts on June 19, 1979. The club still had seats then.

Joey Ramone and the notorious bathroom.

Fans in front of CBGB at a DMZ show on April 8, 1978.

CHAPTER FOUR

"Merv was one of those guys, the more you hear about him, the less you really know. He gave the club amazing stability. He was the rock."

— BILL SHUMAKER

By the spring of 1975, Television and the Ramones were pretty regular at CBGB. Blondie and Talking Heads were getting themselves together, and bands like the Mumps, City Lights, Rainbow Daze, the Demons and Teenage Lust would be there, as well as the Shirts and Tuff Darts. But it was a very small scene at CBGB. Fifty paying customers was a big night. Often one of the 50 was Patti Smith, who would be there to see Television and specifically Tom Verlaine. At the time, she was already an underground celebrity in New York as a poet, performing at Max's and Metro and a few other places around town with ever-growing musical accompaniment.

"We played maybe about once a month, if that," recalls Lenny Kaye, Patti's guitarist. "Of course, it was still more of an art thing; it wasn't even a club circuit. We played with Television; I think we shared a bill with them at Max's around the end of August in 1974. And then we went to California and played the Whisky, by which time we were actually becoming a real band. There wasn't a steady drummer at the time. We had a drummer, I think, one time we played in San Francisco at a Winterland audition night. Jonathan Richman was on drums, I think. We were always experimenting with different ways to do what we did. In a certain way it was me and Patti and Tom Verlaine, because that was like the improvisatory element. As soon as we started adding Ivan Kral [on guitar and bass] and then started adding Jay Dee Daugherty [on drums], we became more of a rock band. But we needed them because it was getting hard to carry the rhythmic load on my shoulders. When we got Ivan, it was hard for me to really cover the fretboard with all the things that needed to be covered given where we were going."

Obviously, the Patti Smith Group needed time and a place to develop its new direction, and what better place than CBGB, where Patti was a regular already, giving at least moral support to Television. Hilly says it never happened, but things were pretty loose at the time, and Clem Burke remembers Patti sitting at the door collecting admissions for Television. "She said, 'I know who you are, but you have to pay.' I was in total awe of Patti Smith at the time anyway," Burke recalls.

"Jane Friedman asked me if they could play here [in early 1975]," remembers Hilly. "First we did one or two nights, and the idea was, let's see what happens. And we did. And, of course, it was packed. It was the first time the whole group played together. They played well and simply and Patti was very forceful. I think they were here four days a week. It was four, five, six or seven weeks in a row, with Television opening. It was two sets a night, and it was just a very good thing. The crowds were not packed, but there were crowds for every set. It was a very joyous thing. Every time Patti played here it was a special night."

Recalls Jane Friedman: "The only reason we went to CB's at the time — besides the fact that Patti liked it because she had seen Tom there and stuff — was that we needed a place to play that would give us the door. I mean they didn't really have a stage set up. But I wanted the door. Up to that point with Patti, most of the time I had to rent a room we could have. We had very little access to a regular venue, probably none. It was all some fluke, some stroke of genius, to be allowed to perform when

CB's just became available. And when it became apparent we could take the whole door, and we could say how many nights we wanted to perform — no one was going to tell us that you have one night and that you have to open for so-and-so — it was very lucky for us. The time was right and everything.

"But to clarify it, Patti was already an incredible star in New York. She had already developed an incredible following over a number of years, from a few hardcore fans who never missed anything, to a few more, and finally she got taken over by a large audience. The thing is that she was at the point where she was packing places, doing amazing things. CB's was the first time that we played so many times in a row. We didn't just pack CB's, we had people literally standing around the block who couldn't get in. It was a tremendous triumph for her, it's true. But it really wasn't a break. It was just proof to all the people who for so many years said, 'She's a mockery' or 'It could never happen' or 'I don't really see what it is' or 'She can't sing and her band stinks.'"

The Patti Smith Group played four nights a week, two shows a night, for seven weeks in March and April 1975. The extended date could not but solidify the sound of the band. Says Lenny Kaye: "We had a couple of songs, all of them really, like 'Free Money' or 'Land' or 'Gloria' especially, which we would call fields, something we really went and explored when we played together. We would just spin off on them and jam on them and see where they took us. Our credo as a group was that we would never define anything. We never defined what type of band we wanted to be, we never defined the type of music that we made, we never defined our own sense of gender. We wanted to be free to move beyond any definitions. And playing someplace for seven weeks, you can really explore. For instance, I remember we would do 'Land,' and one night Jonathan, the dog there, got hurt, got run over by a car, and we incorporated that. There was always something new to incorporate. Patti would just look over the audience and let it take her off. It was very improvised kind of stuff, before our songs fixed themselves firmly in the modus operandi with which we would play them.

"By the time we finished at CB's it was interesting, because I'm not saying we helped create it or anything, but what happened was that, as we played there, more and more people came down. CBGB became not only a place for them to come and check us out, but it sort of got into the New York consciousness. By then we had gotten a record deal. [Arista Records founder] Clive Davis came and saw us there, and in a lot of ways it started the ball rolling, not just for CBGB, but in a sense for us. The experience of playing night after night at CB's kind of hardened us, so that when we played for Clive, we sounded tight."

"Patti's stay here was one of the most memorable seven-week periods the club ever had," adds Hilly. "She was good right from the beginning. She was very sure of herself, without being overbearing, and it was beautiful music. When her first record came out, I wished it was as wonderful and dynamic as she was live. Every show was a joy. It was a happening that went on for a period of time. Clive Davis came a number of times and a lot of other record people came, but mostly it was newspapers and a lot of people on the periphery of theater and the arts. Those first dates put us on the map, at least initially. A lot of excitement was generated.

"It was an interesting mixture of people who came to see her. When I managed the Village Vanguard many years ago, one person there who created the same sort of excitement, because he had a whole mixture in the audience, was Lenny Bruce. He generated a scene where all kinds of people came. There were doctors, lawyers, Leonard Bernstein, all kinds of comedians. Patti was not quite the same way, but in a subtle way she was. There was a nice mix. She said things in her own way. I think she was really the first of, I don't like the word, the punks. Not that her music was punk. It was poetry. It was her style of poetry. We got along cordially — warm, I guess. We were always friendly. I haven't seen her in years. But we always got along. She came back here many times. She wasn't very communicative, but she would talk every once in a while. She would say something, and I would say something, but she was very quiet. She wasn't a small-talk person and neither am I. So there was a limited thing you could say. And she came here not to talk about herself but because she liked it here." In later years, Patti Smith performed at the club in a neck brace after being hurt in a fall. She was the main headliner when Hilly opened his theater, and her last show in the U.S. before her (hopefully temporary) sabbatical from the music industry was at CBGB.

One group who did not need a map to find CBGB was Talking Heads. They had a loft nearby. "It wasn't that hard [to find CBGB]," recalls David Byrne. "I stayed about a block away from the place. And there was not that much to do in the neighborhood. So, we were thinking, let's go and check out this bar. I think Television was playing. I was writing songs, but we hadn't started [Talking Heads] yet."

Fellow Rhode Island School of Design students Chris Frantz and Tina Weymouth moved to New York and into David Byrne's loft in 1974. "I think it was more at their urging that we started rehearsing our songs, the songs I had written. I was writing these things, but I didn't know what they were for. I didn't have any plans to put a band together, but there were the songs. When we started rehearsing, we would go over to the club at night and have a couple of drinks.

"We had been like a dance band before that, but CBGB was the first place [we played as Talking Heads]. Chris said something to the effect that a lot of kids in our generation had an ambition to be in a band. And I guess we felt that, since we had our songs and could play our instruments, we should at least give it a shot. Otherwise, we might be kicking ourselves for the rest of our lives if we didn't. Whether it would succeed or not we didn't know. And so we thought, let's give it a try and see what we can do. And we thought that rather than try to do something mainstream and then do our own thing later on after we cracked the marketplace, our feeling, and some of the other bands' as well, was to do exactly what we wanted to do to begin with, and if nobody was interested, then we would have to work on it.

"There were small crowds at first. There were some people we didn't know about who were local celebrities, people like Lenny Kaye and Danny Fields who were around at that point, and they seemed to like us a lot. They were generally encouraging. The audience reaction was kind of bewilderment. Then they would decide they liked it during a performance."

"The Talking Heads and the Shirts auditioned the same night," remembers Hilly, who later managed the Shirts. "There were three of them then: Tina, Chris and David. I loved them right off. I thought they were great; they were one of my two or three favorite groups. They wrote well and had an interesting sound. It was very angular music, and David looked like a chicken with its head cut off. But I kind of liked the wild flow they had when he sang. It was an emotional quality. Tina played whatever she played as well as anyone could play it. She played very exactly. In other words, she played certain notes that she learned how to play, and she played them very well. It was clear and simple. Chris was a very good drummer. Whatever they had to play, they played proficiently. I don't see how any professional musician could have played it any better. I booked them from the first show. They, through their contacts, and I, through mine, invited people down and they were immediately well received. The *New York Times* especially liked them."

"Nobody had a lot of equipment, but the Talking Heads had the least equipment in rock and roll," recalls Mike Scopino, then the road manager of Orchestra Luna and later the night manager at the Ritz, New York's most successful rock club. "The Talking Heads would play out of the trunk of a cab. I remember David Byrne carrying his little amp through the front door. It was about three feet by two feet. Once we had to borrow an amp from Tina, and she made the guy sign a note. They were real neat about their equipment. They were a very neat band. Their clothes were pressed, and they would clear up the beer cans where they were staying. They would clear a little space where Tina could do her makeup. It was like Camp CBGB. If you needed a mirror, you brought a mirror. If you needed a heater, you brought that. You could camp out there for a day and start getting comfortable once you knew your way around."

Many fans felt that Talking Heads did not really hit their stride until a few years later, but there is no denying that they made some friends early.

"They were the best of the whole batch, easily them and Television," says Joel Webber, then an independent promotion man and later director of A&R at Island Records in the U.S. "But definitely there were three bands I thought were really great. The Ramones were totally earthshaking. There was nothing in the world like them. But more people hated the Ramones without ever having heard them than any other band that has ever existed. The Heads were great and Television were great, but on a sort of intellectual level. I can't say that Television ever made me crazy with rock and roll fever. But you would sit there and say, 'God, these guys are good.' But the Heads were so quirky and weird that they set much of the stylistic tone. Not punk, but a transition period."

Seven weeks with Patti Smith certainly brought a few people down to 315 Bowery; it was nice that such a hot new band as Talking Heads should walk through the doors, but the attention span in New York City is very short. As spring turned into summer in 1975, Hilly had an idea: "I could see that the media got all excited about Patti, but they were not paying attention to the other bands. They acted like there was nothing here. Yet at the time nothing else was happening in New York. It was just after the *Newport Jazz Festival*. From asking around I learned that nothing was going on for the next couple of weeks after the festival. Nothing was really being booked in the theaters and there were no big concerts. But the papers had to go on and they needed something to write about."

So why not have a festival of his own? The June 23 issues of the *Village Voice* and the *Soho Weekly News* carried advertisements for a Ramones/Talking Heads bill (maybe a hundred people came to that). But underneath there was a notice for "CBGB Rock Festival Showcase Auditions." Who is to tell what the casual reader thought about this, but new and prospective bands took notice. The phone at CBGB began to ring. And the bands came with their tapes.

"I weeded out the worst bands and picked what were the best bands," says Hilly. "What I tried to do was get a combination of what I thought were the most interesting bands, the bands that were playing pretty well at this point and had a little bit of direction that was their own. There were a lot of others that were just nothing yet. Whether they were just beginning or not, they weren't saying anything. These we weeded out."

Three weeks later, the preliminary lineup for the festival, set for July 16–27, appeared, listing the bands in alphabetical order: Antenna, Blondy [sic], City Lights, Day Old Bread, David Patrick Kelly, the Demons, Jelly Roll, Johnny's Dance Band, Mad Brook, Mantis, the Marbles, Movies, Mink DeVille, Planets, Rainbow Daze, Ramones, Raquel, Shirts, Silent Partners, Sting Rays, Talking Heads, Television, Tuff Darts, Trilogy and Uncle Son.

A week after that, the *Village Voice* made the festival one of its music picks, recommending it like this: "London's *NME* [*New Musical Express*] called CBGB 'a toilet' and intimated that the owners kick holes in the walls and urinate just to provide atmosphere. Actually, it's not that exotic. From July 16 to 27, it will house the best of the New York underground. Among them there are ex-Doll Johnny Thunders' Heartbreakers, ex-Stiletto Blondy [sic] with her group, numerous acts I never heard of like Movies or Uncle Son, and don't miss stuff like the Ramones, Talking Heads, Television."

The schedule for the Festival then looked like this:

July 16–18: Ramones, Tuff Darts, Blondie, Talking Heads, White Lightning

July 19–20: Jelly Roll, Pretty Poison, Mink DeVille, Sniper, Antenna

July 21–22: Planets, Day Old Bread, Rainbow Daze, Mantis, Ice

July 23–24: Patrick David Kelly and Toivo, Demons, John Collins, Johnny's Dance Band, Trilogy

July 25–27: Heartbreakers, Shirts, Stagger Lee, Mad Brook, Second Wind

After that, the festival was extended. On July 30, Uncle Son, Sting Rays, Johnny's Dance Band and Hambone Sweets played. On July 31: Ramones, Blondie, Sting Rays, Johnny's Dance Band, Hambone Sweets, Silent Partners. On August 1: Ramones, Blondie, Talking Heads, Punch, Dancer.

"The festival originally was to be eleven days, but we extended it," Hilly recalls. "We had it through three weekends and two weeks. I repeated

THE STORY OF CBGB

some of the groups, since there was a demand for them. The Ramones, Television, Talking Heads, the Shirts, the Heartbreakers and Johnny's Dance Band from Philadelphia were the most popular. The Marbles were so-so. Mink DeVille wasn't yet popular. My favorites at the time were the Shirts and Talking Heads, while Television was also getting exciting."

The festival itself, with so many bands playing every night at a small club, created its own dynamic for the musicians and for the audience, both during its run and afterwards. It was also a bit of an ordeal.

Willy DeVille recalls it this way: "I may be exaggerating, but I swear to god, 20 sounds like the right number to me, 20 bands in one night. Everybody played like three songs and that was it. Three songs and you came off. It started about ten o'clock every night and it usually started late. Everybody went on about 11:30 and it went on until five in the morning. Of course, the equipment wasn't like it is today. Everybody just had to change their little amplifiers by themselves and go on and off stage and people were borrowing each other's equipment and stuff."

"We had six bands a night during the festival," says Hilly. "It was pretty hectic. Nobody wanted to open. But it worked out pretty well. It was harrowing, though. It was new. And when things are new, no matter how much work it is, and how many people come, and how they enjoy it, it is quite good. It was quite pleasurable. The crowds at the festival were not great, but they were good, better on the weekends than during the week. But the festival did get a lot of attention. The *Times*, with John Rockwell, came down. Christgau of the *Voice* was there a few times. *Rolling Stone*, then on the West Coast, came down a couple of times. *NME* was there, so was *Melody Maker*. So were the *Aquarian* and the *Soho Weekly News*, who were very important. There were lots and lots of photographers. The papers wrote about it. It was a really big lift. It wasn't just a lift to CBGB, but to this whole new scene in music."

None of the bands that appeared in Hilly's *Festival of Unsigned Bands* got a record deal immediately. But the bands were beginning to get press. Two weeks after the festival, in the August 18, 1975 issue, the *Village Voice* cover story was entitled "A Conservative Impulse in the New Rock Underground," talking about the return to rock basics as practiced by the acts appearing at CBGB. In his story, James Wolcott, who was most partial to Television and Talking Heads, and who advised Blondie that "someone ought to tell the guitarist that the way to sing harmony is to sing into the microphone," wrote this:

"CBGB resembled some abattoir of a kitchen in which a bucket of ice is placed in front of a fan to cool the room off. To no avail, of course, and the heat had perspiration glissading down the curve of one's back, yeah, and the cruel heat also burned away any sense of glamour. After all, CBGB's Bowery and Bleecker location is not the garden spot of lower Manhattan....

"So those who stayed away are not to be chastised, except for a lack of adventurousness. And yet they missed the most important event in New York rock since the Velvet Underground played the Balloon Farm … The very unpretentiousness of the bands' style of musical attack represented a counterthrust to the prevailing baroque theatricality of rock. In opposition to that theatricality, this was music that suggested a resurgence of communal faith. Rock bands flourished in the '60s when there was a genuine faith in the efficacious beauty of communal activity, when the belief was that togetherness meant strength. It was more than a matter of belonging: it meant that one could create art with friends. Playing with a band meant art with sacrifice, but without suffering; Romantic intensity without Romantic solitude.

"What CBGB is trying to do is nothing less than to restore that spirit in rock and roll. One is left speculating about success. Will any of the bands who play there amount to anything more than a cheap evening of rock and roll? Is public access merely an attitude to be discarded once stardom seems possible, or will it sustain itself past the first recording contract? I don't know and in a deepest sense I don't care. These bands don't have to be in the vanguard to satisfy...

"Flashes like the way Johnny Ramone slouches behind his guitar, Patti Smith and Lenny Kaye singing 'Don't Fuck With Love' on the sidewalk in front of CBGB, the Shirts shouting in unison in their final number; Tina Weymouth's tough sliding bass on 'Tentative Decisions,' the way Tom Verlaine says 'just the facts' in 'Prove It.'"

The *Soho Weekly News* and the *Aquarian* also did big spreads on the festival. The *Village Voice* began to cover the Ramones seriously; the *Times* liked Talking Heads.

"There were not that many people at the festival; people remember it as being more crowded than it was," says Hilly. "But the coverage of the festival started making things happen. Some [local] publications, and later national magazines and television, were supportive when it was expedient for them. Robert Christgau of the *Voice* and John Rockwell of the *Times* went beyond what was expedient, because they thought good things were happening. This also was a photographer's haven. I let every photographer come in, and it worked well. When I managed the *Ford Caravan of Music* and the Village Vanguard there were certain restrictions on photographers, because when somebody like Nina Simone performed you couldn't have flashbulbs all the time — it would be really distracting. But with the kind of rock played here it added to the energy.

"And since it was summer and it was hot, people would be going in and out and hanging around outside, leaning on the cars. Soon it became a scene. It was this place on the Bowery, and in a city of more than eight and a half million it was the only exciting thing that was happening. The press really got into it, and as they started reading each other's articles it got so more and more. Then the record companies started coming down, mainly Sire Records, but also others."

Hilly and his little bar on the Bowery had been discovered, at least by the rock print media in New York. Fans would follow. A scene was being made.

A rock and roll club, as any institution, is defined by the people who run it and work in it. CBGB was and is Hilly's baby, of course, and it is also a family operation with ex-wife Karen and the kids getting involved, too. There is daughter Lisa, now an attorney, who helps out in the business. There is also son Dana, who isn't so closely involved with the club, but who has been the pool champion at the place when there was a pool table.

It is acknowledged by virtually everybody that, whatever faults it had, CBGB always boasted a dedicated and professional staff. There was

Bill Shumaker, Susannah Eaton Ryan, Carol Costa and Connie Barrett and, more recently, Louise Parnassa, Connie Hall and Luther Beckett in administration; Roberta Bayley, deerfrance, Liz Kurtzman and B.G. at the door; Richard Billet, Barbara DeMartis and Maureen Nelly at the bar; and Charlie Martin, Cosmo Ohms and Norman and Dennis Dunn on the technical side.

Through the years some staffers have come, some have gone, and some have come back again. B.G. is still at the door, now with Mike, Rick and Eddie. (Probably only the accountant, if anyone, knows the last names of all the people working at CBGB.) Carol Costa sometimes comes in to tend bar, as does Lisa Kristal. Her husband Ger Burgman is at the bar as well, as is Cindy. Perennial sound and light experts Norman and Dennis Dunn still add their expertise. Recording and mixing during the days are Ronnie Ardito and Reggie Allen. At nights there are Judy Marianiss, Tommy Victor, Steve and Joshua. The opening of the CBGB Record Canteen next door has reactivated Bill Shumaker on the food side, while Curtis Cates runs the record department.

"There was a big circle there," recalls Cosmo Ohms. "Liz Kurtzman was at the door and now she's dealing with fashion. Roberta Bayley was one of the charms of the Bowery. I respect her. She always got great photographs. She was a classic. Between her and deerfrance, they were really the classic door people. After them you had to fall in line. She had the best way of dealing with people: 'You are not on the guest list, get out of here.' But she was friendly to all the right people, and if people were assholes she called them assholes." (Bayley later worked as the publisher's assistant at *Spin* magazine.)

"Richard [Billet, one of the first bartenders] was a pisser," recalls Maureen Nelly. "Richard didn't have any sense of smell. He seriously couldn't smell. When I worked with him, he used to eat constantly behind the bar. I was amazed. He was real nasty and mean to everybody, but when it came down to it, he was one of the sweetest men on Earth. I was so afraid of Richard when I first started working there. And working behind that bar with those two huge men, him and Merv, you have to understand that you are rubbing bellies constantly. Whenever I had to come near Richard I said, 'Oh, God, let me shrink six inches.' Until I knew him. Then he used to come back every Christmas after he left, and he would bring Christmas presents to the girls like myself. He would bring us little presents like scarves and mufflers and socks. He really cared and was very nice.

"I don't think he had very much respect for musicians. Richard had a good set of values and manners. But a lot of musicians take things for granted. Sometimes I wouldn't like musicians, myself. If somebody pestered me too much to give him free drinks all night, I would say, 'Fuck you. I don't need you. You are not God's gift to the world. I respect your work, I like you, but…' I think Richard was there so long that it got to the point where he had enough. And he didn't want to be bugged any more by freeloaders. If there were people who were nice to him every once in a while, then he got along with them. But I think he just had enough. He wasn't a mean bastard. He just got to the point, where, okay, this part of my life is over. Because musicians can be very uncaring, egocentric, and they expect everything to be handed to them on a platter. Some are very talented, but most of them are not. A lot of times it was, 'This is my image, this is what is going to make me great.' 'Forget it,' I said, 'If you don't know how to play guitar, go away.'"

Says Connie Barrett: "My first impression of Charlie Martin: He had long flowing hair and a gray beard, so he looked like Moses and acted like him. He wouldn't let anyone stand next to him at the sound booth. He is now more relaxed, but also they didn't have that wall there built up around the sound booth. That went in shortly after I got there. The crowds were pressing in so much that the guys just couldn't work. And the equipment was in danger. Charlie would sit down and roll up his shirt sleeves and you would think he was playing the grand piano or something. But Norman Dunn was totally different. Norman would sit there, and everybody would crowd up and ask questions and interrupt him. He would draw diagrams and pictures and explain all the setup. So right away it was a very strange scene with Charlie doing 'I am an artist,' while Norman was doing 'Hi, I have some Chinese food, do you want to sit down?' Charlie's thing was always, 'Don't worry about it, we'll fly it,' which always meant total disaster. He was good at that. His major talent was walking into a situation where everything was fucked up and saving the day. But God help us all if everything worked well that night. Then he was in a dreadful mood. Norman was a real techie, very consistent and a sensible human being. But together they could do great things with that system.

"One thing you have to learn about CBGB is that if something doesn't have to exist, it doesn't. Hilly always says, 'This doesn't have to happen. This doesn't have to be. You don't have to be here.' Surprisingly, a lot of people there are quite intelligent. Most of the people that Hilly has collected during the years have been very intelligent. But they don't last. People who work there don't really work there for the money. I think the pay has gone up to $25 a day, so nobody gets paid that well. The bartenders do not do well with the tips, and everybody who goes there thinks they are God's gift to the world. A lot of people need the job to pay their rent. So Hilly does keep a number of people going. I remember one of our waitresses got very sick and she came into work. She went home and I spoke to her on the phone and she sounded so awful that I felt really scared. I told Lisa, who got on the phone and called an ambulance. It took her two hours to get an ambulance out there at the other end of Brooklyn. It's a funny kind of place. Sometimes people think they don't give a damn, but they do. Of course, when Merv was there, he certainly gave a damn."

Merv. If Hilly was the sometimes-unwitting driving force of the place, for many years, the heart, soul and glue that held CBGB together was the late Merv Ferguson, best known to staff, musicians and customers alike as just Merv.

Merv was easy to spot at CBGB. He was a large, big-boned man, standing about six-foot-four and weighing close to 280 pounds. In his late 30s and early 40s, when he worked at CBGB, he wore his blond hair in a pageboy, and looked even more imposing than he was because of the yellow construction helmet he always wore on the job.

"Merv was a customer of mine at Ninth Street," recalls Hilly. "He managed another nightclub, and we would talk every now and then. He first started working for me at the place on 13th Street as a bartender and a night manager. Then I opened CBGB, and at first he didn't come here, and then he did. He worked the bar as a bartender and manager, and then he worked strictly as the manager three or four nights a week: Thursday, Friday and Saturday, and he stopped by on Sunday to see everything was fine, sometimes opening and closing. He also did other things. He was a buyer. If somebody wanted something, no drugs or anything like that, but commodities and they couldn't find it, Merv would find it. He bought odd lots of things and sold them. He was a collector who bought and sold old movies. Anything he thought was interesting. I don't even know. He was a very private person. He didn't even have a telephone at one point. His personal life was his own. He was a very loyal friend. He was loyal to everybody.

"He was a former athlete; I think a discus thrower. He was Scottish but spoke with an English accent. He had taught in schools in the UK and then he came here and taught English and history at a college in Connecticut and a college in Virginia. He knew a lot about a lot of things. But he gave up teaching. He just hated it. So, he became a bartender and manager and did whatever he wanted to do."

"I remember every time I got into a fight, he'd kind of break it up and stuff," says Joey Ramone. "One night, the guy who owns the Bleecker Bob record store — I didn't really know him or know his sense of humor, but I found him very obnoxious — he was getting on my nerves. I was fucked up, and I just took a beer, poured it over his head, and said, 'Let's go outside, I'm gonna kick the shit out of you.' Then people told me he was a black belt in karate. But Merv broke that up. Or if Merv caught you stealing beer from the bar, he wasn't a prick like a lot of people are. He knew how to handle things."

"Merv was kind of like a stepfather to me," says Dana Kristal. "Though I am kind of ambivalent towards him. I loved him, but after he died my mother said not to make him into a saint if that was not the way you felt about him when he was alive. He used to save me when I used to get drunk. I didn't get drunk very much but whenever there was any trouble he would always help me.

"One time, I was working in the kitchen and these two big guys, one guy looked six-foot-six, a muscleman, started taking food. I said they couldn't do that. I told Cosmo to get Merv, but he got Richard, which was a mistake. Richard used to work behind the bar. He was not bad-tempered — everybody in this place has quirks, and it's not fair to say that Richard had a bad temper. But he didn't like to put up with the bullshit from some of the musicians, who were kind of pushy. Merv was really big and he could handle things, but Cosmo got Richard, who came and said, 'What are you doing? They said, 'Get the fuck out of here.' I couldn't let anybody talk that way to Richard. And I said, 'Who the fuck are you?'

"Meanwhile, all the Ramones are around the pool table and the giant guy starts dropping cigarette ashes on my head. So, I grabbed him and we spun around, where the ladies' room used to be, and we crashed through the door. His friend charged in, and I am fighting with both of them. Richard jumps in and they punch him in the eye, so that was the end of Richard. Cosmo is hiding in the corner. Charlie Martin comes in to help, but they throw Charlie six feet.

"And the Ramones are just standing there by the pool table. I thought they might help me a little bit. But they just stood around. After they threw Charlie, I tried to lift one of the big guy's feet, but he was so big I couldn't budge it. He just pressed his foot down. Then Merv comes out and starts walking toward them. They see the size of Merv, and that was the end of it. Nobody took a swing at him. It was just his presence and the way he walked."

Says Connie Barrett: "If Merv asked somebody to move two or three times and they wouldn't move, he would be very nice and just wrap his big arms around them, pick them up off the floor with their feet dangling, and he would deposit them on the sidewalk outside. I used to work several jobs to support Sun when I managed them, and I wasn't always around when they needed money. I would give Merv ten dollars to hold for me to give to the band if they needed it. I called him First National Merv. And the band knew. They didn't have to give a reason, they just had to ask him for ten dollars, and he would give it to them."

"Merv was very special, and I think a lot of people probably have similar stories," says Maureen Nelly. "He was different things to different people. He was usually a father image. He was my father in New York. He helped me. He talked to me. He would lend money to people if they needed it for whatever. Like, if a girl had to have an abortion, if somebody was in trouble and couldn't pay their rent, they would go to Merv and say, 'Listen, can you help me?'

"Late at night he would discuss philosophy. He could be very elitist at times. He was an intellectual. He was very much above the crowd, I think. He was compassionate; he empathized. He was warm and caring. He brought in cats ... these stray cats. Each one had a name and a personality. And he took care of the cats. He took care of the people who worked here. He took care of the band members. And then, when he left, he did it in a way he felt he should do it. Some people felt disappointed that they couldn't say good-bye to him.

"One thing I found out through talking to different people who worked there was that he let certain parts of his personal life be known to certain people. He would open up to one person about how he was an actor. I think he was a professional football player. He was a scholar. These are bits and pieces that I have picked up from various people. I knew about Alexander, his son. I knew his baby's first word was 'flower,' the second one was 'fuck.' These are the things Merv told me. And then there are other things.

"Merv would relate to people at a personal level. He would talk about certain things. If somebody had a drinking problem, he would talk about drinking. He had done so many things in his life that he related in certain small ways to everyone. In the beginning he was very fatherly to me. And I was very naïve. He protected me from being stupid and vulnerable. He protected me from men on many, many occasions. And after I grew up a little bit he was more like a friend. But we weren't that personal then. When I was younger, we were more personal.

"Financially he didn't have to be at CBGB. I don't want to say anything negative about him. He had been through many, many things in his life, some of them negative, and when people sometimes experience hardships or bad periods of time, they pull themselves up. I think working in a bar for Merv was sort of like therapy. He liked people very much. He was special.

"Merv was a philosopher. He was worldly, knowledgeable and a jack-of-all-trades. And it wasn't that he was a master of none, he was probably a master of many. He was masterly at most everything. Why was he there? Because he had a passion for life. He liked to see life and experience it. He was a voyeur in some respects. He listened to everybody's problems, he commented and he cared, but he never got too involved. Yet he really cared, and he was always open-minded. He never let himself get old. He may have been opinionated, but he was open to everything. And I think the CBGB scene kept him in touch."

Remembers Annie Golden of the Shirts: "There is a beautiful story that I want to tell about Merv. We were doing this really big night. I was making [the film] *Hair,* and my picture had come out on the cover of the Sunday magazine section of the *Daily News.* It was a beautiful, beautiful spread, and I have it framed in my house. It was the first key piece of publicity that I had and the Shirts had. Hilly had booked us for a weekend at CBGB, and we went down to do our usual gig to our usual following, but people were hanging from the rafters to see this band with this girl in the Sunday papers.

"We are onstage, and I notice this girl who was a friend of my sister. She had done drugs, climbed a tree and fell down when she was stoned, and she had snapped her spine. She is in a wheelchair now, and I'm singing, and this kid made her way to the front in packed CBGB in her wheelchair, and she's still getting high, she's still a mess. After the set, she makes her way to the dressing room, what there is of it — it looks like a bombed-out bomb shelter. The girl is telling me how I'm her idol and how she's going to straighten out, and she really thinks it's great that I'm getting all this attention.

"All of a sudden, she starts weeping. I think she's overjoyed or too stoned or something, but she grabs me and says, 'I have to go to the bathroom. It's downstairs and I don't know what to do.' I don't know what to do, either. I could get down there, but I didn't want to. The bathrooms were the most social thing down there because the guys would kick a hole through the wall and talk to you. So, she was in a predicament. I went to Merv. He was the strongest man I knew, and I told him the problem. He just picked this girl up in this wheelchair, which had to weigh 80 pounds with all the paraphernalia on it, and carried her over his head, wheelchair and all, down those stairs and into the bathrooms. All he said was, 'Please don't ask me to go in with you. I don't even go there myself. I piss on the Bowery.' Then he waited for her and carried her back. When she had to leave he led her out the back way, which was unheard of because that alleyway is just … But he carried her over the debris and got her into the street from where she could go home. The girl has since gotten herself together through the brilliant kindness of Merv, that he would do that for her."

Former CBGB bartender Patrick Hartigan says, "My relationship with Merv was that of student to teacher; Merv gave me reading lists, the books which have provided the cornerstones of my philosophy and morality.

"The man was a mystery. This secrecy was born perhaps out of necessity, as many people conjectured. Or perhaps it was just Merv's fantastic sense of perspective and decorum. Amongst all these floundering children, should he have dwelt on his own past? Nonetheless, we were somewhat skeptical of some of the awesome (to us) tales Merv could relate. There were clues from another life altogether, stories of combat and of athletic feats, stories of his family life. His father, I believe, died before his eyes. There was pathos in his life and an occasional victory, but always related with an uncommon ease and gentleness.

"Some of us at the club had difficulty understanding why Merv was there in the first place. But it always seemed enough of a reason that Merv enjoyed the company of youth, and even perhaps the chaotic and ribald atmosphere of CBGB. I do know he enjoyed a good laugh and Bach. He liked pretty girls and the philosophy of [18th century Scottish philosopher David] Hume. He disliked rock and roll, or so he said, but he was more than willing to acknowledge those with talent. He had an intense dislike for drug dealers, at least with regards to their presence in the club. All in all, he was a pure Scottish empiricist, a true skeptic, distrusting with his soul all that which seemed greater than it was.

"Merv was at ease with all types of people, a testament, I believe, to his experience, knowledge, humility and charm. I can only admire his deft manipulation of conversation, of language and all the shades of its meanings. Merv could make you laugh, he could upbraid you or he could leave you with thoughts in your head that could change your life. And all this was done with ease, gentleness and the confidence of a man who, after having known him for only a few insufficient years, I can say was truly wise."

Karen Kristal remembers Merv this way: "He was a very private person. Shortly before he died, I asked him why he worked at CBGB. 'You don't make enough money here to make it worth your while.' He said, 'It keeps me young.' And he wasn't that old himself. He was only about 42 when he died. He had cancer of the colon, a tumor the size of a grapefruit.

"He treated all the employees as if they were his children. In a way, I didn't like it too much because sometimes it is a little difficult to discipline somebody if you are close to them. Sometimes they do things they shouldn't do. And I'd catch them at it. Sometimes I would catch the employees smoking pot, and I'd say, 'You, at least, should know better. You work here. You are hurting the place.' They would go running to him for comfort. He said, 'You have nobody to blame except yourself. If you do things that are wrong and [Karen's] around, then you deserve everything that you get. You know she never misses a thing. Then you deserve everything she gives you.'

"In a way I felt that he coddled the employees. I was on one end of the scale and he was on the other. They used to write terrible things about me. I know it wasn't our customers who wrote the graffiti about KK. I'm sure some of it was written by employees. I get along much better with the employees now. Maybe because I don't stay there.

"It was in the summer, in 1982, that Merv died. In the spring we bought a large amount of some French cheese and invited the staff to help themselves, and Merv came. I told him to have some. He said he was constipated and couldn't eat cheese. He said he didn't feel well because of it. I didn't think much of it, but several weeks later he said again that he didn't feel well, and I asked if it was the same thing or something new. He said it was the same thing. I asked him what his doctor said. And I said, about that time, that if you are still sick with the same thing, maybe you should change doctors. But Merv hadn't been to a doctor in about 15 years. He didn't believe in doctors. He thought they were all idiots. Until this thing started. Then he went to a surgeon, who was going to put him into St. Vincent's Hospital for exploratory surgery. It was on a Sunday night the last time he worked. He was sweating profusely, and I thought he was looking scared. That made me scared, too. But I reached up and kissed him on the cheek and said, 'You're too big and fat to have anything seriously wrong with you.' But he looked very sick. I never saw him again. They operated, and then his girlfriend told me that he had a tumor that was malignant and inoperable. They did a colostomy, and after that he wouldn't let anyone near him. He didn't want to speak to anyone or to see anyone while he was in that condition, and finally they released him [from the hospital] and gave him chemotherapy.

"That year I wasn't going to go to Europe [Karen normally tries to take a European vacation every year], and in July, one night I couldn't sleep, I kept thinking of Merv. He and I used to tell each other that you should go on with your life, you shouldn't wait. That is what he would say to me and I would say to him, and I was thinking that. Maybe it was too late for him, but what about me? I want to go to Europe and I'm going to go. Because who knows when it may be too late for me? It was almost as though Merv was telling me. I turned on the light and made my reservations. This was Saturday night. Tuesday, when I got into my office late in the day, my boss said that Ailene was calling through the whole afternoon. That was his girlfriend. I called her back: 'Karen, he's dead, he's dead.' I was in shock. He died on Friday, about 4:15 p.m., and Saturday night when I started thinking about him he was dead but not buried. I had a feeling that he was telling me something. Because that was the best trip I had up till then. I did what I wanted to do, but he never did. He put things off too long."

CHAPTER FIVE

"Everybody was as accommodating as could be as long as the favor was not too much. Right from the beginning it was as in all rock circles: You wished everybody well, but not too well, not better than yourself."

— MARTY THAU

Sometimes irreverent sometimes irrelevant, sometimes annoying in its celebration of Marxist chic, the *Village Voice* is and was during the history of CBGB the self-proclaimed but still respected weekly arbiter of popular entertainment and culture, at least in the southern half of Manhattan island. A club or a restaurant or an off-Broadway play that doesn't find approval in the pages of the *Voice* more than likely won't last too long. The *Voice*, and the now defunct *Soho Weekly News*, grew to be one of the biggest supporters of the nascent scene developing on the Bowery, but in the very beginning the *Voice* wouldn't even take Hilly's ads. The reason was simple: "When I sold out my place on 13th Street, I still owed the *Voice* money. And I didn't have any. I got checks that all bounced. So, I paid the *Voice* when I could.

"I had been taking ads with them since 1966, and when I started CBGB I still owed them some money. They said they wouldn't accept any ads until I had paid all my bills. I wanted to pay concurrently, but they wouldn't do it. So, I said fuck you and went to the *Soho News*."

It wasn't until halfway through Patti Smith's stay at CBGB in 1975 that Hilly finally made peace with the *Voice*'s advertising department, and his ads have appeared there almost without interruption ever since. Before then, some of the bands that played CBGB took out ads in the *Voice* on their own, though the story goes that the *Voice* wouldn't allow them to print CBGB's phone number in their ads. Among them were the Ramones, and it was a series of Ramones ads that lured [Connecticut native] Willy DeVille back [from California] with his band, Mink DeVille, several months before the CBGB festival.

"It was the *Village Voice* that put me in touch, because I was in San Francisco at the time, putting a band together," recalls Willy DeVille. "There was really nothing happening in New York after the Mercer Arts Center fell down. It seems it got so trendy in New York that nobody was playing this freak kind of show. So, I went out to try to find some good players and come back to New York later with some good players and a good band. My main line to New York then was the *Village Voice*. I was living on Bush Street in San Francisco near the old Fillmore and out of homesickness I would pick up the *Voice* to see what was going on. One day, I saw this ad that was maybe two inches tall. It had the name of this club, CBGB, and the name of a band playing there, the Ramones. And when I saw the ad for three weeks, I said it looked like this place is going to stay open. I was looking for a bar to play, and any place that would have a band called the Ramones could have Mink DeVille. I convinced the guys in my band I knew what was going on enough to get us a booking there, and I conned them into coming to New York. I told them they were going to get a record deal, and the four of us jumped in a car with a U-Haul trailer in back and drove to New York."

It has been pretty much axiomatic in the music business in the U.S. that the press, the written word, does not sell records. It may help establish an image for an artist, but the common wisdom is that nobody buys a record because of something they have read; they buy what they hear on the radio or, nowadays, see on video. However, for live performances this is not quite the case. As in film and in theater, reviews do sell seats.

Folks may not buy the record based on a review, but they will go see a live show on the basis of a recommendation from a journal or critic they trust.

In the case of CBGB, a 300-capacity club, consistently favorable press could not help but draw the curious and adventurous who form the nucleus of any trend. Fortunately for CBGB, and for all lovers of new rock and pop music since, the rock journalists who came to CBGB were able to appreciate the music and musicians on a socio/philosophical level, as well as just liking the music.

Robert Christgau explains the former:

"For a lot of reasons, rock writing, or rock criticism, which I prefer to call it though it includes other kinds of writing, has had a greater influence in the last ten years than it did before, because as good music came out that radio refused to touch, people had to learn about it in other ways, as they do in England, where radio is limited. In addition, whatever small effect rock criticism has on the popular success of any musician, it tends to have more effect — to choose a pre-punk example — on a Randy Newman, who is literate and appeals to people who like to read, than it does on the success of a Black Sabbath or a Van McCoy.

"Punk as a whole was a very aestheticized movement. These were very aesthetically conscious people, even if they took an anti-arty stance. And the writers, most of us, it seems to me, had been waiting for something like this to happen for a long time. I think punk responded to some real mainstream assumptions of rock criticism, which were not mainstream assumptions of rock and roll. Rock critics are much more interested in rebellious music, in new music. They are much more in-terested, despite what people say, in short catchy songs with a hard beat. I know people think of rock criticism as a wimp profession, when in fact most of the great critics really liked, and were really weaned on, pre-Beatles stuff, and they really liked the approach of the '50s. And punk is really not a recapitulation of the '50s at all, but in certain kinds of formal ways — its brevity, its attack — it is a modernization of that kind of idea. But the beat is entirely different, for instance, and it seems to me the beat was very attractive to all of us.

"There was an aesthetic, what John Piccarella called the 'forced beat' [in] writing about the Feelies in 1978. It took what we liked about rock and roll and it did something with it that we always wanted to hear. And that is what we responded to.

"I think in specific terms the writing of Alan Betrock in the *Soho Weekly News* was incredibly important and preceded anything the *Voice* did. But we were on it early. I came in here still believing in what I called pop. And I still do believe in what I call pop. Not in the sense that it means Wham! now, but in the pop art sense. And I trusted the media. I was not anti-mass media, and I am still not, but clearly CBGB, and what happened in the wake of CB's, changed my feeling about that a great deal. And so very early on I decided that Patti Smith and the Ramones, to choose two examples, were worthwhile writing about before they had records out. I think [critic James] Wolcott did the first Patti Smith story, and I believe he did the first Ramones piece. He hung out there. He was a lot more of a hang-out type of guy than I was, though I did see Patti there at her first gig, and in fact I was there at the bar before it was a rock and roll bar. It was one of the few bars I ever went to.

"I wrote a piece where I went to see the Who at Madison Square Garden and then Television was playing down at CB's. It was a Friday night, and I went to see what it was like. I wrote a piece about the two places. And at that time CBGB was the place where I was most comfortable. As I said, I'm not a hang-out kind of person, but for a while I came close to hanging out there. I was there three or four times a month. I would drop by from any gig in the Village and see what was happening there for a few minutes. If it was a band I liked I would stay, if it wasn't I would leave. And I have always felt comfortable there. I had one of my first deep conversations with my present wife at CB's, then called Hilly's, after a Cockettes show, which was in 1970 or 1971.

"Very, very rarely do I do something that will get somebody on the map. And I was there for Patti, not for Hilly. But insofar as it helped Hilly, I'm delighted. The club deserves its reputation. My philosophy has always been that a good club builds up its own clientele, and if it can't survive on word of mouth, pretty much, it is in trouble. Certainly, we were instrumental in turning CB's into a scene, which it became for a while. But it seems to me it is still living on that reputation. It is not a scene anymore. But it does seem to do okay, and it does have its own reputation. But that has very little to do with what kind of coverage we give it or don't give it. I'm happy to say nice things about the club because I like its vibes, because it has a very good sound system — though I hear bands complain about what a dive it is and how hard it is to play there, which in certain physical respects is obviously true. But it does really get the music lovers, and you really can get the music. And those are very, very important things in a club. And it is unusual in a club today."

There were other reasons why the rock press adopted CBGB and the bands that appeared there so quickly. By 1975, post-hippie, post-'60s music — represented by such acts as the Jefferson Starship, the Eagles, Fleetwood Mac, Led Zeppelin, the Who and others — was nearing its potential in the marketplace, with multimillion sellers still in the future. But the excitement, at least for critics, was gone. The new superstars could now be only glimpsed in passing as they grew more and more commercial and remote. Older critics, who knew these new celebrities when they were only scruffy musicians, began to feel left out and bypassed. They started writing about the death of the '60s rock dream and the irrelevance of arena rock music. Yet there was only that on the radio and disco, which then was worse. And as for younger rock critics, they had no music of their own.

It was very easy to recognize rock writers at music business parties and functions. They were the poor, shabby looking guys in the corner who nobody else wanted to talk to. After all, they didn't sell any records. As for their exposure to the artists, that was always carefully monitored and controlled, as impersonal as a half-hour session at a stuffy whorehouse. There was no hanging out with the stars. Then, at CBGB, for a while, things changed. Here was a group of bands, as good as anything on the radio, and you could buy a beer for Richard Lloyd, or chat with Dee Dee Ramone, or crash at the Dead Boys' apartment, and it was cool. You could even help make the scene happen.

"It seemed like every week there was something there to cover," remembers Roy Trakin, then a regular music writer for the *Soho Weekly News*. "Who knows, I wrote maybe 25 to 50 stories at least, if not exactly about CBGB, then about the scene around it. The most important thing was that here was something you could really reach out and touch and be a part of. For someone like me, who basically missed the '60s — I was 18 in 1970 — and didn't have a culture of his own, it was certainly a chance to feel really a part of something. I was even a member of a band called the Corvairs.

"The feeling of CBGB was that it was like a basement or a recreation room that you sort of took over. Every night you would meet someone else who was involved, a lot of artists and students in this great melting pot. There was a real feeling that here were new ideas, something happening, like Paris in the '20s or London in the early '60s. It was a scene you could really call your own, and I literally stumbled onto it. In many ways, I forged my professional identity on what was going on there. The new wave, punk and all those things were our way of taking it over and taking it for us. It was the next generation, and if it hadn't happened at CBGB's it would have happened somewhere else. But it happened at CBGB on a level you could reach out and touch. Here were musicians who between sets would hang out.

"And also here was the best music that was being played anywhere, on any stage. There were nights here, when Television was playing, that were magical. Television seemed to have the goods because I was a big Grateful Dead fan, too, and there was that guitar interplay and a whole combination of things. You could sit up front and touch the people. Everything was right in front of you. I would always sit up front and laugh my fucking ass off. I thought the Ramones were hilarious. To me they were the logical successors of the Dolls. They just brought what the Dolls did to its lowest common denominator. They were great. Television was great and to a lesser extent Talking Heads, which I began to get into. Then I realized Blondie had a lot of potential. I think it was shortly after Jimmy Destri joined the band and added a new keyboard sound. But Television was always the tops for me. I remember seeing

Television with Richard Hell and I remember seeing Tom Verlaine and how they looked so cool onstage, the juxtaposition between Richard Hell's sort of chaos and Verlaine's neurotic uptightness, and the interchanges between Lloyd and Verlaine on guitar, just their styles and the way they meshed. And, like I said, I began to meet the various people, and became involved."

"In my mind, the goal was never to make it," recalls Ira Robbins. "In fact, when the bands were signed, it was very much like they were taken away from us, not that they were going on to greater things. It would have been fine if all those bands stayed local, when we knew that the bands playing on the local scene were a hundred times better than those other bands playing out there. Certainly, we felt that they could get signed and justice would be served if they did get hits. But I don't think anybody in the audience really wanted to see them get signed, because it wasn't going to do us any good for them to get taken away from us. I certainly remember feeling that way about Blondie. Blondie was great. Then they got signed, and it was like goodbye. They got harder to reach on the phone, and they moved out of New York a little bit and they were never around. It just wasn't the same."

In the first few months of 1976, a record contract was still just a dream for most of the acts playing at CBGB. It is true that *Horses*, Patti Smith's debut album, had just come out, and though Patti would probably have been signed whether she had ever played at CBGB or not, it gave the other bands a psychological boost. It was obvious that something big was happening when, on a weekday night in January 1976, Hilly booked a typical CBGB double-bill: Talking Heads opening for Television. No special advertising or anything. But the place was packed.

"Hilly was kind of like the P.T. Barnum of the scene," recalls Willy DeVille. "He had everyone down there from the Ramones to Mink DeVille to Patti Smith to Cathy Chamberlain's Rag'n'Roll Revue. He was trying every hook he could, and it was working. The press were coming down in droves, and everybody wanted to know what the scene was all about. And now maybe they would go down there to spot Willy DeVille or Joey Ramone or somebody. At the same time, people were going down there to see if they could see Lou Reed at a table. It was the place to be."

Says Legs McNeil, staff writer for *Spin* magazine: "In 1975, what was great about it was that New York City was broke. No one wanted to live here, so there wasn't anything like yuppies and stuff. And there weren't that many places to go. There was CBGB, Max's and later the Mudd Club. You would go into CBGB and there would be 300 people — and you knew 200 of them. Now you go out and there are 50,000 people, and you're lucky if you know one.

"CBGB was a juvenile delinquent hang-out. Everybody I knew was [one], except [*Village Voice* writer] James Wolcott, who was in the back taking it all in. Even David Byrne was, to some extent. Now he's being imitated in television commercials, but back then he was thought of as a weird psycho. But there was a real sense of community, because everybody was so broke. Richard Hell's song 'Down at the Rock and Roll Club' was what CBGB was all about: 'Sweetheart, will you buy me one…'"

It was around this time that the CBGB "punk" look began to be defined. It never got as wild as it later did when the English kids discovered the "Blank Generation" look, which was first adopted by Richard Hell, original bass player and singer for Television. Hell later formed the Heartbreakers with ex-New York Dolls Johnny Thunders and Jerry Nolan before embarking on a solo career.

"Richard Hell was the first one that I ever saw wearing a ripped T-shirt and his hair looking like he just got out of bed. And it really gets me down when I hear stuff like 'England started this whole movement,' when this was such a while ago," says Elda Gentile, who certainly was there in the beginning.

As Richard Hell explains, "My look was sort of a strategy. I knew I was really against the hippie music, so I wanted my hair to be short. It was actually a combination of a lot of factors, if you want to analyze it. A lot of the appeal of the Beatles and the Stones was that they had haircuts that looked like children. The Beatles had their bowl haircuts and the Stones this shaggy look. And I wanted it to look like do-it-yourself. Everything we were doing at that time had that element, from having ripped-up clothes to not knowing how to play instruments. The whole thing was partly a reaction to the hippie stadium music. And we were saying any kid can do it.

"The haircut came from just taking scissors and violently testifying. Then you get those kinds of results. In my generation, little kids tended to have haircuts that looked that way. Eight- and nine-year-olds of my generation had these butch crew cuts that would get ragged because they wouldn't go to the barber every two weeks.

"Then there were some artists that I admired who looked like that. Rimbaud looked like that. Artaud looked like that. And it also looked like the kid in *400 Blows*, the Truffaut movie. I remember I had a picture of those three guys. I really thought all this stuff out in '73 and '74. I wanted the way we looked to be as expressive as the material on the stage, down to what the posters were like. It was all of a piece. The ripped T-shirts meant that I don't give a fuck about stardom and all that, or glamour and going to rock shows to see someone who pretended to be perfect. The people wanted to see someone they could identify with. It was saying, 'You could be here, too.'"

"Many people walked into that place from Bayonne, New Jersey, saying this is hell," says Clem Burke. "You could see the look on their faces. They would walk in and see a sea of black leather jackets, which was the de rigueur outfit. That was the CBGB look. There were no safety pins. It was more like Debbie Harry wearing a wedding dress onstage and the famous quote, 'This is the only dress my mother ever wanted me to wear.'"

Punk magazine, which started in January 1976 and lasted through 16 issues until 1979, when lack of advertising put it out of business, helped give punk rock its name and defined its look in a highly stylized manner. "It codified the imagined image," recalls Ira Robbins. "One kid might be wearing a leather jacket. Another kid wore torn jeans. And a third one had a spiked haircut. They put it all together in *Punk*."

"I came up with the name *Punk*," says Legs McNeil, who was the "resident punk" of *Punk* during its brief history chronicling the lives and times of the nascent scene around CBGB. "John [Holmstrom, the editor of *Punk*] wanted to start a rock and roll fun magazine. He was really influenced by *Mad* magazine; one of his teachers was Harvey Kurtzman, who had come up with *Mad* with William Gaines, but later left over money disputes. John was mulling over various titles, and I suggested why not call it *Punk*.

"Lester Bangs had used the term before, but I didn't really read rock and roll magazines; I got it from watching television. Kojak, instead of calling people 'you fucking asshole,' would call them 'you lousy punk.' That is basically where the term came from. I don't know if we'd seen the Ramones yet, but we certainly studied the Dictators [first album's] inner sleeve, which showed them in black leather jackets in front of a White Castle. There's also a line in a Dictators song ["Weekend"] where somebody is called a 'local punk.'

"The pins in the cheeks were after the Sex Pistols, but at CBGB there were mods and there were rockers. The Gary Valentine [of Blondie] art crowd would be in their jackets and skinny ties, and we would be in our leathers. There never really was any friction, nor anyone offended. There was also the leftover Dolls crowd, but mostly it was the Ramones: leather jackets and pegged pants, stolen from Brando and James Dean.

"The first time I was at CBGB the Ramones were playing. Lou Reed was there; they started doing a song but Dee Dee's bass strings broke and they walked off the stage after two minutes. [Dee Dee says that was because the band was too poor to have any spare stings.] And it was fantastic. I remember I was wearing a *Creem* [magazine] T-shirt and a blue denim jacket, looking like a complete nerd. The next day I went out and bought a black leather jacket."

Dee Dee Ramone recalls the Ramones were still a glitter band like their inspirations, the New York Dolls, at their first CBGB date. That soon changed. "We were always very fashion-conscious, but when we got into rock it was punk rock, anti-establishment," he says. "We were getting so fanatical about being anti-establishment that we even forsook our own [post-hippie pop] music culture and decided to just make up our own. We wanted to do punk rock, and we decided the punks were people from the '50s like Eddie Cochran and Elvis Presley. You would always see them walking around in motorcycle jackets. We thought that was the coolest thing, to have a motorcycle jacket, to really prove you were in the groove."

Recalls Carol Costa, who did bookings at CBGB: "I lived on Long Island, and I heard some pretty wild rumors about this place, but I had never been here, though I was going out with a guy who was a regular. One night we came here, and the Shirts were playing. We got here and the place was jammed. I looked around and people were wearing, to me, such strange clothes. The first person I saw was some girl wearing red and white striped tights, green shorts and an orange jacket. Her hair was black and it was going in a thousand different directions. There was nothing like that on Long Island. That made me really like the place. Everybody could wear whatever they wanted to and nobody was looking at them as though they were from Mars. Even in Long Island I was dressing differently from other people, and everybody would look at me strangely, so it was great to come to a place where I was nothing compared to everybody else here dress-wise."

If ever there was a time filled with golden potential at CBGB it was during 1976. A look, a sound and an identity were developing. The top bands could make a couple of thousand dollars for a weekend's work; record company interest was beginning — maybe ambitions could be realized after all, and there was still the pioneer spirit of camaraderie. CBGB was this little island for a still relatively small group of people, a second home in a mostly indifferent world.

"There was a whole lifestyle situation," says Chris Stein of Blondie. "One night we did our set using the Ramones' equipment, guitars and all. The whole scene was crazy. Hilly lived in the place, and there was a whole living room environment. You could just come in, sit on a rocking chair and read books. Clem Burke used to call up the phone booth collect when he was in England. There was always this possibility that somebody would drive a car through the front door. That never happened, but it was constantly discussed. It was quite nice hanging out in front. Some of those warm summer nights were quite wonderful. And I remember Legs McNeil hopscotching parking meters down the Bowery, tripping and falling on his head. He was okay, but you could hear the crack down the street."

"I was the baby there and I was treated as such," recalls Maureen Nelly, who was then a 19-year-old barmaid and waitress. "There were a lot of crazy things that happened, but I think there was a kind of meeting of the minds. There were poets there, there were musicians, there were actors. I met Frank Zappa, Mick Jagger, Paul Simon and so forth. And in a situation like CBGB they became like real people because they were there to enjoy the music like everybody else. It was not a pretentious place at all. It was a place to hang out. It was when *Punk* magazine began. I used to live with one of the girls who also worked there, Liz Kurtzman, who was very much involved in punk. Her father was Harvey Kurtzman, the inventor of *Mad* magazine. And [*Punk* editor] John Holmstrom was Harvey's protégé. All these people would come to our house at night and joke. Legs McNeil would sleep over on the many occasions he was too drunk to make it home.

"In 1976, there were still 20 people in the audience, except for certain bands like Television, Talking Heads and the Ramones, who would always draw. Patti Smith, when she showed up, would always draw. But the place was tiny. Four people could barely stand on that stage. That's when it was very intimate, and the only people who came were those who really knew what was going on. Then it started opening up, and the bands — not all of them — started catering to the commercial thing. Their attitudes changed, and the whole feeling of the place changed. I remember when Steve Forbert would be working at one o'clock in the morning on his stage act with Hilly. He would ask, 'What did you think of this one?' and 'What did you think of that one?' It was a very personal experience.

"During one of my birthdays, when I turned 20, it was the first time that John Cale played a long stint there — four days. It was the first time I had seen any of the Velvets live, outside of Lou Reed, and it was a big thrill for me. After the set, John Cale, Lou Reed and Allen Lanier [of Blue Öyster Cult] and maybe somebody else got up on stage and jammed well into five or six in the morning. And a couple of the Shirts, who are my good friends, Hilly, and maybe about five or six other people were there. That is what the club was all about.

That was very special. And when that stopped, it stopped for me, and I had to leave.'

"I can't even remember the number of times the Dictators played at CBGB," says lead singer Handsome Dick Manitoba. "When we started playing we started meeting the people personally. I got along fine with the Ramones, Chris Stein and Debbie Harry, the Talking Heads. Regular people. And I must say these have been the fondest memories of my life so far. When I want to feel melancholy and good I look at the memorabilia of those days. CBGB was like a home place. No class, on the Bowery, but the same people who worked there were the same people who came there. It was a rock and roll club, and I'm really glad a bunch of legends came out of there, because it wasn't fancy or anything. Everybody could afford a drink there. It was a nice place to hang out."

"It was actually pretty comfortable," says David Byrne. "It was always kind of run down, and there was never any intention of cleaning the place up, except that Hilly did put in a great sound system, probably the best club system around. The atmosphere, the people created. I would come in the evenings and have a drink no matter who would play, even if it was a band I didn't particularly care for. A lot of regulars would be hanging around. After working our day jobs and then rehearsing for a while, it would be nice to stop by and say hi to friends."

"The audience on any particular night at CBGB was the Ramones and Blondie and Television and whoever was onstage," says Clem Burke. "For an impressionable young man, which I was at the time, it was a real magical place. I had my apartment at the time on Christopher Street, and going to CBGB was like being carried on a magic carpet. You turn the corner on Christopher Street, go on to Bleecker, buy a beer and walk from the West Village to the East Village, winding up in front of CBGB. And the closer you got, the more magical it became. When you got there, you would see Richard Hell or Joey Ramone or somebody looking about ready to get in, or whatever band was playing, and it was a real feeling. It was something that was really happening."

"I remember hanging out there a lot in '76 and '77" recalls Lenny Kaye. "We would go down there every night. It was where you could go see everybody and just kind of sit on the sidewalk and chew the fat, or whatever. I think every scene needs a place like that just to go and keep in touch with everybody."

"CBGB's really became the focal point of an entire generation's growth," says Richard Lloyd. "Within the confines of that you'd find people coming from Paris going, 'Zees eess CBGB,' walking in shit and acting like this is where Christ resides. We were not Jesus or anything like that, but there was something so powerful emanating from that place, and so many people spun off it, that they became not millionaires of money, but millionaires or zillionaires of the spirit of music. There was a time when I would say we were 60 people strong, and out of that came Television, Patti Smith, the Talking Heads, Blondie, the Ramones. And it didn't end. It does go on and on."

And what really made it go was the music. It obviously wasn't the prettiest club around, and beyond the musical interest there really wasn't much going on. Certainly, there is going to be sex and drugs where there is rock and roll, and CBGB has had its share of both, with scenes in the phone booth, in the alleyway, in the lighting booth and in the bathrooms — especially the bathrooms. But in 1976 that was just beginning, and it didn't really happen until later, when the club became more of a punk scene.

"The wild, glamorous things that happened elsewhere were never really the order of the day," says Jim Wynbrandt of the Miamis. "It was not conducive to that sort of carrying on. The ambience of the place was not like that. There were a lot more dark corners at Max's or Club 82 where things could happen. There was perhaps more of a sense of privacy in other places. CB's was never the wild kind of hangout."

"That was the major complaint— there were no girls at CBGB," recalls Clem Burke. "Until 1976, there were a bunch of guys, Debbie Harry and a couple of Ramones girlfriends. It was ridiculous. From a male point of view, we realized that something was happening when women started showing up at CBGB. It was a very male-dominated scene, a bunch of guys who had nowhere else to play. It was a major breakthrough when a couple of girls would show up by themselves."

Tish and Snooky, between dates with the Stilettos, the Sic F✳cks or sometimes a pickup band, were among the first. "We would take a train down to CBGB in the middle of the night," recalls Tish. "We would leave home around midnight and take the subway in from the last station in the Bronx. It took at least an hour for us to get there. We would put on our party clothes and fancy dresses, then put our jeans over them. When we got to within a block of CBGB, we would take off our subway shoes and put on our spiked heels, put on our dresses and tease out our hair a bit more. We would put on our makeup the whole way down on the train. That's the way we prepared ourselves. A block away, we would do this quick change in the streets and then always walk in with shopping bags. We were like these teenage shopping bag ladies."

"And when we were doing shows at the Bouwerie Lane Theater we would run across the street in these real skimpy outfits and blonde wigs. We used to be allowed in for free," adds Snooky.

There were also some more worldly female creatures of the night coming into CBGB at the time. "A lot of my friends at the time were not hookers, because I think of hookers as these girls with no lives who stand on the streets all night," says Dick Manitoba. "But a lot of my friends were heavily into drugs and prostitution and all kinds of rock and roll. For a lot of people on the scene that was the only way they could make money. Probably it still is."

But of course there were other women right at the beginning of the CBGB scene. Recalls Annie Golden: "It was really exciting, the women who were down there at the time: Patti Smith, Tina Weymouth, Debbie Harry, the Stiletto girls, Helen Wheels were all hanging down there. That was exciting, because whenever I would be with a band I was the only woman, and there never was anybody else. And now finally there was. And each one of us was different; that's what I loved. Tina was not vocal at all, but very visual, very rhythmic. And Patti was so poetic and esoteric. She was fantastic. Then Debbie was like the rock and roll Marilyn."

It wasn't just the women who were all different from each other. The reason CBGB succeeded may have been that all the bands that came from there were different. "Tom Verlaine always said an interesting thing, that each of the bands at CBGB was like a little idea," says Lenny Kaye. "It wasn't that kind of style of punk rock that happened when England took over. Here it was all like little art projects. And when you look at the bands that came out of here, they were all different. There was no one dominant thing. We were all different, and that gave CB's a vitality that really sparkled."

Annie Golden describes it this way: "There were so many kinds of bands. There were bluegrass bands, rhythm-and-blues bands, like the Rice Miller Band and Blue Sky, psychedelic bands and left-over glitter bands. Even Mahavishnu-type bands. You could go down there on any given night and there would be rockabilly with Robert Gordon or punk with the Tuff Darts or punk-posing bands or real devastating punk bands like the Ramones, the Heartbreakers or Richard Hell. And then you would go there another night and you would have Willy DeVille doing Otis Redding, and it would just be so soulful and musical. Then the Ramones or the Heartbreakers would play, and it was energy, energy, energy. Then you'd get the Planets and it would be English rock night, and then there would be the Shirts, and I don't even know what we were. Then the Talking Heads were real artsy rock, Television real cerebral rock, the Laughing Dogs real pop lunatic rock and Manster trying to be real inventive. Then you'd come in on another night and there would be these people from a commune in Long Island dressed all in white and putting these little incense sticks all around. They would be playing this esoteric psychedelic spiritual rock, or something. And you would say, 'Oh God, only at CBGB.'"

Robert Christgau recalls some musical nights at CBGB this way: "I remember the shows that were the most remarkable physically, because they stand out. They give me a visual memory. Like the Ramones policemen's vest gig. [The Ramones did a benefit to buy the New York police bulletproof vests.] I literally hung, not from the rafters, but from some other thing, hung for the entire set. And it was worth it. I remember seeing Blondie when Debbie Harry was complaining about the heat messing up her hairdo. I remember a great Feelies gig, where I was sitting in the second row. It was the best gig I ever saw them give. I heard

Tom Verlaine play a lot of great solos in that club. I think of it more as Television's club and Patti's club than I do the Heads' club. The Heads got better when they left. I think they managed to evolve and become less minimal, and it has really improved their music.

"There is another gig I remember: the first Ramones show I ever saw. This group had been sending me handwritten notes and lyrics — maybe handwritten and then xeroxed. And they looked intriguing; something about the way they presented themselves appealed to me. I went to some kind of gig at Soho with Tom Johnson, who was our big apostle of minimalism, our avant-garde music critic. So, we went to this gig in Soho, and I said I heard of this band playing at CB's and I just wanted to check it out. Except for the Patti gigs it might have been the first time I ever was at that place to see music. They played a 25-minute set, and I was utterly knocked out. I said these are people who figured out everything that the Stooges did that was a mistake and left it out. And that was what was left. I loved them. Tom Johnson thought they were great. Their conceptual intelligence was obvious to him immediately. And there could not have been more than 20 people in the bar. It was a weeknight, and Danny Fields sat at the end of the bar. I remember that gig. That was a real moment in my life."

Even at the beginning, with the great music and pioneer spirit, not everything was always smooth and happy. "It was real competitive also with a lot of people shunning each other," recalls Ira Robbins. "It was as bitchy as it possibly could be, even when there was nothing to protect. Everybody was really wary of each other. We were avoiding people we were in competition with, or bands we didn't like. We would make fun of them mercilessly. I remember one Ramones show where we were mocking them, shouting 'one, two, three, four,' along with every song. I made a tape of it and in the background the Ramones are doing this brilliant 20-minute set, and we were making these inane remarks. It was really nasty."

And for a musician who felt underappreciated from the first time he came to CBGB, it was nastier still. "We walked in the door, and I said, 'Hi, we're here to audition,'" recalls Willy DeVille. "And this guy [Terry

Ork] said, 'What's the name of your band?' 'Mink DeVille,' I said. 'Great,' he said. We went onstage, played a few numbers and the guy said, 'Well there is nothing really interesting in another white blues band.' So right there it was really disheartening. And then I learned from somebody else that this guy didn't even book the club. He was just the manager of another band. So, I realized what was going on. This guy and probably a few other managers wanted an exclusive on the club. But I wanted to get in there, too. I went to Hilly and said, 'Hey listen, this guy says you work for him.' Needless to say, we got in after that.

"We started playing and then we started pulling on Hilly's cuff, saying, 'We want a headlining date, we want a headlining date, we want a headlining date.' But to do that with Hilly you had to make him smell that the A&R record people were coming down to see you. It was a real mindfuck. When you start to think that Hilly is not such an innocent old folkie type of guy, it starts putting a bad taste in your mouth and you start feeling a little bit used. But that's New York, and I think that if you can get through that training, you can do it anywhere. 'Cause I'll tell you, with all the bullshit I have been through, I don't think I have been through anything as rough as that whole scene. It was like a school of vampires. It was about as exciting as having a vampire come to your room at night."

CHAPTER SIX

"At the time there was a lot of political play down there, especially between Hilly and Peter Crowley, who used to run Max's Kansas City. Let me see if I can get the facts straight here. I am trying to remember which guy was the one who was threatening us."

— MARTY THAU

By the spring of 1976 it was becoming obvious that this whole new music scene that had been gestating at CBGB for the last two years was finally about to break out and make its mark in the larger world. In England, once it got started, it happened very quickly. It took a lot longer in the U.S., but not for want of talent and effort. The reasons were mainly economic and social. Much of the new music coming from CBGB was dark and pessimistic, if not anarchistic. With the Vietnam War finally over and the country prosperous, Jimmy Carter's warnings of malaise notwithstanding, kids in the U.S. were relatively satisfied with their lot. They wanted to dance at the disco or get high at the arena and not worry about "Psycho Killers." In Britain, however, there was a severe economic recession going on, racial tensions and, more to the point, there was "No Future" for the English "Blank Generation" looking forward to little more than a lifetime on the dole. The music of the Sex Pistols, the Clash, the Jam and the Damned made immediate sense to British audiences in a way that the music coming out of CBGB did not to their American counterparts.

Also, the club, radio and press scene in the UK was much more receptive to new music. English clubs (I know from experience, having briefly managed a band there) do not pay much. But neither do they normally demand that a band play only covers of hit songs. Very few clubs in the U.S. book unknown bands that insist on playing their own new music. And radio is neither so pervasive in England, nor so conservative, nor so important to selling records as it is in the U.S. Instead there is a very aggressive music press that constantly hungers for the new. But there is no American counterpart to *Melody Maker* or the *New Musical Express*.

In the middle months of 1976, Hilly was able to jingle a few coins in his pocket; his enterprise on the Bowery was finally making money. The fans were coming in. He didn't have to move furniture anymore to pay his bills. This meant it was time to expand, to shepherd his scene to greener pastures. How to do this? Over the next couple of years, Hilly tried a number of ways. He recorded and marketed an album. He put his bands out on tour. He started managing a couple of acts, put in a new stage and sound system at CBGB and opened the CBGB Theater. (Most recently, he started the Record Canteen.) Some of these enterprises were more successful than others.

Hilly wasn't the first to see the recording possibilities of the CBGB bands. Seymour Stein had a small record label, Sire Records, whose biggest acts at the time were Renaissance and the Climax Blues Band. But Seymour always had a good ear and an eye for an opportunity, and he was the first record executive of any note to visit CBGB to check out its new acts. He signed the Ramones first.

"We got Linda Stein, Seymour's wife, who saw them before Seymour," says Danny Fields, then the Ramones' manager. "Then we plotted to get Seymour to see them, and he loved them. They were signed to Sire by the next summer [1975]. The Ramones' commercial potential was not really tried at that point, but their press was so incredible that no one could fault anyone for signing them. Even in those early days, the *Voice*,

Soho Weekly News and *Aquarian* were there, and the Ramones were the darlings of the press.

"Seymour was very supportive," continues Fields. "We didn't get much [of an] advance, but whenever we needed money or tour support or equipment or stuff like that, he was always there. That never stopped; when we were hard up it was forthcoming. He never said no. I didn't go crawling to him every week, but almost every month. The debut record was made very cheaply. It literally cost $6,200 to make. I have been involved with him for many years, and to this day I don't think he was ever gloating over getting something cheap. The commitment was always there. There were bands, like Richard Hell, where he pulled out after one album, but he didn't do that with the Ramones. And the Ramones are still beloved and they are professional. And that is their job. They don't have to work as waiters. They are the Ramones, and they made history. And Seymour gets a lot of credit for that."

In 1976, Seymour was looking for other opportunities as well, later signing Talking Heads, Tuff Darts and the Dead Boys from CBGB. Current acts on his label (which has since been sold to Warner Bros.) still include the Ramones and Talking Heads as well as the Pretenders and Madonna. Punk rock has been very good to Seymour Stein. He still comes down to CBGB, but not as often.

"Seymour Stein, who had been his partner, contacted [producer] Richard Gottehrer, whom I was talking to," recalls Marty Thau. "We went out together and scouted around, and we came upon this idea to do a compilation album. That got recorded, but not through us. But we talked to David Byrne and Willy DeVille and Blondie and some other acts. I do feel that if our casting had taken place it would have been a superior album. But it did come about that Hilly owned the place; he held the upper hand once he got the drift of what was going down. Maybe he had the same idea simultaneously. He cast what he did and the acts that he chose were different than the ones we chose. He couldn't get some of the acts we could have gotten."

"I know Marty Thau and Richard Gottehrer used to come around, but they never let me in on anything," says Hilly, who organized the recording of his compilation album in June 1976 on his own, as he had his festival of unsigned bands the year before. He advertised that he was going to do it, he auditioned and negotiated to see what bands he could get and then he had them play brief sets for five nights before a live paying audience. The only difference was that he had a mobile recording truck parked outside and he had Craig Leon, who produced the Ramones' debut album, as the producer.

Not every act that was recorded appears on *Live at CBGB*. Those who do include Tuff Darts (with Robert Gordon still their lead singer), the Shirts, Mink DeVille, the Laughing Dogs, Manster, Sun, Stuart's Hammer and the Miamis.

As Hilly explains, "The Ramones were signed and Television were about to be signed, so we couldn't do anything about getting them. I didn't have any choice. Blondie didn't define the scene then. They were not known; they were more popular as the Stilettos. They recorded and it came out badly. We went over it, and we wanted it to happen. They may have recorded for two days; we had them do it again, and it just didn't work. We couldn't even overdub. We couldn't do anything. And it was not fair to the band to do something that wasn't good.

"We did Talking Heads, too. But my agreement was that they could bow out if they didn't want to do it later. I got a little bugged by that. They did mixes and remixes and then David or his lawyer or whoever felt that they didn't want to do it. So, they didn't.

"I put up $15,000 for it and the guy who managed the Tuff Darts put up $5,000. The album was released on the CBGB label. I sold the albums out of here. A French company bought a few thousand copies and some record stores and distributors bought a hundred here and there. I sold three or four thousand copies. Then Atlantic Records bought the rights. Jerry Greenberg and Jim Delehant over there liked it. They gave us some money, and I paid every band, based on a track thing, gave them their percentage. I think it eventually broke even. Everybody got their publishing. I think worldwide it sold 40,000 copies, which is not so bad for a double album."

Needless to say, there was some serious jockeying for position, not only as to who would be on the album, but also who would be playing when. Since it was a live album in front of a paying audience it was important to be able to play near the middle of the evening. Too early or too late and there would be no one there. And there were other ego-related considerations as well.

"It was like people trying to line up for the Preakness horse race," comments Cosmo Ohms. "There were maybe a hundred bands rehearsing in their lofts. It was really underground loft music, and everybody wanted their shot. Here it was and they all wanted record contracts; they all wanted their piece of the cake. And the CBGB album became the realistic vehicle for achieving that. Who was signed around then? Patti Smith, the Ramones. The Talking Heads weren't signed yet, but Seymour was watching them. And Private Stock was watching Blondie. So, it was really a wide open thing. There had been no interest, and all of a sudden there was interest. There were writers, there were players, there were actors, there were people in clothing, major merchandising, marketing. People started to realize, hey, this is more than just a local thing. It has an ability to happen. So, yes, there was a lot of bickering, hankering to get a shot."

"This is how silly this whole scene got," says Willy DeVille. "This band called the Tuff Darts showed up. Now you have to get the right perspective on this. Everybody at CBGB is trying to play their songs, get their sets, 'cause it's like the place to be, right? Now this band shows up, maybe for an audition or something, but they have their own limousine. And I'm wondering who the hell these motherfuckers are. I know what they are getting paid because they are not getting paid any more than I am. It ended up that Tuff Darts' manager hired the limousine to make his band look like somebodies. He was financing the album. It kind of made everybody wonder, 'How the hell are these guys on the album when they have been playing here only two weeks and we have been here two years?'

"But they got to doctor up their guitar parts and some of their vocal parts. I'm sure it's true. That's why the two Tuff Darts cuts had that polish. I don't think that was fair to the rest of us bands, because we just recorded it straight and it's pretty shabby sounding. But if you listen to the other bands and then you listen to the Tuff Darts cuts, you can tell they've been doctored up." For whatever it's worth, Hilly says that Mink DeVille was asked to play two sets during the recording of the album — one more R&B flavored, the other more rock — because the stuff they were getting from the band was so good they wanted to get as much as possible.

The album was not a critical success, and at a time when production costs for bands like the Eagles and Fleetwood Mac were hitting seven figures, the $20,000 *Live at CBGB* LP was not quite up to par. "The album was totally bizarre," says Ira Robbins. "To me it was not representative of the bands that were happening at the time. They were one whole rung below the bands that people went to see at CBGB. Nobody knew about bands like Manster and stuff like that. Even bands like Laughing Dogs and Sun were nothing. Some of them I had never heard of. I remember really hating the album and reviewing it very negatively. I am sure a lot of bands declined to be on it. The only good track was a cut by the Tuff Darts, and a week after the album came out, Robert Gordon left the band."

"The technical part of the equipment being used to record the album was what you found in any recording studio," says Norman Dunn, long-time sound engineer at CBGB. "But there was no pre-production. There was no one to go up to the drummer and say, 'Your drums sound like shit.' You have to work with each band for three or four days beforehand if you want the drums to sound human. As it was, a lot of the drums sounded horrible and a lot of the bass guitars were farty as crazy. Seen live, there was an incredible amount of excitement in the music. On the album it sounded alright, but kind of sterile; it didn't know if it was going to be punk or commercial."

Neither did the record companies at the time. Seymour Stein with the Ramones and Clive Davis with Patti Smith notwithstanding, the initial music business reaction to the bands from CBGB was hostility when it was not indifference. *Frampton Comes Alive*, which sold some 14-million copies that year, was the big item. Other big sellers were ELO and Kiss. Heart was up and coming. And disco was breaking into the

Top 10 regularly. Two of the biggest hits of the year were "Disco Lady" by Johnnie Taylor and "Play That Funky Music" by Wild Cherry. Who cared about some grungy music coming from the Bowery?

"I taped stuff I liked and took it around to record companies and some of the people at the record companies were not very nice," says Hilly. "They didn't like it and they used very bad language. That becomes upsetting, and I may have told some people to fuck themselves, too, when they started talking about people who were good and creative. It was ridiculous. Why couldn't they be open to other things? They didn't have to buy, but there were some bands that were good."

"In those days, from a business point of view, the album was an especially adventurous thing to do," says Joel Webber, who helped promote it. "There were only two record companies doing anything like that. One was Beserkley in California and the other was Stiff in England. And there was Ork Records, which was putting out at the time seven-inch singles. So, to put out a double album was an amazing statement of faith on Hilly's part. It did a lot to solidify the scene. And it also showed how bad a lot of these bands really were. But there were also some bands of quality on that record, certainly the Shirts and Mink DeVille. There were a couple of other acts that were obviously going to get signed. And it may have been a ploy, Atlantic's way of getting in on one of those bands, I don't know, but Atlantic took their time taking over that record, and by the time they took over distribution it had been sold in the city to everyone who was going to buy it, which at that time represented 90 percent of the new music scene.

"About record companies and CB's, you should note how completely impossible it was. This guy who ran ABC Records, which was distributing Sire at the time, once came down with a bunch of his cronies. He literally had on a powder-blue leisure suit. I know that is a cliché catch-all phrase, but I am not making this up. This guy comes popping out of his limousine in this fucking powder-blue leisure suit and we were all in hysterics. Here comes Mr. Mogul. It is really funny the first impressions some of these guys would have of this place. They didn't understand one thing that was going on. They would come in usually with the local

A&R guy, and they would look around, dust off their suits and try not to put their elbows on the table.

"It was kind of cool, because we were getting these guys to come down to our turf. Then it was like us against the world. And we were not going up to their offices to sing for them. They were actually coming to our natural habitat, next door to the Palace Hotel, to see some band play. It was a great feeling that we were beginning to develop that kind of power that later took over the record business."

"The record company people don't like to go to places like CBGB," confirms Marty Thau. "Many of them were literally afraid to go down there. The place was not some polished neon venue. It's funky and there are all types around that the record company people don't know how to relate to or understand. Leather jackets, strange names and high energy music were counter to what they were signing. And these guys don't necessarily have their ears to the street. They want you to go out and find the new movement, make it happen and then they will go out and buy it up. I always used to say, why can't you go out and get it earliest, it sure would save a lot of money. But that is not their concern. Saving money is not a concern."

Nonetheless, Marty Thau was instrumental in getting Blondie signed, the second band after the Ramones (or the third after Patti Smith) to get signed out of CBGB. "Debbie Harry was a friend of the New York Dolls," remembers Thau. "In fact, she came up with them the day I invited them to my house in 1972 shortly after I signed them for management. I figured if I was going to do serious business with these people, I might as well get to know them socially. She drove them up in her car.

"Later, Howard Rosen, the promo director of Private Stock Records, who was a close family friend, invited me up to his house for dinner one night. I brought up with me the newly completed demo of Blondie's 'Sex Offender' and played it to him about 30 times. And he said, 'Look, it sounds like "Born to Run," and if that was a hit for Bruce Springsteen, why shouldn't this be a hit for this group?' And I said, 'Tomorrow, when you go to work, why don't you tell your boss you want to buy this record?' I knew there would be some difficulty in selling it because of the generation they would be appealing to, which was the burgeoning new wave generation. So, I concluded that the thing to do was just get the record out and have an option, make it possible for Private Stock to exercise that option. I knew that Private Stock and the other labels at that point were not fully aware of the feedback they would get. But once they got the single out [as 'X Offender'] they would get this amazing press response and they would then just have to pick up the option. And that was how we got the first Blondie record going."

Frankie Valli of the Four Seasons, the principal owner of Private Stock, went down to CBGB to check out Blondie on his own and liked what he saw. Now, with Atlantic picking up the CBGB compilation LP and Private Stock signing Blondie, the logjam was broken; it was no longer just the folks from Sire coming down to check out the action. In due course, Talking Heads, Tuff Darts and the Dead Boys were signed to Sire. Television went to Elektra. The Shirts and Mink DeVille went to Capitol. Robert Gordon, formerly of Tuff Darts, went to Private Stock and from there to RCA. And Sun, after changing its name to Mayday, was eventually picked up by A&M.

The days of innocence were over; success was beckoning. The top bands were signing contracts and becoming part of the four-billion-dollar record business. They wanted to get their music on vinyl and into the hands of potential fans without selling out — and do it better than their friends and/or rivals.

"The greatest thing about it in the beginning was that there was no pressure," recalls Elda Stiletto. "We were all there to be seen and have a great time. Everybody felt that they were an important part of what we were creating. Then, after a while, the record companies started to come in. And then people started to be cutthroat about being seen and stuff like that, and it was not the same. As soon as some of the bands started getting signed, everybody started looking at each other, and, hey, what is going on? All of a sudden, there were hands involved that nobody expected. It translated in the sense that some people got on high horses, and then some didn't. But when the record contracts started happening, everybody was under pressure. Artists that were hanging out at

CBGB, what did they know about clauses in contracts and terms and all that stuff about how the record business functions? We didn't have any understanding. And then there was the so-called English Invasion [of new English punk and new wave bands like the Sex Pistols and the Clash], which destroyed what a lot of people at CB's were trying to do. Everybody sort of went with it, but at the same time it was something that turned off the general public to a lot of acts."

"Everybody wanted a record contract, right?" says Willy DeVille. "But everybody got real, real artistic. When it came down to it, and the A&R people started coming around, they realized they had something to protect. They were really throwing their songs out on the railroad track, but when the A&R people came over suddenly everybody got real uptight and got into the sort of mentality that we are not going to sell out, we are not going to sell out."

"That's a great attitude story, but there was very little of that 'we hate the record business' thing," comments Joel Webber. "I think that came mostly from us [the media and the music business] and not the musicians. The musicians were not about to compromise their music, but at the same time they were not going to be turning down record deals and stuff. That's one of the myths about the era."

With the *Live at CBGB* album out in the marketplace, obviously it was time to get some of the bands out on tour. The music was too raw for bland American radio, so there was no way for the bands to get their work heard outside the Bowery other than to take it to the people in the hinterlands themselves. So Hilly, with the two trucks from his moving business, got Tuff Darts, Mink DeVille, the Shirts, Sun and Laughing Dogs out on tour, playing in South Hampton, New York, Virginia Beach, Virginia and in Boston. They were not the most well-organized dates in the world.

"I had everybody on the Virginia Beach show," says Hilly. "I had trucks and rented vans and it was a mess, a real costly mess. One of the guys who invested money with me had all these contacts there, and we thought it was wonderful. But they opened up this club after having closed it for the season and nobody came. It was in September, after

Labor Day. Nobody knew about it, the sound was bad, there was a problem with the motel. Somebody left with the money. It cost me two or three thousand dollars. Nobody gave me tour support. I had to pay for the bands to eat. And then we went to Boston, which was much better. There was a scene at the Rat [the Rathskeller, Boston's closest equivalent to CBGB]. But there was no other scene anywhere else at the time. The Hot Club in Philadelphia had not yet happened. We didn't do any more *Live at CBGB* tours after that."

"Hilly lent us a truck and we went to Boston in a snowstorm," recalls Annie Golden. "It was like the Little Rascals version of a rock band tour. We had to take the *Live at CBGB* albums out of their sleeves and use them to scoop the snow off the windshield, since the windshield wipers didn't work. It was real death-defying, leaning out the window on the Massachusetts Pike. There were no seats in the van, so you had to sit on a folding chair and lean out while somebody was holding on to you. We would sleep in the van with the equipment, and if we stopped at a rest stop and kept the motor running we'd get carbon monoxide poisoning, so we would have to run out and throw up and get fresh air. Either you would be freezing your ass off or you were poisoning your lungs. It was a whole crazy great time then."

Fortunately, not every CBGB band had to rely on Hilly and his truck to tour. The Ramones did it themselves, building a circuit in the U.S. and even crossing the Atlantic, inspiring the English punk movement with their visit to London for a now legendary July 4, 1976 date, which seems to have drawn and encouraged every incipient punk musician in the country. And, back in the U.S.A., "There was Max's, a few places in New Jersey and a few places in Long Island, and then we went to Boston and we played in a really horrible place," recalls Danny Fields. "We would do anything to get into another city and we would do anything to get into another venue in the metropolitan area. We worked for virtually nothing. In the beginning, we went to these other cities that looked to what was happening in New York. In the east, they are obviously Boston, Toronto and Washington. Not so much Philly, although it did happen there. And the promoters there were ready to go out on a limb.

Especially in Washington, we played some weird dates just on the basis of having come from CBGB. Because these guys in Washington thought it would make them hip to present something that was seen at CBGB. It was the same in Toronto and Boston and Chicago, perhaps too, which are important markets.

"We were really inventing a circuit. We inherited the remnants of the New York Dolls' circuit. We were astonished that we would go out to these cities and there would be people waiting in line. There was a hard-core group of people who paid attention but that was about all. It gave you an opening in those places. There were other places where it hurt. There were more provincial places where it just didn't do you any good at all.

"We had to play outside [of New York]," Fields explains. "You can die of overexposure playing one place. When you have an album, you have to get out there, and we were one of the first bands to have an album so we were one of the first bands that had to go out and tour. So, we were testing it, too. We were there for the money, but we were also testing the market. I went to bed every night with the map of the U.S. in my head. Before we got into Premier Talent we had seven booking agencies, we jerked off seven agents, asking them to get us what they could, most of it by word of mouth. Some dates I booked myself.

"There was not that much else going on anywhere else in the world. The Sex Pistols had played before the Ramones' July 4, 1976 concert in London, but the Clash never had — they were still a band afraid to come out of their rehearsal basement. But when they saw the Ramones on July 4, I think a week later, they decided, oh shit, if those guys can do it … and they literally played their first gig in front of an audience. This was inspirational to a lot of people. We heard it, too. Every time we came back to a city, we heard that 15 guys who had been there had started their own bands and a new club had opened up. It was kind of inspiring. It was the same way the Ramones responded when they saw the New York Dolls and they decided to be a band: 'If these guys can do it, we can do it … they don't play any better than we do.' And the same thing happened when people saw the Ramones. It was a nice kind of torch to pass on," concludes Fields.

Meanwhile, back on the Bowery, Hilly was facing his first competition. In the beginning of 1976, Max's Kansas City had adopted a new wave music policy, basically booking the same acts as CBGB. A little healthy competition would have been beneficial to everybody, but it became a personal matter following an altercation at CBGB between Wayne County and Handsome Dick Manitoba, which had ended with Manitoba in the hospital with a broken collarbone and County facing charges for assaulting Manitoba with his microphone stand. This incident polarized the scene, especially since Peter Crowley, who managed Max's, was also Wayne County's manager. Handsome Dick remembers the incident this way:

"It was unfortunate what happened with Wayne County. We got a lot of press out of it, but it was an unfortunate incident. All that I remember is that I probably had a few drinks and I was feeling cocky. You had to step across the corner of the stage to get to the bathroom. And I did that. But I heckled him [County, who was onstage]. I always heckled. And I had a reputation that preceded me. It was not the serious Manitoba side but the fun side. Obviously, some people took the reputation seriously. I was a wrestler, a bully, I hated gays, all that shit. And I was just walking past the stage. I said something, I don't remember what it was, and the next thing I knew Wayne County was saying some very nasty things to me. I guess my brilliant 20-year-old machismo got the best of me ... I was a little intoxicated, so he said something to me, and I said something to him. It was one of those things. Well, fuck you. But I don't care how drunk I was, I would only fight to protect myself or if I felt I was threatened. I didn't start anything. I don't start fights.

"Obviously, because of my reputation, he felt that I, whatever kind of gesture I made, had crossed that barrier, that performer's barrier between him and the audience. This was wrong. But it was the way CBGB was set up. Being by the side of the stage, you could actually be onstage. It was only six inches off the ground at that time. It was not like I jumped up onstage and said come on. I was on the side of the stage on the stage, I guess. But I didn't really feel I was the cause. The next thing I knew I was turned around and hit in the back; somebody hit me. I had to have stitches in my head, and my collarbone was broken. After getting hit once I went after him, but then something was broken, and I had to get out of the place. There was almost a lawsuit after that. There was a lot of publicity.

"But what it did was it made me appear to be a gay hater, which I am not. I had no intention of ever attacking anybody, but their rap was that they didn't know that. I could see that side of the story, but if you know me, it's just not in my repertoire. Peter Crowley, who was Wayne County's manager, also managed Max's. Anybody who played with the Dictators would be banned from Max's. It got all out of hand. It was cleared up over the years and everybody has forgotten about it. But I will tell you to this day people do not like to believe that he hit me. It's always, 'You're the guy who beat that fag up.' I go, 'Yeah.'"

There was a benefit to pay Wayne County's legal fees. (He later left the country and went to England, where he formed the Electric Chairs.) In New York, the result of the altercation was a polarization among bands with some, like the Heartbreakers and the Fast, becoming known as Max's acts, while others, like the Shirts and the Dead Boys (both managed by Hilly), would only play CBGB. Still others, who had a strong enough draw, or were just strong enough, managed to play both places. Nonetheless, the feud even spilled over to other clubs.

Willy DeVille recalls: "How nasty did the feud between Max's and CB's get? Towards the end there, before we got our record deal, we started working with what we called buddy bands. It seemed like a safe route to go. For instance, we wouldn't open up for the Tuff Darts and the Tuff Darts wouldn't open for us, because we were too competitive. We'd kick each other's ass on stage. So, some bands picked up a band that would complement their music and at the same time not give them any problems. Television picked up the Talking Heads, and we kind of liked to work with the Blondies. They seemed like nice people, they weren't particularly ambitious, they were into their own trip as to what they were doing, they weren't threatening and they had okay attitudes. Their audience, I think, kind of went for our stuff, and our audience was willing to accept them. So, it was okay.

"Then we were supposed to play this new club, On the Rocks, owned by this guy Richie Alexander, who was trying to get a foothold on the club scene. But Hilly and Peter Crowley were enough competition for each other and they just didn't want anybody else in there, so they were going to squeeze anybody who tried to get in there. They went about that by threatening bands. I am not saying that Hilly did, but I would definitely say that Peter Crowley was vicious enough to do this. He'd say, 'Lookit, you can't play there,' and that is what went down.

"Now we were going to play On the Rocks, and Blondie were going to open for us. The way I got it was that Peter Crowley threatened them and said, 'Look, you're either going to be a Max's band or you are going to be a CBGB band.' Now maybe they will deny it [Chris Stein says Blondie avoided the Max's–CBGB feud, and they did play both venues], but I know it went down. What it meant was that if you played there, you couldn't play here, and that meant one of your venues for a record deal was cut off. So, Blondie didn't play the show at On the Rocks, and we did. We were kind of pissed off at them, like those candyasses, they are going to be scared of club owners. It was that kind of scene."

"Max's was supposedly more trendy," says Mike Scopino, a former roadie who is now night manager at the Ritz. "It had the people who thought they were following the footsteps of the Dolls. There was no scoring at CBGB. When you went to Max's you dressed up. When you went to CBGB you put on a sleeveless T-shirt. At CBGB it was a dressing room with a curtain thrown up and all the bands shared it. But nothing got stolen. Five in the morning the place would be cleared out and there would be one drunk on the street, but your stuff would still be there. At Max's, forget it. You took your eyes off your shoes and you could forget about them. That was the big difference between the two. You could feel safe at Hilly's place."

"We were friendly with Max's at a distance," says Hilly, now being charitable. "I didn't know [owner] Tommy Dean at all. I probably saw him only once or twice a year. We competed, but we didn't try to hurt each other. It was healthy. It was like when you have two or three networks; it was competition. We didn't socialize. But we were friendly.

And I must say that financially it was very hard. I didn't make that much money there. A couple of times he offered to help me out if I had a problem. I never asked him, but he was very supportive. Peter Crowley worked for him. He was alright. He ran the entertainment, and I didn't agree with his policy necessarily. He had this thing at various times of not letting people play CB's when they played there. I didn't care. I started first and I was a little better known, I think. Max's as a new music thing was a whole new generation. And they made money off food in their restaurant. So, it was different.

"I was in the Bowery, which was a tough place to be. But it worked. They told me that people were threatened [that if they played Max's they couldn't play at CBGB]. I think for a little while they did that, and then they stopped. If they did, and some of the bands told me they did, it was not good, but I couldn't do anything about it. I thought it was terrible what they were doing, if that was what was happening. But I think in principle (and I managed the Village Vanguard — you wouldn't play the Village Gate one week and the Village Vanguard the other), it's not fair to either club. So, there is a good reason. But I think when you are dealing with new bands looking for a place to play you have to be a little more liberal."

To accommodate the ever-increasing crowds at CBGB, Hilly dumped the pool table and moved and enlarged the stage. To remain competitive, he put in a new sound system. Though there were some reservations at first, the result was one of his biggest triumphs. For both musicians and fans alike, the custom-built sound system was (and is) as good as it could be.

"I don't think music ever sounded as good as it did there," says Danny Fields. "We were terrified when he put in that new sound system. They were tampering with something wonderful and they could have fucked it up. We were afraid of overkill. And we all held our breaths, telling him it would be no good. But, no, he had to keep up with the competition and all that. And, you know what? It still sounded great. The sound was perfect."

"The sound system was put in July 1977," remembers Hilly. "We already had a pretty good sound system, which we rented. When I first started, I used whatever I had, and then the Shirts would bring theirs in. And then other people would bring theirs in. It was very tough because we had a small sound system that was being augmented. Aside from the Bottom Line, we were the first club in New York to have its own big sound system. Since this was a place for music and for presenting it, a sound system was what I spent my money on."

The reason musicians like it so much is that the monitor system is the best anywhere. Nowhere can they hear what they play better.

Jim Carroll: "For a small place it actually has a big-sized stage. It goes back deep, and when I was playing there, I realized that I had played in theaters that didn't have stage monitors that good. Because you have the side monitors right there. The front monitors are never as important as the ones on the side. And here the side monitors [which are mounted on the walls] are so close. The stage is deep but not that wide, and you can really hear yourself so well."

Soundman Norman Dunn explains the sound system and how it was put in: "There was a lot of liquor involved and a lot of saying to Hilly, 'Come on, you need this, and you need that.' At the time I was designing custom-made sound systems — I did the system at Grand Central Station — so I was experienced in writing specifications and reading between the lines on specifications. As soon as the industry learned that Hilly was in the market to add $5,000 worth of sound equipment, the proposals started coming in. Then after we started reading the proposals I would say, 'Hilly, they want to charge you $15,000 for this and it's a piece of junk.' Meanwhile, Charlie Martin [who then booked bands and worked the sound at CBGB] would have these little meetings with Hilly and a lot of liquor would go down.

"Finally, it was decided: buy an expensive sound system, get a bank to finance it, charge the bands an affordable price to use it so it would be paid for every day and the bands would get a cassette tape of their performances. I designed the system with Mark Morris of the Record Plant on the West Coast. They came in and we went through three months of meetings on what type of console we would use. They wanted a Yamaha

PM 1000 because it's inexpensive. I wanted a Soundcraft Series Mark II because it has the equalization to take the worst-sounding punk rock band and then be able to exemplify and amplify the one good point that would be acceptable to the general public, to really bring out that one little sweet thing that they have, that one individual note, or something.

"The bass cabinets fit into that room in the one vertical space where one is mounted vertically and the other one horizontally. You have three-quarters of an inch clearance. Those bass bins are custom-made for the club, and so are the mid-range bins. You won't find them anywhere else in the world. It was our belief that we should have 115 to 118 dBs with no perceptible distortion. We worked on this until we got a system that could kill a fly. It might be big and heavy, but you only had to hit it once. Each speaker doesn't really have any big excursions on its linear travel, doesn't produce much distortion. You keep the excursion down to a minimum, you have plenty of amplifier power, then you only have to turn it up.

"CBGB's total system facing the house is a combination of a three-way and a four-way system and it's crossed over [at] 250 and 1,000 cycles. Different areas of the club are served by different speakers. In total there are about 38 speakers with 4,500 watts of power. You could almost run an outdoor festival with that. That CBGB is basically shaped like a railroad flat is acoustically its biggest advantage. The good thing about that is that the stage faces the longest dimensions of the room. And Hilly, in his unknown wisdom, hung all those beer signs and other stuff on the ceiling — they break up any hard reflections and any slap from the back wall. It is basically as close to a plane wave tube or a standing wave tube in acoustics as you could possibly get in a room. Because the stage starts out at the full width of the club with the PA totally framing the stage, it decouples the audience area from the stage area by making a picture frame. Then the room goes back for about 25 to 30 feet till the beginning of the bar, where the room gets narrower, and more dense acoustically. For an unaltered, unscientifically set room, it is the best sounding room I have ever heard. Surely in the U.S. there is no other room that through random chance has come anywhere near this."

In 1982, much of the sound system, including the sound board, the amplifiers, preamplifiers and tape decks — just about everything except the speakers, which were bolted down — was stolen. Karen suspects an inside job:

"We had a $100,000 sound system, and what happened was we had a porter, a very, very nice man and he had a landlord he had problems with. He was evicted from his apartment. So Hilly said he could sleep in the storeroom while he was looking for another place to live. But we couldn't keep the security system on when he was there, because it was comprised largely of motion detectors. It was during that time that, early one morning, the locks on the front gates were cut and most of the sound system was stolen. So, somebody inside had to know that the porter was sleeping there and the alarms were off.

"And people who should have been cooperative were not cooperative. We did not want to take it back by force so we tried to arrange something. Somebody had recognized it. But by the time we got there, everything had disappeared. So, they were tipped off too. That was inside, too, because word leaked out that we had located it. But word leaked out inside the club. I don't know if Hilly thinks that, but I do. Who to suspect? I don't know. But it was impossible for someone outside to have that kind of information. Since then, nobody sleeps there and the alarm is on every night. And we've had no problems."

The sound system has since been replaced and is as good as it ever was.

CHAPTER SEVEN

*"When the Dead Boys played, Hilly asked me to take them
out to dinner, just to make sure they didn't have too
much to drink between their two sets."*

— KAREN KRISTAL

They were one of the first bands to play regularly at CBGB. They made three albums for Capitol Records, and in 1977, when Hilly decided to expand his operation, they were the first band he managed. They lived only a few subway stops away from CBGB, but for the Shirts it was a long way to come.

"We were like hicks from Brooklyn, never aspiring to go across the bridge, but we had read about the Mercer Arts Center, which had just crumbled, and the back room at Max's, and we went down to see Patti Smith at CBGB," recalls lead singer Annie Golden. "After the show, we saw Patti as we were piling into our car to leave. We started screaming at her, 'Hey Patti, we thought you were really cool.' I think we startled her because we were so raucous and so excited by what we had just seen. She backed off at first and then she realized we were fellow lunatics, and said, 'Oh, thanks.'

"Then we got this booking. Our friend, who was an artist, went up to

Hilly and said, 'I manage this band from Brooklyn and we'd like to gig here.' There was no audition and no audition tape. Hilly just said, 'Okay.' At this time, we were holed up in Brooklyn, we all had day jobs, and we were rehearsing eight to ten hours into the morning, saving money for equipment. Bands in Manhattan were doing it another way. They were like artists; they were doing minimalist rock and they were starving. But we had this big light show and a big PA, and we brought all this shit in for our debut. Hilly was like, 'If you're too loud, I'm pulling the plug on you, and that's it.' We said, 'Oh, okay, and we turned our amps to the wall and did this so-mellow rock. Then Hilly was like, 'It's the quality of sound, not the quantity of sound.'"

Golden remembers the Shirts' first CBGB gig as being with the Planets, the second with Television and the third with Talking Heads. Hilly says that the first time they played it was an audition with Talking Heads. In any case, Hilly took a liking to this band from across the river. Maybe he liked their sound system: Norman Dunn, who first worked for the Shirts, still does the sound for CBGB sometimes, between producing hardcore bands. Or maybe he liked the band's songs: the Shirts were the most melodic and mainstream of the original CBGB bands. Or maybe he felt that the charismatic lead singer, who managed the neat trick of being able to do a whole set and chew gum at the same time, could become a real star.

In any case, Hilly adopted the band. In rough times, he had some of the band members help him out in his moving business. He booked them regularly and featured them prominently in his festival of unsigned bands. He gave them three cuts on the *Live at CBGB* album. He put them out on tour, and then he got them a record deal with Capitol and a featured role for Annie Golden in the film *Hair*.

"Hilly was the one who took us through the ropes," continues Golden. "We were down there in the Bowery, playing and playing, getting a following and getting notoriety, and he was our mentor. We went to him for advice. And then Hilly offered to take our tapes around. He said: 'If you want me to represent you to record companies, you know I will, and if there is a deal in the works then we'll talk about management. I can't deliver you if I don't have you.' So, we signed for manage-ment, and then we got signed, not to Capitol, but to EMI in London first, where we did our first album. Hilly was my manager when I did *Hair*, too."

"The Shirts had their own charisma, they had a certain energy, they weren't derivative," says Hilly. "I saw the Shirts many times, and I got to like them. I don't remember if they asked me or I asked them, but I started managing them. The one really responsible for getting the Shirts signed was Seymour Stein, who was very responsible for this scene. He was a great talker, very enthusiastic and he wanted to sign the Shirts [to Sire]. He got Nick Mobbs, who was the head of A&R for EMI in London, and he loved them. Ben Edmonds was at Capitol, and he loved them, too; he wanted them on Capitol. They convinced me that was the way it should be. I was also managing Annie; she got the *Hair* role through me. Milos Forman, the director, and members of his staff came down a couple of times looking for certain types for the film. They were looking for a number of people first. They wanted to see Television for a certain type and maybe David Byrne. When they were looking for a girl, I suggested they come down when Orchestra Luna and the Shirts were playing together, and Lauren Hutton and Geraldine Chaplin came by — Milos was away. They saw them and then he saw them three or four times. Then they said, this is it, and Annie kept going for auditions and interviews. There was a dance audition with Twyla Tharp, which she was very worried about. But she did it."

Recording the Shirts' debut album, *The Shirts*, in London and at the same time working on *Hair* became quite an ordeal for Golden, which made the management situation rocky almost from the beginning. "The film ran concurrently with the making of the album," recalls Bar-bara DeMartis, then the Shirts' road manager. "Annie was jetting back and forth on the Concorde to make her movie commitment and also her recording commitment. And she was a real nut case at the time, really a frazzle. And maybe she was not protected. I think that was what began to sour the management situation, but it was a miracle that they got through it all in one piece, because it was just too much."

Even after the album was finished, things remained hectic. "We would be playing CBGB while filming *Hair* at Central Park," recalls Golden. "We would be shooting at night and I would have a gig. Milos would call a break, give me a car and a production assistant, who would drive me to the Bowery. I'd trash up my heavy makeup a bit, do a set, go on for encores, while the production assistant would be watching the clock. He'd say, 'Take the encore,' and then he'd come back, hand me my coat and say, 'That's it.' We would go back to the park, everybody would have had dinner, they'd resume shooting, and Milos would begin by asking, 'How many encores?' He was a real Shirts fan."

Unfortunately, there were not that many other Shirts fans out there, and the band, despite three albums and a gallant try, never really had any great popular success. The record company lost interest, the press never really adopted the band, and by 1978–79 the radio backlash against new wave was already in full force. Album-rock (AOR) radio consultants and programmers actively blacklisted new wave until the Knack's "My Sharona" in 1979 and Blondie's "Call Me" in 1980 broke through on pop radio. And the Shirts were identified as a "CBGB band," which at the time almost automatically disqualified them from radio play.

Even though there was also a lot of pressure on Annie Golden to go solo and concentrate more on a film career, the Shirts hung together and kept Hilly as their manager until 1980. They did not finally break up until 1983. Since then, Golden has appeared on Broadway and TV.

"I always felt that the Shirts were a band that could go very far," says Hilly. "When the Shirts were hot they were very hot, and they were hot a lot. They were a great live band — and there have been many great live bands here — and their first album was very strong. There were six people in that band and all of them wrote music. But the New York press didn't like them at all. They said they were a garage band from Brooklyn. Meanwhile, Ben Edmonds, who had signed them to Capitol, left the company, and then Capitol was not interested in the Shirts. It is hard for an East Coast band to make it at Capitol. Now they have an East Coast company here, but it is still hard to make it in a company with a regional West Coast base."

"We got involved with Capitol in New York, and New York was really behind us, but they are not the headquarters, Los Angeles is," says Golden. "So we went across country; Hilly helped us finance this ourselves. Capitol didn't want to give us any tour support, so we went across the country in a van by ourselves and we also went to Europe when Hilly was our manager. We had a hit in Holland, so we went there. We did lots of promotion, lots of television, cover girl centerfolds and posters. Very poppish stuff. Meanwhile, Holland didn't want to know about Blondie or Debbie Harry. But in London they hated us and said I was a rip-off of Debbie Harry. In Holland they didn't want Blondie; in England they didn't want us. Strange who gets where first."

"In Holland we did an ad for a chewing gum manufacturer and had a couple of hits," continues Hilly. "We did a tour before the third album of Portugal, France and Holland. Portugal paid an enormous amount of money. It was eight or nine gigs. It cost about $35,000 to do the tour and we made $30,000, so there was a slight loss to EMI, who put up tour support. But at the time Annie's father was dying. So, it was a very nerve-wracking thing for everybody. But we did it.

"Then the Shirts started getting pulled from many different directions. After the third album was over, I got a letter from their lawyer saying they didn't want me to manage them any longer. They looked for other managers who promised them the world. But they never got anything."

"The Shirts were one of Hilly's first projects, and maybe he could have known more, maybe he could have been advised better," says Barbara DeMartis. "We couldn't speak for ourselves; we left everything to Hilly, and I suppose he did the best he could. He certainly cared about the band a lot, so I can't say anything bad about Hilly, because he really did care."

"I think we did one gig at CBGB after 1980," says Golden. "It was a showcase after the contract with Capitol ended, so it was about 1981. Hilly did a really nice night for us. He wasn't managing us anymore, but he just did it. He opened up his club and our lawyer called the record company people, and it was a really nice audition."

The Shirts never did get another major record deal. But for all the trials and never-paid bar bills, the Shirts were never anything like the Dead Boys, Hilly's next foray into management.

"Actually, I was the one who got the Dead Boys a job at CBGB," says Joey Ramone. "We had played Youngstown, Ohio, and that is where I met [singer] Stiv Bators for the first time. We didn't know how to get back to Cleveland, so he said, 'Follow us.' They were driving 90 miles per hour and we were following them. Then, all of a sudden, Bators climbed out the driver's side window — and he's still driving at 90 miles per hour. Then he mooned us, and I thought that was very impressive. I had never actually seen them play, but I went to Hilly and got them a job there for a Sunday night [in August 1976]. I told people about them, and they were great. They became sort of the CBGB house band, Hilly became their manager, and they got signed to Sire Records."

It didn't take long for the Dead Boys to establish themselves at CBGB. Their musical abilities were never that well developed, but — after the Ramones — they were probably the most energetic band ever to play at CBGB, and they certainly had the most dynamic show. Stiv Bators, who later led the Lords of the New Church, would regularly toss his microphone over one of the braces above the stage then wrap the microphone cord around his neck and hoist himself up. Sometimes staffers wondered if they would have to cut him down.

"Stiv would sometimes hang himself onstage. That was real," says Connie Barrett. "And sometimes it would take several seconds before he would get up. I would watch for it in case he would need help. Sometimes it was too many seconds. He didn't bounce up right away. That was a bit bizarre. One night, Stiv pissed in Merv's hardhat. Stiv was onstage, some-one grabbed the hat, passed it on to him, and he pissed in it. Then he handed it back to Merv. Merv wore the hat again, so I guess he dumped the piss out and washed it. It was a sign of love, I'm sure."

A few years ago, Bators developed tennis elbow from banging his fist or the microphone on the stage floor. Hilly says often the major (but not the only) expense with the band was having to replace microphones after the show. The band would make $500, and then $300 would go for mikes.

"I thought the Dead Boys were great, one of the best live bands I had ever seen," says Hilly. "I did some tapes of them, and as I listened back to the tapes I could hear it was a wonderful group. They were very well-behaved in the beginning, they spoke well and I had no inkling of what they would become. They did their first album very quickly; they were prepared, and they did a good job. They were getting wilder and wilder, and [guitarist] Cheetah Chrome was a little bit of a problem, but not really. Everything was fine."

From a management point of view, everything did not remain fine for long. When, in April 1977, the Damned became the first English punk band to play in the U.S., debuting at CBGB, the Dead Boys opened for them. And for many observers, including this one, the Dead Boys just blew the Damned right off the stage.

"The second show I reviewed at CBGB was the Damned and Dead Boys," says Roy Trakin. "I remember being less impressed with the Damned than with the Dead Boys. I thought the Dead Boys were the greatest thing since Iggy Pop and the New York Dolls, while the Damned were a pale imitation of the Dolls. 'Gee, is this the English punk scene?' I asked myself. 'We're ten times better than this, ten times more interesting.'"

The Clevelanders rapidly became a CBGB favorite. As their critical and popular acclaim grew, the Dead Boys started believing their own hype, and started to live out their version of the rock and roll dream. "The Dead Boys were one of the best of all rock and roll groups, but they were their own worst enemies," says former night manager Bill Shumaker. "The funny thing about the Dead Boys is that they were all ex-altar boys, so I could be there with my wife, and Cheetah, who was the crazy one, would come up and have this polite five-minute conversation with us, just as his mother had taught him to have with the slightly older woman next door. Here's this guy with his dog collar and orange hair, having the most polite conversation, not quite how's the weather, but close to that. Then he would go off and be Cheetah Chrome. They were young kids, and suddenly they were thrown into this world and they were expected to live up to certain kinds of expectations. They had heard and read about what rock stars were supposed to do, and whether it was true or not, they tried to do it."

One person who lived the Dead Boys story was Jim Sliman, who grew up with them in Cleveland, went to New York with them and was their road manager through most of their career. He tells his version of what happened:

"I had hung out with the New York Dolls when they came to Cleveland, and I went with them through four or five cities, like a groupie or whatever. So, they invited us all, a group of us from Ohio, to New York for the July 4th, 1976 bicentennial. We came up and spent much of the weekend at Max's. Stiv [Bators] was one of those who came along. It was his first time in New York. He totally worshipped Johnny Thunders and was all over the guy like a cheap suit. Then we went back to Ohio, but we came back a couple of times afterwards. While we were here Stiv dropped off a tape with Hilly. He had chatted up Joey Ramone previously and got an audition night.

"We came to New York for the audition night and then stayed around to see Television, but I was so exhausted I fell asleep at the table at CBGB when Television was playing. When we got back to Cleveland, Hilly offered the Dead Boys a regular date. We came up for that and we thought it was great. That was around August of 1976. Then, in September '76, I packed up everything and moved here, before the Dead Boys. I got this apartment on East Ninth Street with this gorgeous girl who knew Arthur Kane of the Dolls. She was a groupie, but a beautiful girl. I moved in with her and Miriam Linna, who was later a drummer for the Cramps. So, I lived there with Miriam for a while and another girl, Pam Blam, whose brother Gregory was with the Cramps. And around December, the Dead Boys came up and they had nowhere to stay so I offered them my place. After they did so well at their first couple of dates at CBGB, Hilly offered them a management contract. They stayed at the apartment with me and Miriam and Pam, and around January, because they had signed with Hilly, they all moved here.

"Then Hilly said, 'Look, I need someone to take care of these guys.'

He quickly got them signed to Sire and they would be recording soon and they would be on tour, and Hilly didn't know what was going on. So, he hired me and part of it was he paid my rent. The Dead Boys moved in, which I regretted later. It was a two-level apartment, and I had the master bedroom. Many people came and went at that apartment. The Dead Boys lived there and whatever roadies were working for them at the time, usually two guys from Ohio. And my friend Michael Sticca, who was working for Blondie, wound up living there, too.

"So Hilly started paying me to be their tour manager, though they weren't on tour yet. He signed them to Sire and Genya Ravan came in to produce their first album. The album is actually pretty good. We all lived together in that one place as the first album was recorded at Electric Lady in February 1977. Hilly would come in after the club was closed at night and fall asleep at Electric Lady. Hilly was sometimes really cool to me and sometimes he was a real prick. It was really hard because there was no money. The advance money was used to buy equipment. There were times when I started with the Dead Boys that the band made so little money that we had to live on Karen Kristal's famous chili. We would steal the hamburger meat and take it back to Ninth Street.

"When the album came out, the Dead Boys were suddenly the rage. The press loved them, gobbled them up and spit them out later. Whenever the Dead Boys played, the crowds grew and grew. CBGB was packed to the rafters. People would hang from the pipes. We decided to go on a mini tour, up to Boston and elsewhere in the northeast, and then we went on a heavy tour. This was before the serious record company depression hit. And Sire was pretty cool with the money. But our neighbors on Ninth Street started to get suspicious because we were all living in this one place. We took our trip to Boston and the apartment got hit. It got robbed. They took guitars and money and all my camera equipment. At the time I was still wearing platform shoes and all the Dead Boys would make fun of them. And when the thieves came in, they took everything except my platform shoes.

"The Ramones and all the other bands were like one big happy family, and when we weren't on tour, when we were not doing shows, we would hang around CBGB till five or six in the morning. The Dead Boys had an open tab at the bar because Hilly was managing them. They were always big drinkers, and it got to the point that whoever was with us, friends or whoever, would get free drinks. The bartenders couldn't do anything about it. Whenever I had a few nights off from the band I would tend bar at CBGB. Everybody knew that James was bartending that night and everybody from Blondie, the Dead Boys, the Ramones and the Dictators and others would come down and everybody would get drunk for free.

"I went to L.A. at the time and when I came back two days later to the apartment on Ninth Street everybody from every band at the time and all their hangers-on and their girls were at that apartment. It was on the sixth floor, and above that was the roof, where the party was. In my bedroom, the master bedroom, Cheetah had all the umbrellas up, and people were getting blow jobs. The place was ransacked. This party happened the same night that this girl got covered in whipped cream and gave Stiv a blow job onstage at CBGB. She wanted to crawl into a hole. To this day, if you bring it up, she'll hop on a plane to get out," says Sliman.

Not exactly. The woman in question remembers: "It was one night when Genya Ravan was producing their first album. Genya and I are friends. We would talk on the phone and we had a good rapport. At the time I was very, very drunk and she wanted something spectacular to happen onstage. She wanted somebody to go up onstage with whipped cream tits to surprise the boys at the very end of the set. She's saying to me, she's egging me on, 'Do you know anybody with balls enough to do it, do you know anybody who would just get up there with whipped cream?'

"'Genya,' I said, 'I don't think I could do it.' She said, 'Have another Jack Daniels.' Other people say it was Southern Comfort. She was giving me glasses filled up to here. I must have had three or four. Finally, the woman talked me into it. It was 'please' and 'come on, you can do it,' 'you've got the balls,' 'you're the girl.' She dragged me into a dressing room, took off my shirt and somehow she managed to get a can of whipped cream. And she proceeded to decorate me. At the appropriate time Genya pushed me onstage and — I don't have much memory of this, because I was gone, I was on cloud nine, never-never land — I was onstage, pushed onstage, and I landed on my knees, head back, and Steve [Stiv Bators] started having his way with me. I'm pushed back in a very compromising position, as I said, on my knees. The next thing I know he is pulling down his fly. Now people say I gave him head onstage, but I don't believe it. I know Gene [Cheetah Chrome] was having a wild time, and everybody was enjoying it, but Genya got freaked. She immediately told the roadie to pull me offstage, and I did get pulled off. Because she realized that she had gone too far. She was the producer, she was having a good time, and even though there were probably only 20 people who saw this, it turned into something that was too much. Steve was getting a little too carried away. That's the story."

"A couple of other times Stiv would get some girls up onstage and get pretty wild," explains Sliman. "When he was up there, he was a different person. And when I was at the shows, I had to deal with that. I have been on the road with a lot of other bands, including the Heartbreakers, Squeeze, Blondie and X-Ray Spex. But there was nothing like being on the road with the Dead Boys. I literally got tied down by hotel managers, local police sergeants. Because the Dead Boys would trash hotels. We got blacklisted from hotels. Cheetah and Stiv would run around naked in hotel corridors. There were problems with young girls in various cities. I grew up pretty fast. I was only 19 then. I don't think anybody has been a road manager at 19. After a show, the band would do all their business and I would light up a joint to cool out or whatever, count the money, do the paperwork, make a few phone calls and then go to bed. And then two hours later I would get phone calls: this happened or that happened. Get up, there is trouble. So being on the road with them was really an ordeal.

"The Dead Boys were considered hip to hang out with and see. A lot of famous people would come see them. So, a lot of times after the shows, if we were in San Francisco, L.A. or Chicago, I would arrange parties and people would come and have fun. At Swingo's Hotel in Cleveland, the Dead Boys did much damage. Cleveland was their hometown, so when they hit town it was all the families, the relatives, friends, the press. But they did so much damage that I knew something would happen, and by eight in the morning old man Swingo hauled me up — it turns out that he knows my mother and he said, 'Mr. Sliman (I was 19, and he was calling me Mr. Sliman), please meet me down at the lounge in about half an hour.' And he had a list of damages, about $2,800. At the time we were on a shoestring budget. And it was like 'Pay this money or you guys are not getting out of this hotel.' So, I had to call Hilly right away. He wired the money, and I took care of it. But it was all on me. What really got me out of it was that he knew my mother.

"There was a brief hiatus after the first tour and we came back to New York and pretty much hung around until the band got really, really edgy. They played CBGB again and the whole thing clicked fabulously, with the press and everything. Talk about a show. The place was packed to the rafters and the band was really great. Then it came time to go to England. There wasn't much money, but Hilly paid for me to go with them. I had to hook up with the band in Liverpool. This was the Damned/Dead Boys tour. We got back to the U.S. in December 1977 and right after that Hilly sent us all back to Ohio for Christmas. There was a local studio in Ohio where the band did some early tracks for the second album. We came back and did a big weekend at CBGB. Hilly would book them for Thursday, Friday and Saturday. Shortly after that, they decided on Felix Pappalardi as the producer on the second album. Sire arranged for the big bucks and everything, and they booked this terrible hotel in downtown Miami sight unseen. We got there and it was terribly depressing. We stayed at this first hotel for two hours and then I found this other hotel, on Biscayne Boulevard. It was a real cool place. Hookers if you wanted them.

"We rented a couple of station wagons and started our experience with Pappalardi. The album was recorded at Criteria. Andy Gibb and some of the Bee Gees and the Outlaws were there. It was a higher budget than the first album. I was there pretty much to oversee everything.

"Back in New York after the second album, there was this period of limbo before it was released. So Hilly had them do a few days at CBGB, and then up to Boston and Toronto. Then we came back for the second tour and things started to fall apart. It was the second major tour of America. After about the first three or four months they hated Hilly's guts. They were always complaining about him. And, of course, I had to take much of the complaining because they had nobody else to complain to. They wanted to be treated like stars. They got a lot of press and celebrities came to see shows, so they felt like stars, but they weren't. They should have been a lot more practical. Things went too fast and they couldn't deal with it. Another year and a half and they would have had it. A lot of fights started between the band members. They wouldn't agree with each other's girlfriends or each other's habits or stage presence or the way they played. There were a lot of inter-band fights. There were some things with [guitarist] Jimmy Zero wanting more of a spotlight. He wanted to be more like a Paul McCartney. Stiv was getting the whole spotlight. There were a lot of problems.

"The band really hated Hilly at the end and they blamed me for a lot. They said I was his yes-man and all that shit. We had a couple of fights, real fights, one or two physical, especially with [drummer] Johnny Blitz, who hated my guts. He loved me and then he hated me. A very weird relationship."

"And there was the stabbing incident. I get a call at five in the morning from Stiv saying Johnny had been stabbed, and Michael [Sticca] had been stabbed, both of them. Two minutes later, Michael comes into my room, blood on his hand. What happened was that Michael was out with his girl Marsha, who used to go out with the Heartbreakers. And Johnny was out with this girl Danielle. They went to a deli on Second Avenue and First Street. Michael walked out of the place and these five Puerto Ricans drove by and yelled something at Michael. Marsha, with her big mouth, yelled something back. And they jumped out of the car and ran after Michael. Marsha ran into the deli to get Johnny. Johnny comes out to help Michael, and there are these eight Spanish guys who attacked Michael and Johnny with their chains. Michael pulled out his knife. Johnny got stabbed. Michael, trying to help him, stabbed a guy a couple of times.

"I got called because they didn't want to call Hilly. Then I called Hilly, and me and Michael and Hilly went down to the police station. Johnny, of course, was already in the hospital. None of the other Dead Boys were really involved. It was just Michael and Johnny Blitz. But at the police station they arrested Michael, because Michael had to say what he did, and he did stab somebody. Johnny nearly died. Michael was sent to jail at Rikers Island. This was at the end of my commitment to the Dead Boys and I had a commitment to meet Blondie in L.A. Blondie was going to play the Starwood and I could make some money. Michael accused me of deserting him while he was on Rikers Island and Jimmy didn't know what was going on.

"And then real quickly we put together the Blitz benefit [at CBGB]. It was for three days. Because of Blitz, a lot of people called to play at the benefit. John Belushi played drums, and a lot of people got up there to collaborate on the spur of the moment. It was my part that they had a concession in front of CBGB where they sold buttons and T-shirts, flyers and posters. And all the money was to go to the Johnny Blitz legal and medical fund. Michael Sticca never saw a dime of it. And he was the guy who risked his life in the knife fight. Sticca's father was the one who paid for him. Hilly hired the Hell's Angels' lawyer to help Johnny, who lost about thirty pounds because of this. And then he left the rock and roll business. He played drums again on a couple of gigs but he was never the same.

"After that I went to Cleveland and we had a Blitz benefit there. A lot of Cleveland bands came down and played there. And that was about the end of it. It was a very emotional period. For a while the Dead Boys had a mini tour with Iggy Pop. It was like four cities. I had met Iggy earlier when I lived in L.A., but for Stiv Bators it was a heavy gig. Iggy was his idol. One of the opening dates was at Cleveland and we again stayed at Swingo's. It was the first time Stiv had met Iggy in his life. So, me and Stiv, one of the roadies, Iggy and his girlfriend at the time all went to this Chinese restaurant in Cleveland. And Stiv could not deal with being at the same dinner table with his idol. There is that famous story of how Stiv rubbed peanut butter all over himself in the front row at a Stooges concert. And Iggy was such a raunchy motherfucker; he still is. Stiv had promised Iggy some Quaaludes. Stiv passed out in the restaurant. We got back to the hotel and Stiv passed out again. I put him on his bed and Iggy started going through Stiv's suitcases. I said, 'What are you doing? What are you looking for? Don't go looking through his fucking suitcases.'

"'He said the Quaaludes were in his suitcase, and he promised them to me.' He comes to my room and I throw the 'ludes at him. 'You want those fucking things? Take them.' He took advantage of this poor little scrawny weasel. Talk about bursting your bubble. Your idol, right?"

Says Hilly: "After Johnny Blitz got back they still did some things. The end of the band as far as I was concerned was after the second album, when Sire didn't renew the contract. They wanted maybe Stiv and Jimmy Zero, but we could never come to anything. And the Dead Boys were a little upset with the whole thing. They felt they didn't get a decent break. In fact, they were built bigger than life. I got them in *Time* and *Newsweek* and other major magazines all over the place. Video people came down; I used to do videos on them. Wherever they went, I promoted them with videos. It's a shame that Johnny didn't realize how messed up he was. Johnny and Cheetah were the worst. Stiv used one against the other. It was rough, because the whole group was unstable. Although it was a big financial loss, a very big loss, it was a relief not to see them anymore. I was kind of happy for that. They were getting very obnoxious."

CHAPTER EIGHT

"When you are a part of something it can be difficult to realize
how big it has become. You get caught up in it.
People look from the outside and say, 'My God, this is a
real happening place.' But you don't feel it happening at all.
You are too busy sweeping the floors."

— HILLY KRISTAL

If 1967 was the summer of love in rock and roll, with a sea change in music coming from the hippies in San Francisco, then 1977 was the year of punk, with Great Britain at the center of a whole new approach towards pop music. What was a bud at CBGB bloomed to full (if tattered) flower across the Atlantic. Suddenly there were the Clash and the Sex Pistols, the Jam and Sham 69, the Stranglers and the Vibrators. There was all this rude and crude noise, the musicians and audiences alike in black leathers, spikes and studs, pogoing to a new and strident beat.

"There is no doubt that punk originated in New York, though the English press elected to lay claim to everything," says Marty Thau. "I think the Dolls have to get more credit than they have gotten. The Dolls really originated all the ideas that became the Sex Pistols. Malcolm McLaren [who managed the Dolls after Thau], my haberdasher in London, is very fashion-oriented, and he spotted Richard Hell's style and in the Sex Pistols he put that style together with the Dolls' energy.

The Ramones were very much influenced by the Dolls, and so was the Clash. In that whole period I would guess that the great influences were the Dolls, Television, the Ramones, Talking Heads, Patti Smith and Blondie. Those six bands. We all used to marvel how they all happened in this small three-mile radius, with CBGB in the center."

"When Malcolm McLaren was in New York he used to sell rubber clothes, these outfits made all out of rubber, from the back of his car. One of my girlfriends wore one of his full outfits, and she was told she looked like a scumbag walking down the street. I think Malcolm wanted Jerry Hall to model them," recalls rock celebrity journalist Liz Derringer.

Not too successful with either the Dolls or car-trunk fashions, the irrepressible McLaren, a grown-up imp if ever there was one, took his Alice Cooper/New York Dolls/Richard Hell influences back to London, starting a clothing store there called Sex, selling equally outrageous outfits. Then, when semi-musicians Johnny Rotten, Paul Cook, Sid Vicious and Steve Jones (as well as Glen Matlock, briefly) began to hang around his store, McLaren seized his opportunity and created the Sex Pistols, whose nearly incoherent but razor-sharp rock and roll — and genius for self-promotion — made them virtually overnight stars in Britain. They were thrown out of A&M and EMI Records for insulting and attacking staffers, they cursed on the BBC, they sneered at the Queen of England in "God Save the Queen," which created a furor and was banned, and they became instant rock and roll legends.

In this country, Warner Bros. Records released their definitive and only studio album, *Never Mind the Bollocks, Here's the Sex Pistols*, to a generally lukewarm critical reception and no airplay beyond college stations. The album was a bust, it seemed, and within a year Warner deleted the album from its catalog, much to its subsequent embarrassment as the cut-rate priced LPs were snapped up by exporters who could sell them at a premium in Europe. Warner had to sheepishly re-embrace the record, and it has remained a steady seller ever since. It has also weathered very well. A *Rolling Stone* critics' poll in the summer of 1987 put the album second only to the Beatles' *Sgt. Pepper's Lonely Hearts Club Band* among all-time great LPs.

What the Sex Pistols and the English punk scene did was focus attention on the whole new wave/punk phenomenon, not always to CBGB's benefit. The more visual, more outspoken, more controversial English groups, and their safety-pin-through-the-cheek fans in England, in effect stole the media thunder from the more introspective, apolitical and generally less showy bands at CBGB. New wave may have started in New York, but it was the Londoners who gave it fashion and flash.

"When it got to England, it became rigid in a certain way," says Lenny Kaye. "It became very fashion-conscious. Bands [at CBGB] were originally anti-fashion. It was our way, and we didn't think of it as a style. As to the clothes we wore, I really didn't change outfits when I went onstage, so it was not so much anti-fashionable as a-fashionable. The emphasis wasn't on the look, the emphasis was on the content. It was a reaction to the glitter look, but it was also an evolvement from it in a certain way. There was a kind of androgyny and an ability to deal with topics outside the moon-June aspects of rock and roll. Glitter also gave us a literary basis. The Dolls were artistically intellectual as well as being outrageous in certain ways.

"But when it got to England — and I don't put it down, I like fashion as much as anybody — it got a look to go along with it. Along with that look, it got a certain style of punk rock, which meant a Hydra-headed thing became just one certain thing. Patti would always say that we didn't want to have bands come out to look like us. We wanted bands to come out to keep going the next generation of rock and roll. This was at a time when rock and roll might not have continued, when it might have been absorbed into the mainstream. We served as a kind of catalyst to get people moving again. I remember, on our first tour, the *Horses* tour, how messianic kids viewed our coming. There were underground kids in every city. And they didn't have anything else to go to. They would go see Lou Reed, Iggy Pop and the Dolls, and out of that would grow an underground movement that would be called new wave. It was really exciting."

Exciting it was, but in 1977, as in 1978, 1979, 1980 and even beyond in the U.S., new wave and punk were still very much the underground, with the occasional exception like Blondie or Talking Heads later. In

England, relatively lively radio, and an even livelier press writing about the music of a disenchanted youth lost amid economic stagnation, allowed punk and new wave to flourish. In the U.S., all this was a curiosity item on the evening news at best. But even that had repercussions at CBGB, because reporters from the news broadcast networks and the print media would come down to check out the American version of this violent punk rock they were hearing about from London. It was a meeting of two cultures, one looking for sensation, the other trying to maintain at least a measure of musical integrity.

"The press and photographers used to hang out a lot here; there were so many I couldn't keep track of them," says Hilly. "In later years, the TV networks got interested. All three networks came down, as well as the local people. It was this punk thing. We had *Time* magazine, *Us* and *People*. We had *McLeans* from Canada. The Japanese were down here early. And we had a lot of French press and all the English press. We had the Dutch. It was the only thing that was happening. I think the scene was made to look bigger than it was, and the further away you were from it, the bigger a scene it seemed to be. And this was the nucleus."

Cosmo Ohms: "I remember a funny incident. The Dead Boys, who had just been signed to Sire, had just finished a set and they were really hot. One of the major networks — NBC, CBS or ABC — came down to interview Stiv Bators. And there was Stiv, just off the stage, in his leathers and torn T-shirt, sweat dripping down, soaked to the bone, and here was this proper seven o'clock news interviewer coming down to see what's going on with this punk rock stuff.

"She's saying, 'Is it really violent? Is there something that people see in you that perpetrates violence?' And he's saying 'No, this has nothing to do with violence; we are giving people an outlet. We play unabashed rock and roll, and it's a release.' And this woman says, 'Is this really a statement on perverse sexuality? Is this violent eroticism? I see a lot of girls get excited during your performance.' And Stiv says, 'Well I don't think it's so much that, it's . . . And then suddenly some kids behind him, on camera, started yelling, 'Hey Stiv, don't let her give you a blow job.' That sort of put a cap on that.

"Another time, a camera crew came in to interview Hilly. The night before, some maniac had come into the club and out of nowhere punched Hilly in the eye. Boom. So Hilly has a black eye and is wearing sunglasses. He's got on his cut-off plaid jacket, muscles bulging, blue jeans and boots, his hair puffed out. He's sitting on a bar stool, underneath the graffiti. And this interviewer asks, 'What is this phenomenon on the Bowery, what is punk rock?' as if he's expecting a dictionary definition of punk rock or something. Hilly, bulging muscles, dark glasses, leans down to him and growls, 'Punk rock, what is punk rock? You tell me what is punk rock.' He was almost menacing to the guy. It was perfect for the moment."

Hilly may never have been very certain as to what punk rock or new wave were (he liked the term "street music"), but mostly he was very obliging to the press. And though most of America could have cared less about this new music and some, like Linda Ronstadt, ran out the door after ten minutes of the Ramones at CBGB, there were enough fans in the New York area to turn his club into a very happening place. Also, new American bands from outside New York, like Devo, the B-52s, Pere Ubu, the Runaways, Tom Petty, the Cars and others would play the club. From England first came the Damned, soon followed by the Jam, Squeeze, X-Ray Spex, the Police and even [from Australia] AC/DC.

In no particular order, some of the bands that played at CBGB during the summer of '77 were: Slander Band, Sic F*cks, Steel Tips, Tumbleweed, Nervous Eaters, Walter Steding, Mozart's People, Rudies, WOW II, Blondie, Suicide, Elephant's Memory, Alex Chilton, Shooting Stars, Screamin' Jay Hawkins, Shirts, Hounds, Revolver, Avenger, Talking Heads, Laughing Dogs, Sun, Willie Alexander, Mumps, Paul Starfield and the Mutant Kings, Rousers, Just Water, Raver, Spicy Bits, Gary Wilson, Dead Boys, Thundertrain, Plants, DMZ, Roger Bruce Band, Travin, Aalon, Chris Stamey, Stumblebunny, Peter Tork, Machine Suicide, Boyfriends, Feelies, L.O.K., Manster, Uncle Son, Rubber City Rebels, Mars, Bitch, Eddie Paul and the Make, Spit, Kieran Liscoe, Cramps, Viletones, Diodes, Teenage Head, Cryers, Dorien Zero, Fuse, Public Problems, Jasper Hooks, Dirty Looks, Criminals, China and Richard Hell.

A lot of these bands were from the New York area, but as CBGB became known as a mecca for new music, bands would come from all over. Willie Alexander, Thundertrain and DMZ were from in and around Boston; the Hounds were a Chicago band; Rubber City Rebels, obviously, were from Akron; the Viletones, Diodes and Teenage Head were all Canadians. The first mention of the Police in the U.S. was in a CBGB ad for a show on July 17, 1977: they were on the bottom of the bill for a "special showcase" by [the band] Sun. Preceding them were Eddie Paul and the Make and Spit.

Roy Trakin: "I came in one night to see this English band that came in very unheralded and with no record company fanfare. Everybody was suspicious of them because their hair was peroxided. They just had a single out and the place was absolutely empty. I was fairly unimpressed until they hit one song, which I said was a good song, and that song was 'Roxanne.' It was the Police. The applause was tepid, and there could not have been more than ten people in the place, but that was the beauty of it. A band could come in there like that, and you could never know. For that moment they were the best thing in the world, and that was the beauty of CBGB, crystalized, so to speak, Hilly Kristalized."

"With English groups you soon realized that you had to see them on their first night in town," recalls Bill Shumaker. "Almost always they had immigration problems getting in, so sometimes they wouldn't show, but when they did, they had been up for at least two nights, dealing with all sorts of hassles. Then they would get onstage and on the first night they would really stretch out. They would be great. Then on the second night they would just lose it. Once they had gone to bed and slept they just couldn't get back on."

CBGB was in full flower. "I would go there every Friday and Saturday night to make sure nothing was going on that was illegal," Karen Kristal recalls. "I just couldn't trust the hired help to watch over the things that I was concerned about, like marijuana and cocaine. I would go around sniffing. I learned what pot smelled like, a very sickening odor, and if I caught a whiff of it, I could locate it. I didn't even have to smell it. I could tell in a darkened room, the way one person would hand a joint to another. You don't smoke cigarettes that way. And sure enough. I would go over and sometimes risk my own neck. In those days I was not as wise and subdued as I am now. Now I'd call an employee and say that somebody has a joint. But then I would just go and lift it out of their fingers."

But Karen could not see everything. "The girls' bathroom was amazing," remembers Handsome Dick Manitoba. "The guys' bathroom was just as terrible. I remember getting high in the bathroom, locking myself in the bathroom stall, doing various sexual things. You could always see four feet in the stalls. There was always something going on. It was that time of life when you were turning into an adult but still running on teenage fuel. And anything goes."

And did. "Sex and rock and roll, they always go together. The lighting booth was built to hold two people, and only two people. You close the curtain and you could rock and roll," recalls Cosmo Ohms. "And the bathrooms. They had a rating system in the girls' bathroom. Everybody was rated by their ability to play guitar, offstage as well as on. Television, the Ramones, Tuff Darts, Mink DeVille, the Dead Boys, they were all rated, and sometimes actually tested between sets."

"There was this woman who was dating Dee Dee Ramone at the time, her name was Connie and she was sort of a pathetic character, usually pretty wasted and pretty stoned on something or other," remembers Barbara DeMartis. "And then there was this other woman named Robin who befriended Dee Dee. I don't think there was anything romantic, but she was showing Dee Dee that there were other women in the world who weren't always teetering on their high heels, stoned out of their minds. I guess Connie was jealous of Robin and she started to attack her with one of the beer pitchers at CBGB. I was tending bar that night and I saw that Robin wasn't lifting a hand to her defense. Connie was just beating the shit out of her with this beer pitcher and though it was not full and made of plastic, she was still getting hurt. I was screaming at Connie to cut it out, and finally I ended up jumping over the bar. I just pushed her slightly and Connie fell over on the ground like a leaf. She was wearing these heels and she was stoned. She was down and I felt like shit because I had never hit anybody in my life, let alone knocked them to the ground. But Connie was always getting herself involved in some kind of scene or other; she would just follow Dee Dee around and pick on other girls, have cat fights in the bathrooms."

"There were a hell of a lot of times when there were fights that the bathroom walls actually got knocked down," says Maureen Nelly. "Dee Dee Ramone and his girlfriend Connie would be constantly going at it. This is history, what is written on the bathroom walls."

"The graffiti started in the bathrooms upstairs and then moved downstairs," explains Hilly. "I could see on the sex chart that it was always somebody from the Dead Boys or the Ramones in the lead. It was in the ladies' room so the girls would know. I don't think they rated me; it was for the kids. The sex chart was up there for a good three or four years, and then it was written over or spray painted over. There was a constant change in graffiti. That is what the walls are for. That's the decoration. Now it is not as nice as it used to be. They used to use a lot of marking pens and that was better than spray paint because everybody had their own design. Spray paint takes away a lot of individuality. But I never saw anybody do graffiti. They didn't do it in front of me."

Probably what did the most to end the sex chart graffiti was the change in the club from a small venue with an in-crowd that could pass around in-jokes on bathroom walls to a place for the casual fan or tourist. "The scene is not so underground anymore," explains ex-CBGB booking agent Carol Costa. "It doesn't have the same sort of romanticism about it anymore. So, it's not so big a deal. It was also a smaller scene then and it disappeared."

A much wider range of people were coming into the club by late 1977, but due to its own particular ambience and security system, CBGB always remained a fairly secure place. Explains Tish of Snooky and Tish: "We never had any real problems at CBGB, though one night we were doing our Chocolettes number with the Sic F*cks, doing the Supremes in blackface. We were opening for the Cramps. I was standing by the side of the stage in my Chocolette drag and this guy kept putting his hand on my ass. First, I thought it was just coincidence and he was brushing past me or something. But after the third or fourth time I realized he was just doing it. So, I took him by the collar and threw him into the set of drums. Security came and carted him away as he was screaming, 'I'll remember you, I'll remember your face.' But I was in blackface so that didn't threaten me too much. That was the only time I had any trouble there. It is actually a tame crowd at CBGB. If you play before a college crowd, or where they are very frustrated and their lives are so straight that they can only do outrageous stuff if they are really bombed, then those are the crowds you get into trouble with."

Sometimes the biggest problems came from the acts themselves. Cosmo Ohms remembers: "Hilly used to let just about anybody play. Anyone could get a shot. There was this one guy, this magician, who was into black magic and fire rituals. He brought this band in there and they were kind of jamming around, a real New York jam with congas and bongos and saxes and guitars and synthesizers, with everything kind of out of tune. And this guy is going through his black magic ritual. He's preparing these magnesium mixtures and throwing them out into the crowd. He's tossing javelins, real spears, at the wall. It was looking like this guy was genuinely getting out of control.

"Charlie Martin saw this going on and he tells me to get a bucket of water. 'Look,' he says, 'stand by the side of the stage and if I say go, just douse the stage and don't worry about it. The electric amps and all, just put them out.' Meanwhile the guy on stage is raising the devil. He was throwing fucking sparklers at the audience and firecrackers. It was getting to be real dangerous. The place was filling up with smoke. Suddenly, through the clouds, Hilly appears, beer mug in hand. It was the only time I saw him pull a band: 'Stop the show, you're burning my place down. I've seen enough. I've seen enough. Cosmo, throw the water.' It was wild. I had to throw the water. It was well out of hand. Hilly was in complete panic. We had to clear the whole club, open both doors.

"Another time I remember a band getting pulled off the stage was this band from Boston. Hilly used to have these weekends where he would feature all Boston bands. I think the Cars played on one of them. And this one band ended up going on really late, a little shy of three.

They didn't like that, or the production, or the whole thing. They started yelling and screaming at Charlie. The bass player was really getting out of hand. The show started, it went on for about 60 seconds and the guy just finally pissed Charlie off. 'Fuck you,' said Charlie. 'Just pack it in.' He pulled the plug. They were not too enamored with that. And then they got bounced around a bit in the dressing room. I remember jumping on people to stop them from getting creamed. They got out of hand.

"There also used to be this one band from the Bronx. They were really a hard rock and roll band. They were like ex-convicts, skinheads before it was cool to be skinheads. They were skinheads courtesy of the state. They had one little guy, the drummer, who was a real brute. One muscle from head to toe. And they used to come in on the nights they weren't playing and beat up on people. No one liked their music so they weren't booked a lot. A lot of people would get very offended if they didn't get booked; they would threaten to firebomb or call the fire marshal or whatever. But these guys would come in, and they would bloody a whole lot of people, so you needed the deterrent. There were a couple of big people around the scene who were like arbitrators, who were good with their fists," says Cosmo.

There were always the Hell's Angels, of course. Connie Barrett says, "My band had a crazy [fan]. She took out a contract on my life because I wouldn't let her come and bother Sun, the band I was managing, while they were rehearsing. She had two guys from Harlem come down and follow me around. I came out of the house one day and I saw them lounging against a car. And she was standing right there with them. The three of them would follow me around and then she would call me and threaten my life. I live on the same block as the Hell's Angels. So, I went up to the three of them, pointed to all the motorcycles lined up, and said, 'I think you are on the wrong block for what you are trying to do.' Because generally people who worked at the club, at least in those days, had a certain amount of protection. And certainly on that block. The Hell's Angels are not too fond of people coming into their neighborhood and threatening people who live in it."

Most situations were hardly that threatening. Security at CBGB mostly meant controlling the overflow crowds that would come in as the scene grew. Hilly and Merv were both large men, but the club never really relied on bulk. Unlike most rock clubs, CBGB never had huge bouncers in the corners looking for troublemakers. "We hired security people who would try to prevent incidents, not the kind of people who would break arms or legs or bodily throw people out. We wouldn't tolerate goons," says Karen Kristal. Instead, Hilly tried for a certain amount of finesse. "There is a certain way you have to be," he says. "Never take away anybody's manliness. When I go to somebody, unless they are going to hurt somebody, I let them be whatever they want to be. And that's it."

"When they had the Ramones or Patti Smith or some of the other larger bands, the place would get incredibly jammed," remembers Barbara DeMartis. "We'd have two shows a night and clear the house between them. We'd need security because there was no way that people could get to the bathrooms past the stage. And the waitresses couldn't make any money serving drinks. We would have to keep the aisles cleared and it was incredible mayhem. There were nights when it seemed like the place would explode with so many people there. So, they would have the various waitresses and people they trusted doing security. You just had to hold the crowds and let the important people go backstage: managers, technicians or whoever. You just had to know who was who, and that was a big part of it, just keeping your eyes open and getting to know people.

"It was the fire marshals that were a problem. Whenever we had a really big night we would have to shut down for a while. The fire marshals would come over in the front door and they couldn't even move ten feet inside the club because it was so packed. On those nights the club would look like it would explode, like it was moments from doom. But nobody ever got crushed. People fainted a lot and you would have to take them by the back door and let them cool off. I don't think anybody ever got really hurt. People maybe would drink too much or do too many drugs. But nobody ever died, nobody broke an arm. There weren't even that many fights."

"I remember the Fire Department coming in a number of times, especially during Plasmatics concerts, and closing the show down for five or ten minutes just to hassle," says Connie Barrett. "This went on for weeks and weeks, especially on Friday and Saturday nights, when the place was packed. And Merv would have to come down with a flashlight and open the fire boxes and whatever else they wanted to see and the whole show would stop for 10 or 15 minutes until they would just get up and leave. I always felt that it was political. I don't think it had anything to do with anything real. Because they only did it at the height of a show. There was a period of time when they would come in every weekend, but they haven't come in since. They could have done the inspection during the day if they were so damned worried about it. Hilly, as far as I know, never got citations from that period. But it was mainly Merv who got the hassle because Hilly usually wasn't there."

The police come in sometimes too, but since CBGB never was a rowdy place, despite some incidents, and never a druggie place — at least no more so than any other club in town, and probably less so — there never was much call for the police. Relations have always been very good. The Ramones even had a benefit at CBGB to buy the police bulletproof vests. "At the time there were all these cops getting shot down," recalls Joey Ramone. "New York cops are very good, and seeing how they are in other places, they are very decent. They are not out to lock you away for life or to beat the shit out of you like the gestapo in L.A. So, we decided to do something for them, and we did this benefit. It was the first of its kind."

"Cops occasionally come in. They look around, have a drink and leave," continues Barrett. "Maybe they come for the music, because they never cause any hassles. One time a cop came in while I was working there during the afternoon. He said this was his beat, he introduced himself and we never saw him again. The place by now is such an institution. And it's a decent club. It's not a place for sex and drugs. I remember working a gig with the Ramones that was outrageous. They had their own security and a top-drawer road crew. The night they had a benefit to buy bulletproof vests for the police this big dude came up to me with four or five guys behind him and they said, 'We understand you work here and are the back door security. Since you work here and we don't, tell us what you want us to do.' Which was wonderful. Because some fans got to the alley, pulled up a telephone pole, and were using it as a battering ram to try to break down the back doors. Me and seven guys were leaning on the door while it was heaving in time to the music. They rushed at every downbeat. And they scaled the roof. I don't know where they thought they were going from there because there is no way down.

"I felt the best position I could have was back door security," she says. "That was the back door, the bathrooms and dressing rooms, making sure people threw up in the toilets instead of on the stairs. I remember the first New Year's Eve I worked security. John Cale was playing. I was sitting in the chair in back during the set and there was this enormous guy who was very, very drunk and it was obvious that he was going to throw up. Just as he passed the stage, where there was not that much room, he would bounce off one wall and he would throw up and the vomit would hit the other wall. He hit three different walls as he came toward me. I ducked just in time. That was my first gig there.

"If there was going to be a problem, it was usually apparent by 8:30. You would try to spot the kid who was going to give you the problem. Most of the kids didn't. Most of their problems were they would get too drunk and fall down, and then they were in danger of getting stepped on. Or else they became really violent. I was directly responsible to Merv when I worked security, as was everybody else who worked security.

"I remember one thing that happened. This kid was hassling me and he was just so obnoxious. He was bothering Charlie Martin when he was setting up the stage; he was climbing up on the ladder and he was just being a really obnoxious kid. Finally at the end of the night, at four o'clock as we were getting ready to close, I was talking to somebody, and as he was walking out he grabs me and tries to cop a feel. And without even thinking about it, as it was very close to the doors, which swing out as in a Western tavern, I just turned him around, bent him over, and planted my foot in his ass, and he went flying through the door and onto the sidewalk. Merv was standing there and kind of laughed and said to me, 'I would have given you some help but you looked like you were having too much fun.'

"If I wanted somebody moved Merv was terrific. He would say very nicely, I think you need a little air. Our favorite thing, when we had the side doors that used to open (before they were sealed up), was that if we had kids that were getting too drunk or too fucked up, we would open up the doors and just roll them out. We would slam the door and then ten minutes later we would open up and yank them back in. And that's all they needed really. It was just so intense there, so intensely stuffy when there was a crowd. At one point we had one of those velvet ropes between the sound booth and the end of the bar so as to allow only a few people in at a time. And then there was another aisle in front of the sound booth where the waitresses would go through. Plus, people had to be able to go to the bathroom and back, which was a hassle and a half. There would be a massive amount of people lined up against the wall and you had to make sure there was a foot of clearance that people could pass through. Part of my security job was to walk around and ask people to 'move in, move in.' Because if you left them alone they would go all over the place. I'm sure those kids hated us. It was a thankless job."

After a while CBGB got pretty adept at handling large crowds, even when the problems came from inside the club, but it was getting pretty uncomfortable for bands, patrons and staffers alike. The place was changing.

"We put out an ad for Patti Smith's dates [May 31 – June 8, 1977] and within five days every single show was booked out," recalls Bill Shumaker. "Then on the day of the first show the reservation book disappeared. It was either stolen or we lost it. Only me, Merv and Hilly knew about it, and we didn't let anybody else know because we decided to fake it. It was a regular farce. What we did was every so often we would reject someone, some poor bastard, telling him, 'You're not in the book, maybe we can get you in later.' Others would come in, say they had reservations, and we'd let them in. We had a book of totally fictitious names. And we did it; we were successful. We had the hardcore group of fans, mostly girls for Patti Smith, and they would be there by one or two in the afternoon and they would wait outside the door.

"They were the regular core of fans and we didn't question them. And then we did things like hand out tickets to people in line with numbers on them, and that is how they went in. We tried to keep it well-run."

"When the Dead Boys happened, the club changed, it became punk," says Maureen Nelly. "Pre-Dead Boys it was Television, Talking Heads, Mink DeVille, Shirts, all those type of people, which had a more underground, poet, beat sort of feeling to it. Allen Ginsberg would hang out there. People like that. And then when the Dead Boys happened it was the whole punk English scene with the Sex Pistols, and it became a different crowd. When the Dead Boys came in a new generation came in. That's when the first wave of younger kids started coming around. Previous to that it was all people in their late 20s, people who lived in the city. Though it was only five or six years difference, the older regulars started to maybe not come in as often. Instead, the tourists started coming. And even though drugs were around all the time, I think around the time of the Dead Boys and that whole era it became that much more obvious. If somebody was a junkie during the early Television days, it was much more subtle. It was just a part of your life, whoever was doing it. But with the Dead Boys everything was getting high, being fucked up and fucking in the bathroom stalls. Or maybe I was just more aware of it at that time.

"So that was the first change, but it was still fun then. It was wilder and more extravagant both in costume and in action when the Dead Boys and the punk era happened. People called it punk before the Dead Boys, but they really typified it. The Ramones were like cartoon characters to my mind. As it happened, I thought they were punk, but in retrospect I think they were caricatures. I think Lou Reed was punk, but in a street sense. But what the musical industry termed punk referred more to the Dead Boys than the Lou Reeds and John Cales. Or the Velvets and all that. The whole scene changed and I felt a lot older than most of the kids who were coming in there. I had left home when I was 17, and I made my own life. And when I first came to CBGB it was an intellectual scene. It was something where I felt stimulated and it gradually changed into a more fantastic scene. And then it degenerated into a tourist scene. That was the time when Blondie would play and the place would literally be crammed. The walls would sweat. It was that hot, that uncomfortable, and it was like, let me out of here; this is no fun anymore. And the people came from the suburbs who were rude and stupid. The scene changed from being a stimulating one to a boring place. And monotonous. And then I finally said it's time to go somewhere else."

"It got to the point at CBGB that it was so popular that I used to have images of headlines in the *New York Post* saying '800 people crammed into CBGB died in a fire,'" recalls then-promo man Joel Webber. "I remember the waitresses would light the candles on all the tables. One night when the Ramones were playing, people were literally standing on the tables. I said, 'Jesus, if somebody knocks over these candles and the place goes up, there is no way anybody is going to get the hell out of here.'"

"The last time we played at CBGB it was very crowded and hot," says Clem Burke. "Frank Infante at the time was wearing my girlfriend's leather jacket onstage. And it was so hot that night that his guitar strap melted into the leather. It left this massive indentation in the jacket. It got so hot that the walls would be like in a steambath. If you went to see a Television or a Blondie or a Patti Smith, it was torture. Seeing the Runaways was torture."

"The pinnacle of a bad night was when the Jam played there [in October 1977]," says Ira Robbins. "The place was totally populated by college thugs, sort of like football players, who were very drunk and obnoxious. It was like a Madison Square Garden show."

By the end of 1977, the CBGB scene was literally overflowing out the doors. If Hilly was going to continue to play a major role in the growing new music scene, the venue would have to be expanded in some way. Fortunately (or unfortunately), Hilly found an old Yiddish theater that was empty, for sale and located at 66 Second Avenue, only a few blocks from the club. (In the 1960s, as the Anderson Theater, it had been the site of concerts by the Yardbirds, Animals and others.) It seemed ideal.

"We were doing pretty well here in '77, and I was looking around. I saw there was this theater owned by a Mr. Reins, a very nice man," Hilly says. "I had to put something down, and Seymour Stein contributed some money. I got various people: plumbers, electricians, carpenters, but the costs kept rising and rising. So, I got some people who did theater programs to come in and invest money. They would get a quarter interest in the theater and would do T-shirts and the whole thing. Then we finally opened at the end of December and we did a big week with Patti Smith and Talking Heads. We had lots of bands: the Shirts, the Dead Boys. They were great shows."

CBGB's 2nd Avenue Theater, as it was called, had a legal capacity of 1,734. It opened on a Tuesday night, December 27, 1977, with Talking Heads headlining, supported by the Shirts and Tuff Darts. The next night it was the Dictators, the Dead Boys and the Luna Band (formerly Orchestra Luna). Then Patti Smith headlined December 29, 30 and New Year's Eve. There were problems right from the beginning.

"I was filming *Hair* at the time and the whole cast came down for the Theater's opening," recalls Annie Golden. "The other members of the Shirts were there during the day helping Hilly clean up and get the debris out and get ready for that night, because the opening night was the big thing. And it could have been a wonderful thing. Hilly had gone to England and seen this new concept for a club, which is all the rage now, and that was a big theater-like venue, but with no seats, just a huge space, whether for general admission, standing or dancing. But New York hadn't gotten the idea yet, and the people came in and stood around like, what is all this space for? It should have really gone over but it had a lot of problems, a lot of obstacles to overcome, like no heat, the rent, the sound system. I don't know about the Fire Department, but I think people get your number in New York and they keep busting your chops just because you are trying to do something different. But that may just be my romantic interpretation."

"It was a great concept, but Hilly never really checked out the place," adds Bill Shumaker. "It was in December, it was bitter cold, but the heating system never really worked. I never went down into the basement, but you could look down and it honestly looked like one of the rings in Dante's Inferno. And down there was the boiler. Everybody got serious colds. The sound guys were working with their gloves on because the place was never warm.

"Then, about six hours before opening, some old guy is up on the scaffolding. He started getting dizzy, and what he grabbed was this asbestos curtain release. The curtain weighed a ton, and down it came. Thank God it had a catch on it. It came down really fast and then it stopped, so they could pull out the electric pianos and stuff, and then it came down again, leaving about three feet free from the lip of the stage. Nobody could do a sound check. And nobody had ever checked the mechanism for bringing it back up again. They had to get some kind of special gear. And the place didn't have enough power. The theater was set up for Yiddish theater. And that was about all the damned thing could take. So, they had this noisy generator out on the street."

"I was involved in the attempted rescue of the CBGB Theater," says sound engineer Norman Dunn. "I think at that time Cosmo Ohms and I were only good enough to do the CBGB club in Hilly's eyes. So, he got some professional people to do the Theater. And we were hearing horror stories from the musicians who were practicing there. It was an exercise in how many things could go wrong. In 27-degree temperature you don't spray soundproofing under the balcony. It doesn't dry. At the first note it started falling down.

"The boiler room was under 11 feet of water because the water mains broke. One of the plumbers put in a weak pipe. The generator outside was running the electricity for everything and it was driving the neighbors crazy. It was a huge, unmuffled diesel generator. There were threats, the police were there; but it would have cost $15,000 and Con Edison would have had to rip up the street to make things right. And this thing was opened on a shoestring. So, every time the lights would go full blast, the sound would die to a whisper and then slowly the volume would come back up. There were other things. The chandelier hadn't been cleaned in 18 years and the mixing board was right underneath it. Every bass note, I was being rained on by 18 years of soot and grime."

"On the first night, I got there about 10:00 p.m.," remembers Joel Webber. "It was about five degrees outside, bitter cold, but there was some problem and they wouldn't let anybody in. We were getting pissed off out in the street, looking at this big warm theater, saying, 'Oh man, I can't wait to get in there.' After about an hour and a half they let people in. And the place was disgusting. It made the CBGB club look like the Rainbow Room. We were talking about 80 years worth of dirt. There was popcorn left over from the last performance of the Yiddish theater in 1925. It was unbelievable. They did manage to clean up the entryway, and make it look like a subway station. They also had a little store where they sold punk paraphernalia. I bought my first skinny tie there.

"Then I remember sitting down [there were seats along the side and in the balcony] and the Dictators were doing a sound check in front of the people. And it's like 20 degrees inside. This place had no heat at all. It was colder inside this place than it was out on the street, which is physically impossible, but it was cold in there. And we are sitting there, booing, until finally the band sort of started in the middle of their set from the sound check. It was totally not together.

"Hilly's instinct was right, because the Ritz came along later and basically did the same thing. But Hilly was too early and needed maybe another half-million dollars to invest. So, the place got a real bad rap on the street. It is legendary how negative that was."

Then came the three nights with Patti Smith, notable in one regard because Bruce Springsteen joined the band one night for "Because the Night," the hit he wrote for her. But even more notable was the fact that the Theater made the front page of the *New York Post* for getting closed down by the Fire Department during Patti's performance the next night.

"The fire commissioner came out onstage to close the place, and everybody started to boo," Bill Shumaker recalls. "But Patti goes into this five-minute rave about how great the Fire Department is, and this guy is up onstage lapping it all up. Then she says, 'Listen, we only have a few more minutes, can we finish up?' And there was nothing he could say."

"Those shows at the CBGB Theater were Hilly's great idea, and it was actually very good," says Lenny Kaye. "We had a great time at our shows there. I always have felt that it was a good thing with the Fire Department because we were so good. The first night we played we had not played for a long time and I remember that we all felt that we stunk. So, the next night we were really primed to play good, and we played really great. We peaked at 'Ain't It Strange,' which was like our penultimate song. Then we would do 'Radio Ethiopia' and whatever after that. But we were so hot in 'Ain't It Strange' that I really didn't know where else we could go. And then, kind of fortuitously, the Fire Department came and shut down the show, which was pretty incredible. But it was nice. The next night I smashed the only guitar I ever smashed and it was on the stage of that theater on New Year's Eve, just for kicks, just to do it and see how it felt."

"In the Theater I had a lot of problems with the Fire Department," admits Hilly. "We had licenses and everything, but they demanded more and more. It didn't matter when the Theater was built or the grandfather clauses. I took out every piece of wood in that place. There was no wood in it as far as structural things. But it had to have a standpipe. And then it had to have a new standpipe. Then there was a standpipe inspection. It was unbelievable all the things you need for a theater.

"And then the Fire Department came in during the Patti Smith show because of overcrowding. But that was ridiculous compared to what goes on in other places. The CBGB Theater had a limit of 1,734 and they figured I had a couple of hundred more people in there. Think of that in terms of the other big clubs that have a capacity of 1,000 or 1,200 and then overcrowd by 400 or 600. And we had street exits. Everybody could have been out of there in five minutes, there were so many exits. So, I felt that I was being harassed. Different people said different things, which I will not repeat. They said other people instigated it, and I leave it up to your imagination."

The Theater closed after the Patti Smith dates. The place was briefly used as a rock and roll flea market, and there was a show with the Jam the following March, when Mick Jagger showed up.

"The Jam show was when I met Jagger," recalls Maureen Nelly. "He came to see the Tuff Darts and the Jam. I was taking tickets at the door, and some guy was trying to crash the gate. And I was saying, 'Get out, get the fuck out of here.' He was obviously on downs or something. I pushed this kid out the door. I pushed him right into Mick Jagger. He is much slighter than I thought. He was laughing with Jerry Hall. He was very, very nice and he sat down, but the people started noticing him and eventually he had to go backstage. His chauffeur came up and asked me if I could help him get Mick out of the theater, people are beginning to hassle him. I said, 'fine' and went backstage and asked, 'Would you mind waiting until the performance is over? I can't open the fire doors right now since we would be shut down immediately because of the sound. We've had a lot of problems with the police.' He said, 'If you don't mind, I'd like to stay to the end of the show.' I said, 'Sure, stay. I'm not going to tell you to leave at all.' He was very nice. He was a very sweet man."

There were obvious physical problems with the Theater, and neighbors on residential Second Avenue were not happy with it or its generator, but there were also other theories and explanations for the Theater's quick demise.

"I think what happened was economic," says Robert Christgau. "I think basically Hilly got outbid when he tried to start that place. [Established New York rock promoter Ron] Delsener just creamed him. Delsener said this upstart needs a lesson and I'm going to give it to him. And he started hiring all of Hilly's best bands, filled his now defunct hall [the Palladium] with them, and said, 'Fuck you, Hilly. This is my bailiwick.'"

"I think Hilly was a little early in terms of some of these bands really peaking. We were probably the only band that could sell it out at the time," says Lenny Kaye. "People say Talking Heads, but they couldn't sell it out then. To make a theater like that work you couldn't just book CBGB bands grown up, you had to book every bozo who came through town. And that's a music business commitment I don't think Hilly was prepared to make. Also, this is a pretty tight town where Delsener and at the time Howard Stein were promoting."

"I was underfinanced, and at one point the program people became equal partners with me in the building and the real estate and the production, the whole thing," explains Hilly. "They put up a certain amount of money. And then a lot of things were done, but they disappeared. They wouldn't pay, so I was the only one that the plumbers, electricians and carpenters came after. I owed all these people money for years. And then the building was taken away from me.

"When I had the building we were constantly building, renovating, though the neighbors were not happy because of the sound. At one point there was a huge generator. We put in a whole lighting system. The stuff we bought was ridiculous. New ropes, new this, new that. And I was in debt for years and years. At some point I couldn't pay the taxes and I couldn't pay the mortgage and Mr. Reins said, 'Look, we'll foreclose and then we'll rent it back. I can't let you go this way.' I said fine, and then on the day of the foreclosure my partners, the program people, who were unreachable until then, came and plunked down $150,000 cash and they owned it. It's what you call legal larceny. They now own a piece of real estate that they are asking two million for. They got it for $150,000 plus whatever else they put in. And they sold everything, gutted the whole building. All that stuff that we did they sold.

"We ran the Theater as a flea market for a while with all sorts of music — classical, string quartets, rock, we mixed it up. It was fun. We ran it for a few weeks until I couldn't do it anymore. That was the time I was going back and forth with the Shirts and we had to go to Europe.

"With certain acts we didn't have problems booking them into the Theater. But there were also people who manipulated it so we couldn't do it. I found we couldn't book enough shows to keep it going. The only competition was the Palladium, so I'd say they imagined the CBGB Theater would do shows all the time and wouldn't do them any good. But I wasn't into doing big acts as such; I wanted to further things. I also couldn't get a liquor license for the Theater. It was a viable theater, the sound was very good. And a lot of these acts, like the Ramones, were not getting good money at the Palladium. I could have paid more. But I just didn't have the money to carry it off. And I didn't have the help from a lot of people I wish I had gotten help from. I wasn't into just staying here at the club. It isn't such a wonderful thing to be here. You have to move on. And that really cost me a lot, that and the Dead Boys and the Shirts. I didn't have any money for years. For years I was paying people back. So that was my adventure. It cost me about $150,000 or $160,000 loss for everything, including the Dead Boys and the Shirts. But suppose I didn't go into the Theater? Maybe at that time it was a mistake to do it underfinanced, I might have been a little bit too soon, but if I had the money, I might have done it. Some say it may have been better to start another CBGB in L.A. or London. People have suggested all those things, but you have to run a new enterprise and at least it was easy for me to run it from here. You have to have a certain perspective on how you want it run."

CHAPTER NINE

"CBGB is a rock and roll club that has remained
a rock and roll club. I want it to be rock and roll and
I want it to be what it has been. I want the music to be good.
And I know that as long as there is good independent music,
it will be at CBGB on its way up."

— ROBERT CHRISTGAU

The brief rise and fall of the CBGB Theater and the failures — at least the commercial non-success of the Shirts and the Dead Boys — were heavy blows to Hilly. Though he managed two other bands for a short while after that, it wasn't until 1984 that he again embarked on a managerial career, signing Crossfire Choir to an aborted record deal with Geffen Records. But with a large debt and new new wave clubs opening at a rate of almost one a month, there was going to be no more expansion of CBGB until late 1986, when Hilly opened a small record store, followed by the Record Canteen next door to CBGB in the summer of 1987.

Nevertheless, the club kept on going. There were always fans who kept on coming, and the phones kept on ringing with new bands pursuing their rock and roll dreams. Nor was Hilly the only one there with a band or two in tow. Other members of the staff had their own musical connections.

"I won't deny that various people in the club were involved with different bands," says Maureen Nelly. "Most did get involved one way or the other. Or else people in bands got involved. Jim Morrison of the Tuff Darts was a bartender for a while. Also, Tony [Jones] from the Planets. B.G. [Hacker] was the lead singer of a band called Spicy Bits. He used to be one of the kids that hung around the bar. I would occasionally slip him a free Coke or something. It is sort of interesting how much he has changed to be a straight man from being a singer. Sometimes it happened the other way. Allison, who was a waitress, became Cheap Perfume. Deerfrance had her own band, Floor Kiss, and Carol Costa had Costa Rocka."

"Everybody had a band in 1978," adds Connie Barrett. "Charlie Martin [later with Connie herself] had Sun, Cosmo Ohms had Startoon, Susannah Eaton-Ryan had the Rudies and Greg, the bartender, had the Revlons. Vicky [Rose] from the Toasters was working security. It was a very competitive scene. Everybody was trying to bring up their bands. Everybody in Sun hated everybody else, but that was okay, everybody hated them.

"One night, Hilly put Sun in as security for the Theater then he turned around and fired them, because it didn't work out. They thought the Theater was a great place to practice, which is why Charlie Martin put them there, and they would guard the Theater. Except somebody invited them to a Who concert and they all went and left the doors open. And that was the end of that."

It wasn't the end of Connie Barrett's managerial career, though. In the mid-'80s, she became the virtual den mother of the nascent hardcore scene, managing Agnostic Front until a breakup in August 1987, as well as the Crumbsuckers, Carnivore and Whiplash.

From 1978 on, in addition to his debts from the Shirts, the Dead Boys and the Theater, Hilly faced formidable competition as the new music dance club scene developed. In a way, it started with CBGB, even beyond the then-revolutionary dance space at the CBGB Theater. When Blondie played the Johnny Blitz benefit in May 1978, they surprised everyone with a rendition of Donna Summer's "I Feel Love." It was arguably the first time in New York, in the middle of the great rock versus disco split, that a rock band had played a disco song. Blondie went on to record "Heart of Glass," other groups recorded other danceable songs and dance rock was born.

"The Johnny Blitz benefit was pretty wild," recalls Clem Burke. "That was probably one of our best times. We were really getting to enjoy success and enjoy CBGB. We had played the Palladium before that and sold it out; we announced from the stage that we would be doing the benefit the next night. It was great to be able to play the Palladium and then be able to play at CBGB. So many great things have happened at CBGB. They may have been appalled by us doing ['I Feel Love'] or maybe they were shocked. That's always a good idea. It was the first time we did the song. We were trying to play all the synthesizer and sequencer parts on guitar. It was a weird set. I think we also did 'Denis, Denis' and a Ramones song. I think it was a four-song set."

It was inevitable that out of the 20,000 discothèques that were operating in the U.S. in 1978, someone somewhere would find business not so hot and would take a chance on this new punk rock stuff. And it happened, first in Chicago with a place called La Mere Vipere, and then in New York, where, by the end of 1978, there was a new place competing with CBGB and Max's. It was called Hurrah, and it was on the Upper West Side, near Lincoln Center. Hurrah's capacity was not much greater than CBGB's, but it had certain advantages. You could dance there or not, even the seating arrangement was more comfortable. It was willing to give bands cash guarantees instead of a percentage of the door. Every act likes that better because it means they will be paid whether anybody shows up or not; the risk is the venue's or the promoter's. It was clean, in a cleaner neighborhood. It was easily accessible and it went after the new trendy English bands. And people were beginning to want to go to someplace new.

"I really got tired of CBGB after a while," says Joel Webber, who is a regular there again. "There were better places to go and better acts being booked in other clubs. Hurrah sort of took over from CBGB as the venue for bands to play, especially after [new music club impresarios] Jim Fouratt and Ruth Polsky started booking all those English bands. Laker Airlines was around then, and they would fly in for a few dates and fly out. They would come in every week, and what it took CBGB three years to build, Hurrah did in five months. But at the beginning, even at Hurrah, they would play records and nobody would dance. The people would more or less slink on the couches, listen to the music and drink the night away. It became a place where people wanted to hang out. I guess, as a lot of people got older, they sort of got disenchanted with going to a real seedy part of town and hanging out in a real funky place."

The success of Hurrah caused an explosion in the New York new music club scene; by the time the '80s rolled around, Manhattan had such places as the Ritz, Danceteria, Peppermint Lounge, Privates, the 80's, Heat, Savoy, Rocker Room, Bonds, Mudd Club, Mr. Laff's and a couple of others playing the same new music that Max's and CBGB played. (Only the Ritz has survived into the late '80s.) Even the Copacabana did new wave shows for a while. And most of these clubs were larger than CBGB and able to pay talent a lot more. So CBGB had to rely on new acts who didn't draw many fans. Except for the Plasmatics.

The Plasmatics were truly original. Led by Wendy O. Williams, an Amazonian former exotic dancer who dressed in virtually nothing at all onstage while barking out lyrics about "Butcher Babies," the Plasmatics also featured a six-foot-six guitarist with a blue mohawk hairdo who wore a dress, a chainsaw that Wendy would use to cut an electric guitar in half, mock executions, a shotgun, falling scenery and other mayhem. After the band got more popular, it would blow up automobiles onstage. There was nothing halfway about the Plasmatics.

"After doing all sorts of career projects, I was interested in becoming involved with a rock and roll band," says Rod Swenson, manager of the Plasmatics, who was also one of the first to do videos of new acts at CBGB. "I was going to clubs, CBGB was one and Max's was another, casing out things. I saw hundreds of bands in 1976-7-8 and videotaped many. But I never saw exactly what I was looking for. I was looking for something that was just the ultimate: very excessive, that if somebody would walk in when the band was onstage they would never turn away, whether they hated it or loved it. They would watch it and remember it. They would know they saw that band. Coincidentally, Wendy was looking for a vehicle for herself, and to expand her career. So, what I wanted to do and she wanted to do coincided, and by 1978 she debuted her chainsaw, and kids started lining up around the block.

"CBGB had a lot to do with what we did because there was a certain freedom that was very nice. There is a Hilly school of making a rock and roll band happen. There are certain dues, certain procedures and certain techniques for making it happen. But it is a sensible one because it makes sense for everybody, for him and for a band to learn about itself. CBGB is a great laboratory for creative expression. Hilly is very much helping experimental ventures. He will give everybody their shot, and then give you your next shot depending on how well you did. Hilly starts you out with a low profile and his thing is that if you can bring the people in, you have another gig, which to me is a democratic, fair deal. And that's what happened. We tried out the band one night with absolutely no profile, because nobody had ever seen this thing, even though we rehearsed for a couple of months. But we had never done anything onstage. We didn't know what it would be like."

"We knew five or six songs," adds Wendy, "All of them about a minute long. 1-2-3-4, 1-2-3-4, and we were off. That's all we could do."

"The first time we played it was one of those Monday night audition nights," continues Swenson. "I had known Hilly a little bit from hanging around and videotaping, and I think he had the confidence that if I was involved with something, it wouldn't be totally perfunctory. But we wanted to play on an audition night, which meant we would play for nothing, but that was alright because it was a trade-off where you have a chance to try something out, and they could sell a couple of drinks, or whatever. There may have been 30 people there, milling in and out. But that was fine. We went on, did our thing, and everybody who was in there came forward. And I could tell that we made an impression in their minds. And that is what I wanted to see. I wanted to see if these jaded people down in the bowels of this club, who had seen it all, if we could get them going. And they were going, 'Who's that? What's this?' And we felt that we had something going.

"So, after our audition there was the next step. We opened for this one band, and there were a few people there and the response was real good. Our next date was for a Wednesday night as headliners. But that Wednesday night was the Wednesday before Thanksgiving. Which meant there was almost an equivalence in my mind to a Friday night because people didn't have to go to school or work the next day. Thanksgiving is a notoriously slow day in any kind of entertainment business. But the night before is not bad. The philosophy is that people are kind of uptight about being with their families the next day, feeling that they're going to be stuck dressed up, sitting with grandmother. So, the night before they are ready to raise a little hell. It's a good night to get people out wailing and boogying. So, we got that night and sure enough there was just enough of a buzz brandishing that chainsaw around, and enough buzz from the previous show. I heard people going out from the show, saying, 'That's terrible, that's not music, when she pulled out that chainsaw I knew it wasn't music.' At that point I knew we had them. I knew that person would not sleep without thinking about it and that person would have to tell everybody he saw: 'That's terrible. You should see that woman out there, she pulls out that chainsaw. And they are also doing this and that and the other.' And I knew that he would tell everybody. And next time around they would all be in line.

"Getting that Wednesday night was a real plus for us, because with the buzz from the last time, the place was totally packed. And I think Hilly felt the same thing. There was something happening in what we did and the word got out that we packed the place on a Wednesday night and now everybody was interested, everybody being Max's at that time. But Hilly was asking, when are you coming again. Then we went on for two nights on a weekend. And then ultimately we got to four or five days in a row, playing two shows. By then you would come around the corner and the line would go all the way around the block. It was gratifying.

"CBGB is a very special place, a real American dream kind of a place. Anybody could come in, and no matter who they were, if they had something to give Hilly, they could get their shot. And I think that's been proven by the people who were there. The Ramones and Patti Smith had already passed. It had hit its peak and it was dying down, and we kind of pulled it back. For about a year we were almost the house band there. Every five weeks or so we would be in there and it was always full. There was a cult of people who kept coming back so there definitely was a feeling that we had to surprise people a little bit and make it exciting, not necessarily to top what we did before, in a sense of escalating — though there was that, too — but after we did X number of shows at CBGB, the feeling was, let's get to the Palladium and blow up a fucking car. We were onto something on a different scale. Certain parts of it became almost ritualized. Like the chainsaw. You knew you'd see it, but you wanted to see it. And when it came, everybody was waving their fists and screaming. It was part of the ritual of a Plasmatics show. But then we wanted to interject things. Like Wendy would pull out a shotgun and fire. Or a speaker cabinet would blow up. It was to startle people, and thoroughly interact with them.

"It's the spaghetti in the face principle. We didn't use spaghetti, but sometimes so-called ceiling plaster would fall down, and people would come out covered with white. I liked that. Some people got angry, but most felt that it was a part of it. Otherwise, stay back and be a spectator. And sometimes Wendy would go out on the tables, when she could. People were not going to be sitting comfortably when Wendy was on-stage. But the first time she did it, it was a spontaneous thing and the table collapsed. After that we would put supports under the tables. But it was part of the whole thing, to give her a framework where she could be spontaneous.

"Hilly never put any bounds on what we did, not in the slightest bit whatsoever. So it was nice, because when we started taking the show out on the road we found that club owners were very happy to book us, because invariably we sold those clubs out. But they would ask, 'What are you going to do?' and say, 'Don't scratch the floor,' or something. But CBGB was a laboratory. We would go in and the restrictions as to what we could do were very wide. Very tolerant. I suppose there would be an intolerance ultimately if you were damaging the place. And if we were not bringing in business, they would probably get very intolerant.

"Wendy is a wild person like myself, but she is a committed wild person in the sense that her thing is to get as much going onstage as possible and not put her fist through the wall in the dressing room, which is a waste and doesn't mean anything. She would rather do it in front of an audience, and really get herself off, and get other people excited. So, we are respectful of a person like Hilly with a club and an asset. The thing with the holes in the ceiling with the shotgun: obviously there were blanks, we were not firing off live ammunition, but a blank shoots a big hard wad of something and you can hurt someone or go through a thin wall. But we would sometimes use theatrical effects to exaggerate what we did. Occasionally we put bags of flour in the ceiling. We saw it happen once and a little trickle of plaster came down. So, the next time we put a bag of flour up on the ceiling and our effects guy would have little fishing lines and he would yank those and extra debris would come down. We would exaggerate," explains Swenson.

"If there is one thing, we have been very lucky [with our stunts]," says Wendy. "And the audience has been intelligent enough to realize that a chainsaw is a chainsaw and they never put their hands in front of it. Also, I was careful. I think that I'm pretty good at being able to hold on to the guitar and chainsaw and keep it away from people, keep it on the edge, but far away from people."

"People have different perspectives," comments Swenson. "She has her perspective, and so do I. We will continue to do things together that are fairly hair-raising. Her sense of where to draw the line is a little different from most people's. Audiences would sometimes get very excited and sometimes would be inches away from the chainsaw. And there was some concern, though she claims she was always in control, and apparently she was, but we did try to keep the chainsaw out of reach and had people in front to keep the audience away from it. I think it has been our specialty to do things that you might see on film, but you would not normally see live. And when I look back, sometimes it seems to me impossible and insane."

"CBGB let us know that we could do it." says Wendy. "It was a laboratory and it was great. It was a place for experiments. From the production point of view, I remember we had a high-end speaker that we used to run at the back of the club. Part of what we did was that when we did the chainsaw we said that we just wanted this thing to pierce people's brains, so we amplified the sound of the chainsaw and we put it through the PA. And that wasn't bright enough either, so we had a special speaker at the back of CBGB to pick up essentially the high end of it, the screech, to give it a kind of quadrophonic effect. I don't know if people were aware of it, but we had a lot of fun with it even though doing four shows a week, two shows a night, was grueling. We went on to become one of very few bands that essentially made a living off their touring. The way the record business really is is that groups are signed if they feel there are one or two songs they can get on the radio. And then if they sign them and they don't get a hundred adds [to radio station playlists] in the first week, then they move on to the next project. During those first several years we were making music that could not be played on the radio, and we did not intend it to be. We did not try to get on the radio. We were just doing what we were doing. The main thing was to play as fast as we could. And then once we got tired of that we would go on to other things. For us, CBGB was a proving ground and then we were able to go out and tour the country and make a living off it without being on the radio or having a hit record."

In the late '70s and generally through the '80s, it wasn't just that commercial American rock radio wasn't playing bands like the Plasmatics, it was playing very few of the "CBGB bands" outside of Blondie and later Talking Heads. Album-oriented rock radio is the home of traditional guitar-oriented bands, which means heavy doses of '60s and '70s classic rock: Yes, Genesis, Jethro Tull, the Rolling Stones, Bruce Springsteen and his imitators. It wasn't until the rise of disco radio, contemporary hits radio (Top 40) and MTV that new wave music could be regularly heard. For CBGB, in the late '70s and early '80s, this meant that, after their initial interest, record companies cooled to bands playing at the club.

There were other factors as well. Some thought it was actually a plot, that other record company presidents chastised Sire's Seymour Stein for even allowing these types of acts in the door. There was even a theory that then-president Jimmy Carter, a fan of Bob Dylan and the Allman Brothers, suggested at one meeting with record company execs that they not support this new music. But the fact is that new wave and punk were never popular enough or threatening enough to warrant much attention. The first albums by the original CBGB acts were all commercial failures by the standards of that time.

"No other record company was paying attention to what Seymour Stein was doing in the early days at all," says Danny Fields. "He was then affiliated with ABC, so it wasn't like everybody's eyes were on Seymour. I can't imagine anyone in any record company saying, 'You idiot.' That sounds apocryphal to me. Nobody cared about $6,000 deals, or whatever it was."

Then, after 1978, the U.S. record business slid from $4.13 billion to $3.69 billion in total yearly sales. This meant there was less money to invest in marginal new acts. Despite some disastrous multimillion-dollar superstar signings (the Who, Paul Simon, the Beach Boys, etc.), it was easier to stick with the tried and true than to invest the $250,000-plus necessary to turn a U.S. garage band into recording stars. It was (and is) much easier to import new artists already developed from England, Australia or Canada. And maybe some of the new American bands coming into CBGB were just not that good, or at least not that original and fresh. In January 1979, Hilly recorded *Live at CBGB, Volume II*, featuring Quincy, 2 Timers, Excalibur, Pets, Reptiles, Model Citizens, Come On, Nervus Rex, Decks and Bloodless Pharoahs. The master tape is still on the shelf at CBGB, among the beer cases behind the bar. The album was never released.

"Radio always hated [the Ramones, among others]," says Danny Fields. "There were 35 stations in the country that played every album all the time and that was it. There were no others. It just showed you how provincial radio was, how disgusting it was, because none of these bands had anything in common. The Ramones and Television had nothing in common. There was nothing remotely similar about what they did. They had totally different approaches to music. Lyrically, musically and physically — every which way. And they all got called the same thing, and that was so dopey. Certainly, Blondie and the Talking Heads were something else entirely. There were a bunch of very interesting entities coming out of New York at the time and as we look back on it, it was really a golden age. And nobody would take it seriously. The general feeling was of vanilla."

"Because they were the Shirts, a band with a 'the' in front of the name and one syllable after that, and they came from New York, and the CBGB scene, everybody had a real misconception about them," says Joel Webber, who promoted the Shirts, among others. "It was always an uphill battle to get anything played on the radio. It didn't matter what kind of music they played, these radio program directors, music directors and consultants knew better. I know these guys that would not play Tom Petty and the Heartbreakers because they thought they were punk. The Shirts, unfortunately, were cast in the same mold. But they were hippies from Brooklyn, that's all they were."

The wild looks and attitude of English punk, as well as the rapid rise and fall of the Sex Pistols, did little to add to new wave's commercial appeal. Punk was poison even as far as the record companies were concerned. Says Legs McNeil: "When the Sex Pistols came along nobody wanted to be called a punk band, because that was considered commercial suicide. Sire Records wouldn't [even] advertise in *Punk* magazine and didn't want the Ramones to be called a punk band, which was stupid."

For a while in 1978 in New York there was a commercial radio station, WPIX-FM, that did play new wave music, even broadcasting in the afternoons from the CBGB Theater. The station was ahead of its time, the ratings were never there and the format lasted less than a year. A few forlorn punks picketed the station when the axe fell.

"One of the last things that they tried at the CBGB Theater was the live broadcasts with WPIX," continues Webber. "I remember one day when disc jockey Jane Hamburger was a live DJ at the Theater playing for a bunch of kids, while actually broadcasting, having contests and stuff. Then we would all take off for Hurrah and she would spin records at Hurrah during the night. The WPIX era was short and sweet."

"We did some radio from the Theater and the club as well," recalls Hilly. "We taped things and gave them to WPIX. We also did a few things for French radio, Italian radio, Danish radio, Swedish radio, Japanese radio and TV from all over. The BBC came in once. We did the Dictators live to France and I think we lost the line, so it went on later. We also did a few live shows. We did them around noon and they went on at 6:00 p.m. over there."

Then there was video. To his credit, Hilly never hung TV monitors all over his club, but here too, CBGB was a pioneer. If the bands allowed it, Hilly let videomakers shoot at his club. Rod Swenson was one of the first; around, 1980 Hilly would sometimes have evenings where Swenson's early videos of the Ramones, Blondie, Talking Heads and others were shown. It was also a place where such videomakers as Amos Poe, Pat Ivers, Emily Armstrong and Ed Steinberg were able to learn their craft. Hilly even got the video production bug himself, attempting *TV CBGB*, a musical situation comedy centered around the club.

"We tried *TV CBGB* twice," says Hilly. "The first time we tried to build a situation comedy with music. I wrote some scripts. Then we went into more of a musical concept. It was good, but nobody bought it."

As the '70s turned into the early '80s and on into the mid-to-late-'80s, CBGB just kept going. The competition withered away; one by one, all the clubs that featured new music died off, replaced by glossy discos which once in a while attempted new music without much success.

In the early 1980s, the demise of Laker Airlines and its cheap fares, as well as tougher visa restrictions, made it more difficult for small pioneering bands to come to the U.S. from Britain. The energy seemed to be flowing toward video and the melding of new wave and disco into dance music. Typical were such angst-ridden but pretty and stylish acts with a beat as the Human League or Duran Duran. They weren't Bowery fare, and Talking Heads were too big now to play CBGB. But a new scene, beyond punk, was developing in California with Black

Flag, the Circle Jerks, Dead Kennedys, Minutemen and others. In New York, there were new bands like Youth Brigade, Major Conflict, Bedlam, Violent Children; later came the more popular Agnostic Front, the Cro-Mags, Murphy's Law and the Crumbsuckers. This is hardcore, the music of the hard-bitten little brothers and sisters of the punks of 10 years ago. Hardcore, too, had its roots in CBGB. The Ramones inspired the Plasmatics, who inspired...

"We started that whole hardcore crowd," says Plasmatics guitarist Richie Stotts. "The Ramones played fast, but they played different chord progressions. The Plasmatics played these oddball chord progressions which were really hardcore. I'm not really sure how I feel about the whole hardcore scene now. I know a lot of these hardcore kids and some of them are really great people, but some of them are real assholes. The attitude they portray is 'I hate you but I don't even want to tell you why I hate you.' So what's the point?"

"Why would I go see hardcore to see a bunch of dumb kids jump on top of each other?" asks Legs McNeil. "Sometimes it's fun when the band is a Gang Green or somebody, but sometimes you just want to watch the show. I'm all for audience participation, but guys are just trying to get onstage and then act like morons and jump off. It's been done, and so what?"

These hardcore bands faced a problem familiar to Hilly Kristal: no place to play. But there were some very good reasons for that. The music was very primitive and wild, with a reputation for violence not belied by a wardrobe of studs, chains, and heavy boots worn by skinhead teenagers. And their slam dancing could put the fear of God into anybody over 25. Worst of all for club owners, mostly they don't drink. So, what club would want these acts? CBGB, of course. Every Sunday, Hilly takes the seats and tables out for hardcore afternoons, where the faithful can slam dance to their favorites.

Says Connie Barrett, sometime mother figure and full-time manager of a number of hardcore bands: "Hilly in his infinite wisdom developed all this. He's hardly ever there; he doesn't particularly understand the genre or care for it. But his whole philosophy was to provide a forum for something happening that he saw as a mode of expression, that was not only healthy but essential in developing the musicians. He started [putting on] hardcore in 1980-'81 because here was a group of young kids who were 16 to 19 who wanted to play but who had never picked up an instrument. But they would have friends who would come and see them, mostly people in other groups. And Hilly would open the doors for them, for very little money, maybe $5 for four bands on Sunday matinees. And it became an institution.

"Now it's a bigger scene, but he started with maybe one person at the door, and 25 kids at the club. And he kept running it and running it, and it picked up. It caught on eventually and the scene had a group of about 300 to 400 devotees for the bigger bands, the bigger bands being the ones who finally learned to play the C scale. And the hardcore shows were once a week. Though there were other people who did shows once a month, CBGB was a steady venue. When you're talking once a month, you are talking about a big venue, with a big band that has to draw because there are a lot of fees. But with CBGB, as usual, you are talking about any band that can come in and play and work their way up."

"When anybody asks me what is happening, what is new, the only scene that is happening is hardcore," said Hilly, a couple of years after starting the hardcore scene at the club. "It has its fanzines all over the country and England and Holland. And it is a scene. It is word of mouth, word of pen. Where it will go, I don't know. It is more recited, more poetry, or theater composed to music. It is acceptable to college airplay. And it is growing."

Hardcore, at least in New York, is now pretty much centered around CBGB on Sunday afternoons. Hilly admits that he still doesn't particularly want the bands to play at night, basically because of security problems.

Hilly's former assistant Carol Costa: "These kids don't drink and sometimes the door makes $2,000 on a hardcore show but the bar makes $200. And the staff gets paid from the bar. But you have to be paying out more for the staff because you have to have extra security with the slam dancing and all. Sometimes the kids get crazy. Not much hardcore gets booked here at night, most of it is during the hardcore afternoons. It works out the best that way. You don't want to scare off the other people who might come in here at night and think, 'My God, what is going on?' Here the kids come in on a Sunday afternoon and they know what they are going to find. That's the audience, that's the show, and the only people here are the ones who want to be here. So, he doesn't mind them on Sundays."

"There is so little destruction now compared to the way it was during the punk era," says Hilly. "Initially there used to be quite a bit of thievery, but I don't think that anything has been stolen here for a while in terms of people stealing from one another or stealing instruments. Why this is, I don't know, but it's true. It says something about this society in this place. We started hardcore here in '80 and '81. Then we stopped it for a few months because it was getting a bit too wild. Then I sat down with a few kids, and they are nice kids and have something to say, and after I talked to them we started doing things in the afternoons. So, we have had the shows now for a few years."

What Hilly told the bands basically was that they had to post a $150 bond every time they played because they and their fans were destroying the toilets. No security back, no pay. That ended damage to the club. Besides, where else could they regularly play? And Hilly has Karen to help out.

"We can't sell any alcohol to anybody under 21, they can only buy soft drinks. But even the older ones don't drink. They do their drinking outside or try to sneak it in," says Karen. "They don't want to pay for anything except the admission. So, we have to watch them. They used to come in on the hottest days with sweaters or jackets rolled up. Then I found out. They were smuggling alcohol. And I have to work during every hardcore matinee to make sure nobody under 16 gets in because I can't trust any of the employees to enforce that. The law insists on an ID. So the little kids, 13, 14 and 15, are starting to bring their parents with them.

"Another thing the kids try to get away with is to get their ostensibly older friends to pretend they are their big brothers. But I don't allow that. These are not the parents, and besides, how do I know this is the kid's brother? One so-called brother was in his 20s and had a note from the parents that said, 'I allow my son so-and-so to accompany my son so-and-so to CBGB, thank you. And here is the phone number in case you need it.' So, I decided to call the number. The mother had only one son and didn't know who the other one was, and, of course, did not want her little boy to be at CBGB. I sent him packing.

"Once I went out, because it was a little slow, and when I came back who did I see sitting in the musicians' dressing room but this kid, who is 14. I knew because I had kept him out every week. And he's sitting in the dressing room. I said, 'What are you doing here?' And his friend said, 'I'm responsible for him, he's with me.' 'You are not his father or his mother. You are not responsible for anyone. Out.' And the kid said to me, I'm working for them. I'm their roadie.' 'Nobody under 19 can work here anyway. So, out.' He could put me in jail. He is not supposed to be on the premises. And what if something happens to him?"

What may have happened to him was that he became the charismatic, profuse and energetic lead singer of Murphy's Law, among the most popular of the hardcore bands from CBGB, and he admits he used to sneak into the club when he was 15. Now with an LP, *Murphy's Law*, out on Profile Records, Jimmy Gestapo swears his alias is a childhood nickname. Says Jimmy: "People just started calling me Gestapo since about eighth grade. Just the way I am, I guess. Some people are called Spunky or Pookie, and I'm called Gestapo. It's a name that opens people's eyes. But no way am I a Nazi; I'm an American."

This is a sentiment echoed by many involved in the CBGB hardcore scene, reacting to the scene's Nazi notoriety. "Most of these kids don't even know what it means to be a Nazi, or even what the word means. But they know it and swastikas shock people, so they use it. That's where it ends," is an explanation heard in various forms.

"Murphy's Law is basically a rock and roll band that started as a goof," Gestapo continues. "Me and Harley Flanagan from the Cro-Mags started the band about four years ago. One day we went to an S&M club called Paddles and we used Multi-Death Corporation's equipment but people liked us so we kept playing. CBGB was basically our first big club show. I like going there: the beer is cheap and the PA is the best in America. It's the best place to play. We played 15 to 20 shows there, at least. Just looking at the crowd is not like the Ritz with bouncers in front of you. At CB's you are on the stage and it's a whole different atmosphere. When I was on tour with the Beastie Boys I played 50 or 60 shows in the biggest arenas in America and I still wanted to play CB's shows. I've done the arena circuit and the club circuit, but if you play at CB's you get the best live tape. They have a great board, great outboard equipment and a great stage setup.

"We never had a negative response from straight-edge kids or anybody. Basically we don't label ourselves as a hardcore band or a party band. We're a rock and roll band. Everything we do onstage goes with rock and roll: drinking beer and doing all the stuff like that. They tried to have bruisers at CB's, but they found they couldn't or the kids would go crazy. That's the wrong thing to do, basically. Because when you try to stop it, something like that, it will get out of control and you will have more trouble on your hands than you did in the first place. If you book a good band like us or Agnostic Front or War Zone or Underdog, a band that has slam dancing will control slam dancing. And they'll control the fights and all the craziness that goes on, you don't need a bunch of big goons to do it.

"Basically, slam dancing is an outlet for aggression. If they didn't do that, they would be hitting on each other on the street. I'd much rather have it in a controlled situation with music playing, on a dance floor, than on the street. I've seen a lot of articles on hardcore. It's a lot different around New York and CB's. There are a lot of gangs in L.A., like the L.A. Lads and the Suicidal Boys, but in New York it's basically a lot of kids who hang out together. Gangs are not really cool in New York, not in the hardcore or punk rock scene, never. It's just not allowed. I won't allow it for one, and I have a lot of friends. The kids are united and the kids stand alone. Gangs are a bunch of kids that can't stand up for themselves. In New York there has never been a gang of hardcore kids. Gangs are stupid.

"But Hilly won't book hardcore at night. I think he keeps the scene separated between the hardcore and the other stuff. The hardcore scene is getting a lot bigger than his pop scene. And he could make a lot better money if he started doing some night shows. It all depends on how you handle things with underage kids."

Nevertheless, there can be problems. Not only do members of the audience climb up on the stage and leap off headfirst, so does Gestapo. At CBGB with a knee-high stage, a sprain and a few bruises are about as bad as it gets. But the danger increases with neophyte dancers, higher stages and crowds that don't always catch the divers.

Jimmy Gestapo: "It does happen all the time [the crowd doesn't catch you when you dive off the stage]. That's why they have a barricade set up at many places. In one place, some kid who didn't know what he was doing but tried to make it look like he did got up on the stage, dove and landed on his head and broke his neck. The kid is now paralyzed. But everybody at CBGB on the dance floor knows how to dance because the kids who don't know how to dance aren't allowed to dance. Or at least won't be able to because they will get destroyed. But there are never really any injuries, though you've got to wear steel-capped shoes.

"The only thing wrong with CB's is the bathroom. Hilly just should use steel and diamond plate. The thing is you have to conform with the atmosphere you are dealing with. When we play, everything is in a state of craziness, but we keep everything in control. It's not destructive. It's more of a fun atmosphere. There are not bad vibes when we get onstage and we say that's it, the world is going to end, but we are not there to talk about it. We are going to have a good time and talk about positive things. We don't like to preach gospel to kids who are paying $6 to $12 to come in. I'm sure they hear enough shit from their parents. Why should they listen to us?"

Not that things can't get a little intense with Jimmy. Connie Barrett had her finger broken protecting the sound board from a chair thrown by Gestapo. He says it was an accident: "Somebody messed with me and Connie got in the way and was hurt. Somebody hit me with a beer mug and I hit him with a chair. I don't often get into fights, only when people mess with me."

"From what I hear from the kids, you just wind up getting addicted to hardcore," says Connie Barrett. "The thing that made hardcore unique was that it wasn't patterned. It didn't have the obligatory high note at the end; it didn't have the eight bars in, and verse/chorus/verse/chorus/guitar solo/last verse and chorus. With hardcore you never knew what the hell was happening. They all would start and stop at the same time if they were tight. How they did that is beyond me, but it's a form that has become an established form for a lot of reasons."

As hardcore has progressed in the last seven to eight years it has also had its effect on heavy metal, while branching out into subgenres of its own: now there's hardcore, metalcore and thrash metal, the latter two a hybrid of hardcore's sheer manic pace and metal's power chords. Distinctions here vary.

Barrett: "I think the New York hardcore scene has changed the face of metal. Open up a *Kerrang!* or *Metal Forces* magazine. When I introduced underground metal here, the hardcore kids hated me. Though the night I did Carnivore, which was the first underground metal show done in New York City, at CBGB in January 1985, a few of the hardcore musicians fell in love with them. The flak was never from the musicians. They all know each other.

"What they, the establishment, call heavy metal, is nothing more than hard pop rock. To me hardcore is the heaviest heavy metal. To the kids here the word metal is death. That's Bon Jovi. But I've seen hardcore change a lot. The kids have gotten older, bands have moved on, though they will come in once in a while. It almost looks to me now as a second generation and a third generation. These are the kids who got their chops here initially. They grew up hearing what their big brothers were listening to, Ozzy Osbourne and the Ramones.

"Thrash metal to me is a mixture of heavy metal chords, with a hardcore bass and hardcore vocals. It's a very different kind of music than hardcore. Now there is a thing called metalcore, which means the hardcore kids are going into metal but not thrash. Mosh and skank are hardcore terms for the slow part of a song. Hardcore songs are very, very fast and then they have a slowdown when the kids can crawl up the stage again to throw themselves off like lemmings during the fast parts."

Adds Connie Hall, who books the hardcore bands: "There's also that mesh of metal and hardcore bands, there's metalcore bands; I would say even the Cro-Mags aren't hardcore, they're metalcore now. Bands that are metal are getting into hardcore and bands that are hardcore are getting into metal. And I see that happening a lot and where, back in the early '80s, the question was punks against the skins [skinheads] or skins against the punks, now we're having to deal with the metalhead kids and the hardcore kids. The metal kids have a tendency to come from suburbia and the hardcore kids, wherever they came from, basically live on the street or did at a certain period of time."

Barrett: "It's all part of the dance, which is slamming, but it's more than just slamming. The funniest thing I ever saw was one of the first hardcore shows at L'Amour's, which is a metal club in Brooklyn. And the metal kids were trying to learn how to slam. Connie Hall and I were there together, and it occurred to me that the hardcore stuff we had taken for granted had a definite pattern in the slam dancing. They go in a counter-clockwise circle so they don't bang into each other, and there is a certain choreography to keeping the thing going while flying off the stage. There are certain rules which I found very interesting.

"The kids pretty much police themselves. In other venues where this has gotten big across the country and where they're trying to do a hard-core situation they have run into a lot of problems with damage. But the club does police itself. There are certain rules. You don't come in with a bunch of studs like heavy metal kids do and try to slam dance. You could take somebody's eye out. Nobody at the door has ever stopped anybody coming in like that because the kids themselves do. If you in-sist on leaving it on you will find yourself very quickly out the door wondering how you got there.

"There are really very few fights at hardcore itself. Sometimes it does spill out into the streets. I have watched these hardcore kids when there is an altercation on the floor everybody agrees to go out of the club with it and not trash the club. The point is you do not fight in the club where you have the scene every week.

"But I do remember when we had the great marshmallow fight, followed by the great bagel and egg fight, which got stopped. I remember doing security at the door when somehow the kids got ahold of five thousand bags of marshmallows. Where they got the stuff, I don't know, but I remember going out on the street, then coming home and taking off my jeans which were covered from my ankles to my knees with marshmallows."

The flying bodies, boots and sometimes chairs, fists, beer mugs and various foodstuffs mean that things have gotten very functional at CBGB in terms of attire. Certainly no glamor there on a Sunday afternoon. The two Connies who work with hardcore are attractive and tough, too, but this is not a scene that encourages an influx of sensitive, dainty young women, onstage or off.

Says Connie Hall: "A lot of the girls don't really have fine lines. They tend to wear big shirts and stuff and then slam with the guys. In the beginning it was an equal mixture, but as time went on the slamming became heavier and fewer and fewer girls do it. There are still girls out there slamming and diving, but they are usually the young ones. I think a lot of the girls who have boyfriends in bands tend to stay in back by the drums when they play. Most of the girls do not dress very feminine. They don't show too much flesh, not like back in the punk days, when the thing was to look as slutty as possible. I wore incredibly slutty things behind the bar. But these girls seem to get very uptight when other girls do that. I had a tendency to wear lots of nightgowns. Or I would wear a slip and a bikini top. I noticed at first it made people very nervous. But after they accepted that as being me, a lot of the girls let their hair down and a lot of them are letting it grow back. But the real young ones are still cutting it off. No more real heavy makeup. They still have multi-colored hair. But not like it was. When I first came here everybody had mohawks. I changed my hair color probably twice in a month, but after a while you get to a stage in life where you become incredibly busy. I don't have time to do my hair in the morning."

Says Luther Beckett, who also works the progressive scene at CBGB, "It has become very much more asexual, even the guys." Connie Hall adds, "It's not like in the '70s, when sex was real prevalent. I don't see many people sucking faces — kissing, making out. It's like people no longer have sex. At least in the hardcore scene. The night scene is a little bit different. But you can always tell a chick from L'Amour's when she comes into CBGB. It's almost like she has a big 'L' painted on her. It doesn't go with this kind of music and this kind of situation. In L'Amour's you have [level] floors. I have worn high heels here, and it's like a collision course with hell."

Both Connies are actively involved in the performance and business side of the hardcore scene, but mostly it appears that women's role is to stay discreetly behind the drums, though Amy Keim has been influential with Agnostic Front's Roger Miret's development. Having just had his child, she took the pictures of the band and contributed lyrics to the band as well.

Connie Barrett sounds a similar theme. "It's just not the type of music that particularly attracts women. It's very macho, aggressive. And females can't do it. There are certain female bands around, but not one of them do I feel is as good as the stuff that I've signed." Says Connie Hall: "I see that the women were really excluded a lot from the formation of the hardcore stuff. There are a few girls who are singing that are starting to develop, but they are nowhere near the developmental phase of the guys. New wave seemed to encompass both men and women; now it's more male-oriented. A lot of the girls market themselves as all-girl bands. I feel that's wrong. Did you ever hear of an all-guy band? Then the women limit themselves in the shuffles. Musicians have this wonderful thing called the shuffle. Bands today are composed almost entirely of people from other bands. People in bands have a tendency to outgrow each other and that is when they do the shuffle. But if you're from an all-girl band you have to look for another girl band. In fact, in the hardcore scene, I couldn't give you one good hardcore female band. Not one I would like to see."

The male bands meanwhile keep shuffling along and evolving. People from Murphy's Law were in Cro-Mags were in Agnostic Front were in... And, after six or seven years learning to play their instruments, the bands are also getting a bit away from just the "1-2-3-4 hoy, kick-him-in-the-teeth-boy" song formats. The Crumbsuckers are learning about jazz and funk, while the Cro-Mags are getting into Krishna-type music and philosophy. And a new generation of bands like Letch Patrol, Token Entry, Crackdown and Youth of Today are coming onto the scene, much more straight-edge: no drugs or booze, just hard music for hard people with hard choices in hard times. But at this writing there are still no hardcore acts on the CBGB scene the major record companies even want to consider. This stuff is still much too threatening and off the wall. They are not the pretty-boy clones like Bon Jovi, Europe or Cinderella that big labels prefer to spend their money on. Even the more adventurous small independents have problems relating to hardcore.

Says Connie Barrett: "[Profile label chief] Cory Robbins wanted to hire me to do A&R with the new metal. He said he was looking for a band like Metallica, a little Metallica. I said, 'Why don't you come down to hardcore.' It took Mr. Preppie half an hour to get out of the car. The kids all look like pirates. Nicest group of kids you would ever want to meet, but they look horrendous. Finally he came in. I think it was Murphy's Law he wanted to see, and it was one of the big shows. After the show he looked at me and asked, 'What did I just hear? I have no idea what this is.'

"David Karpin from Shatter Records said exactly the same thing after watching Agnostic Front: 'It's different, what is it?' The labels coming into this had no idea as to what this was. It takes a while. But there is a market. My band Whiplash sold 1,800 demos on their own before they were signed. There are fantastic undergrounds of hardcore and metal that are starting to merge. The majors don't know anything about it, since it doesn't concern dollars and cents."

Certainly not many dollars. Even if the hardcore kids do make a record they enter a world of small record companies, distributors and booking agents, many coming from the early CBGB days, themselves barely afloat in a world of three-million-dollar Michael Jackson promotional videos and two-million-dollar-plus recording costs. If a hardcore band can get $7,000 from a Celluloid Records, a Combat Records, an SST Records, a

Relativity Records, a Prelude Records or a Profile Records, it is very lucky.

It is like 1974 again — but with no Patti Smith or David Byrne or Debbie Harry to lead the way. And those that do try to follow the early CBGB pioneers, almost 15 years later, seem even less knowledgeable about the business side of what they are doing than their predecessors.

Connie Barrett: "Agnostic Front did a record and sold it themselves. When they met me, they looked at me like, what's she doing here? Roger [Miret, singer-songwriter] showed me this album, and I said it's very interesting. It was *Victim in Pain*, their first record, and I asked, 'How many points are you getting?' He said, 'What are points?' I asked 'What kind of contract do you have?' and he said I was all wrong; it wasn't like that. The record company was giving the band 100 records to sell for their own. At that point I looked at him and said, 'You are going to get ripped off.' He said, 'You don't understand, this is hardcore, not business,' and I said, 'You don't understand: it *is* business. And business includes hardcore.'

"If a band is to survive, it has responsibilities, like children, mothers and their lives. They can't come back [after touring] and take jobs again. They can, but it's difficult. You go out on the road for seven months and then you come back to work or you go back on welfare. Music is a very hard business and hardcore started very much like a hippie thing. There are a lot of the same attitudes. Without beards, no hair. But the same attitudes. It's basically a love, peace and tranquility kind of thing, but the way it came out is that it's love, peace or I'll kick your ass. Which is kind of '80s updated hippiedom. But it is becoming a business and losing a lot of its ideology."

It's tough making a living as a hardcore musician: selling a couple of thousand albums at best, playing VFW halls in other little hardcore strongholds on the West Coast and in Texas, Detroit, Toronto, Cleveland and a few other places, traveling from gig to gig packed seven to a small van, once driving 1,200 miles for a show and getting paid for it in ham sandwiches, no money — true story. After that, no wonder CBGB seems like heaven.

CHAPTER TEN

"There are crazies uptown as well, but they are dressed better.
Here we can spot them right off."

— BILL SHUMAKER

"Business is very good actually," Hilly says late in the summer of 1987. "I guess it's good by default with not enough other good places really being around. That's one of the reasons. The other reason is our sound system is really [the best]. It is kept up and even keeps improving, so we keep getting more effects. The bands sound really wonderful here, while there are problems with the sound a lot of other places. So, a lot of record companies have asked me to put people in for them. And, of course, people want to play here because they feel record companies like it better here because it's the best. So, everything helps.

"Record company A&R people come here constantly, more now than ever before. Mark Weymouth, Tina's younger brother, is at Virgin, and he comes down a lot. Elektra comes down, Atlantic, Capitol ... they even put in big bands here. They put in Georgia Satellites, they put them in just as their record came out. And Crowded House was booked here.

"I would say the most popular bands here are the local hardcore bands, Agnostic Front and others. Vernon Reid's Living Colour are popular. They Might Be Giants are doing very well. They are a two-man group, they have a record that's selling, a video that's on MTV. They're good, they're very good. We have the Butthole Surfers here. I guess it's — I don't know what you'd call it — adventurous pop or melodic hardcore, or it's pregnant high energy, just a fresh sounding, high-energy rock. Dick Manitoba's coming back here with a band; Janet from the Wygals was signed to a deal on Rough Trade/Warners. The Brandos have charted. Each band has its own drawing power. I guess our slow times would have been our busy times about three years ago, so we fill the place pretty well.

"We've always had different kinds of pop bands, I think it's a cross section, but it's still predominantly new music. Every now and then we have a straight metal band that's really pop metal, but I stay away from heavy metal unless it's thrash, which I think is kind of exciting. Some is pretty good; it's more or less metal's answer to hardcore. Every once in a while we have a straight-ahead pop band, and it's rather boring, but some of them are pretty good, some of them are so good technically that it's kind of amazing. But unless they have some charismatic thing about them to me it's not our thing," he continues, speaking specifically about Rude Buddha, Crossfire Choir (whom Hilly briefly managed) and Bangaroo. "Bangaroo is kind of a fun pop band, Crossfire Choir is a heavier, more of an R.E.M. kind of thing, pretty up, and Rude Buddha is very esoteric, arty, rhythmic and very interesting, marvelous. They're, I guess, Virginia's answer to the Talking Heads, except that they majored in languages and I think a couple of them studied Russian. They speak Russian and they're from Charlottesville, Virginia. They're quite bright, very young, bright people.

"As for Crossfire Choir, they finished the record and Geffen Records was not happy with everything so they tried to find another producer after Steve Lillywhite. Then they got stuck. They sent three or four new songs and did a couple of the other songs, but Geffen still weren't happy with it, so they just dropped the band. Subsequently the band was on Jem/Passport and they have a record out that is doing well. I don't manage them anymore, nobody manages them. I don't really manage anybody; I don't have the patience to deal with egos, whims and attitudes. It's very hard. People have an unreal view of what this whole thing is about. I don't feel I can be in a situation where they're unhappy and I can't help it, but I think I can actually have production deals and record deals, things I can deal with."

Hilly still has the same system of bands first playing Monday night audition nights on the basis of the tapes they send in, then moving up through the week and up the bill, depending on how well they draw. Not that every band that sends a tape even gets as far as an audition night. One of the things Hilly has to deal with is the job of winnowing out the good, the bad and the ugly, which he does with his assistants Louise Parnassa and Connie Hall. Louise, a 22-year-old former business major, actually attempts to bring a little business logic to it.

Says Bill Shumaker: "The difference between Louise and her predecessors is that they were music people trying to be organized; they were into the music and had very defined opinions about what they liked, not always thinking objectively, while Louise comes at it much more as an executive, someone who is looking at the broad picture. I think she would bring in a band that she doesn't particularly like if she felt it would help at the door, whereas the other people would say, 'This band is shit, I don't care if they brought in 400 people. I don't want to hear this shit music."

Louise Parnassa: "If they bring 400 people obviously they are pleasing these people. Hilly listens to the tapes we get. Today we got eight. One week we had 200 tapes. When Hilly went on vacation he took 285 tapes with him for three days. But he'll also play something in the office and ask opinions. I've been doing this for a year. Sometimes I come here at night, but I see it every day. I see the bands during the soundchecks. After talking to them all day I don't want to talk to them all night. But I like them. I think they're funny. Some of them are pains in the neck, and I don't like that. They bug me for bookings because they think I do the bookings, but Hilly does that, and so they want to talk to Hilly and Hilly can't talk to them, so they bug me. And I feel bad because I know Hilly is very busy, or he doesn't want to talk to a band that's not that hot.

And so I feel bad for them because they want to play, and maybe they will get better. It's difficult. There is nothing I can do about it, and you can't turn back the clock."

CBGB has just kept right on, open usually seven nights a week, presenting a whole new bunch of bands: Agnostic Front, Vernon Reid, the Crumbsuckers, Butthole Surfers, Pussy Galore, Brandos, Big Dipper, Strange Cave, Ben Vaughn Combo, Token Entry, Verbal Abuse, the Toasters, Elliott Sharp, Sonic Youth, Ritual Tension, Nice Strong Arm, Miracle Legion, Lawndale, Deep Six, Dead on Arrival, Dinosaur Jr. and a host of others.

And the best sound board in any club anywhere is still in prime working order, so that any band performing at CBGB, for only a couple of bucks, can have its show turned into a quality demo tape. In the mid-'80s, Hilly took some of these tapes and put them out himself on CBGB Records, distributed by Caroline, one of the independent distributors who make their living outside the mainstream of American pop music.

Hilly was back in the record business. He also rented a storefront in late 1986 on nearby Ninth Street for an office, as much as anything to get away from the commotion on the Bowery. With a little space on his hands, he also opened a small record shop there specializing in new music and independent label records. He wanted to see what records by new bands were selling, he says. This led to a distribution deal with Celluloid, another small independent record label and distributor; the establishment of the CBGB/Celluloid Records label; and the opening of the CBGB Record Canteen, a large record store and coffee shop just next door to the club on the Bowery.

Says Hilly: "When I decided to start CBGB's Records I started with tapes and I put out seven or eight of them by myself. I have Tulpa, they're from Canada; Rods and Cones from Boston; Jing and Chemical Reaction, they're both ex-members of the Shirts, they're very good; Jupiter Jets, Rude Buddha, Ed Gein's Car, Damage, Connotations, Ludichrist, they're on the cassettes.

"Then I was in touch with Jean Karakos [head of Celluloid Records] and made a P&D [pressing and distribution] deal because I find that I really need somebody to market them. I can co-promote. Caroline was only selling the CBGB tapes. They weren't marketing them and didn't plan to. But I think Karakos is capable of doing it. I pay for the production and he pays the pressing and distribution to mom and pop stores and major chains all over the country. He does it on his own and he does a good job. The Golden Palominos [on Celluloid] sold a lot of records, some of the others sell a lot. Some sell less, but as far as independents go, he's growing. I like a lot of the things he puts out, and he needs product. I felt that going with him was best for me because I think that he needs me, and we're close; he's on the other side of Manhattan.

"I have a good deal with Celluloid. If we work at something, and the band starts to move and they're getting a lot of attention, I can take it right off Celluloid and put it on a major label, if a major wants it. Not that Celluloid won't gain a percentage, they will split the percentage with me. I can do that if some band goes beyond what we both think an independent can do at that time for the band that really starts to move and we all of a sudden need to manufacture hundreds of thousands of records.

"First releases [on CBGB/Celluloid] will be by Damage and Ed Gein's Car. They're coming out with album versions of their [earlier CBGB] cassettes. Ritual Tension is a new band, so there will be three releases out initially. After that the next release will be Am Jam, a reggae band, and a group called Deans of Discipline. Then I'll have four or five other bands ready later.

"We will have albums, cassettes and compact discs [at the Record Canteen] and a lot of other things as well. There's a very good reason. The store makes very little money per item; I mean, I make more on a drink than somebody makes on a record. But I pay less, obviously, and realize it's an interesting rationale to put out what you make yourself, because a record store, even a store of this big size, still pays $5.29 to $5.49 for a record that it sells for $6.99."

Hilly originally wanted his new Record Canteen to be open 24 hours a day, but the reality of doing such a thing toned that idea down. With about 3,000 titles in stock at its opening in early summer 1987, the record store and coffee shop do stay open into the early dawn during weekends, containing one of the city's most comprehensive catalogs of new music, especially of bands who have played at CBGB. The Canteen is the same size as the club, 4,500 square feet, with much of the same down-home ambience, though it does look a lot newer and shinier.

The Record Canteen cost Hilly about $200,000 to gut the whole interior of a former shoe-repair supply outlet and set up a new operation, supervising the reconstruction himself. It is 165 feet deep, and at summer's end in 1987, Hilly planned to have art exhibitions in the rear or a mix of video and pinball machines, so that everything will run together in one very long room. The coffee shop starts at the front door, to the right as you walk in. To the left there's a computerized checkout counter and then a longer counter space for T-shirts, cassettes, books and compact discs.

Continues Hilly: "The main purpose was to have a record store that highlights new artists, from the major labels as well as the independents, and imports that deal with new artists or artists that pertain to new music. John Cale may not be exactly new, but we will carry everything. If somebody wants to buy Bruce Springsteen or Madonna, that's fine, too. I also think I wanted to gain a little more leverage in trying to help new artists. I'm actually doing here what I'm doing at CBGB. I found from talking to different people that stores are very vital in starting the new artists with whom independent record companies work. The indies can work with college radio and they can work with record stores; there's not much else. I'm trying to make a record store that can do what I'm doing with new artists at the club.

"This also will be a good place to acquaint people with new music they might not find anywhere else. We will have a DJ playing a variety of new artists all the time. He will announce the artist, play the song and then announce it again. It will be unobtrusive, but at least people will know who they heard if they haven't heard the song before. The coffee shop will have coffee, soda and snacks. There will be an area in front of the DJ's booth where there will be a small stage with microphones where we can have small acoustic acts, poets or what have you."

Two months after it opened, and before it started doing any real publicity or promotion, Bill Shumaker, who helped get the Record Canteen going, said business was picking up in a manner unique to CBGB: "Every week we do a little better than the week before, a couple more hundred or a couple more thousand. We sell more food now. At nights we get a lot of spillover from the club. And we are slowly but surely developing a daytime clientele for food. Some people we see two, three times a week coming in for food.

"Another very healthy scene that is developing is that musicians are coming here at six, seven, eight o'clock when they are not coming to CB's. While we will always be tied to CB's, we will develop our own clientele. The record store in gross figures does better, but that is because of the profit margin. If we did equal sales we would be much more profitable. I don't think we ever will, because our food is very reasonable. [A smoked ham and brie sandwich costs $4.00.]

"We also have entertainment every Thursday night; we recently had a tap dancer, tapping up and down the aisles, literally. Many times it goes down to a '50s or '60s coffeehouse thing. We charge no cover and no admission. The bands pass the hat. I never ask them how much they make, but I've seen a lot of dollar bills in hand."

"When we say there is no set fee or admission, the bands don't mind at all," says Louise Parnassa. "They are really happy to play, to be in there. Audition nights [Mondays at the club] can bring a lot of money." Bill Shumaker adds, "When you have four bands on audition night, each of the bands has a separate quality. There is no overlap. The fans of X band will come into CB's and see their band; then the Y band's fans will see their band. The X band fans might not want to stay around, so they will come to the Canteen for a sandwich or something."

From a financial point of view, the CBGB's hardcore scene on Sundays doesn't do badly for the Canteen, either. For one thing, the Canteen has a first-rate hardcore record catalog. Also, the kids come into the Canteen because they're too young to drink liquor, and Cokes are cheaper at the Canteen than at the club. "The club will do very well at the door, but the bar won't do well. None of them are old enough to drink," says Bill Shumaker. "Before we were here, the kids would just go

THIS AIN'T NO DISCO

to the deli across the street. Now we are hurting the deli since we have 20-ounce sodas for 75 cents. It's funny to look at the sales the next day. The soda proportion will go out the window. The only time we drop off is when there is a weak Sunday afternoon show. But one Sunday afternoon we sold 120 sodas in two hours. We put a girl on the Coke machine and just sold Cokes, a dollar a Coke. So, we tie into what they do on Sunday afternoon. If they have a big show, we will have a big showing. But, otherwise, we have been going steady. We are just working within these restraints."

In the last couple of years, the Gildersleeves rock club up the street closed and became a soup kitchen. That and the downtown crack scene have dragged the Bowery down a bit again. Hilly now calls the area the crack capital of New York, but then Hilly is used to dealing with freaks at his club. Bill Shumaker says even the relatively upscale Canteen hasn't had much trouble: "The Canteen is very mellow and we don't get many crazies. There are crazies everywhere and they can come in anywhere, but the average crack dealer, or whoever, knows what his turf is and what his turf isn't. We don't get them in here. But we do get guys here in the Canteen, in their 40s and 50s, obviously not from here, working-class guys, and the reason they are here is that their kids are under 16 and they are in bands playing next door."

So, what was it all about? After 15 years, CBGB has outlasted its competition, and it is still there, still on the Bowery at the end of Bleecker Street. Hilly still presides over it, most every day and every night, taking care of business, now running a record label and record store, sometimes scolding, more often offering his advice and counsel to any musician who asks. Almost any band, any kind of rock-oriented act, can come in and have a shot, play during a Monday night audition and at least walk away with a tape of its performance at one of the most historic rock venues in the world. And things can start happening for a band. Hilly's rules for building a new act have not changed any in the last decade. Hilly would like nothing better than for a group to come in on a Monday and six months later headline for four straight nights for a month.

"I think it's amazing that Hilly is still there, still trying to give new bands a shot," says Roy Trakin. "I think we have reached a point where kids are not as susceptible to new bands unless they see them on MTV. There is no place to read about them, there is no place to hear them, there is no radio station playing them, so we are in the same position we were when Hilly started. We need a place like CBGB, with creative people. There has to be a new generation that knocks on the door and will not be denied. CBGB has showed that a local scene can be every bit as good as what's played on the national radio. It inspired Athens, Georgia, it inspired London, it inspired Los Angeles. It inspired the world."

Interesting events still happen at CBGB. There have been a series of country music nights (it goes full circle), an acoustic benefit for local derelicts featuring such artists as Steve Forbert (another Hilly discovery), Marshall Crenshaw and David Johansen. There was an AIDS benefit. Joan Jett played an unannounced date at the club just to do it. When the people behind *This Is Spinal Tap*, the film, decided to do some live dates as Spinal Tap, the band, it was CBGB where they chose to play. Heavy metal is no stranger in the club, though it is usually of the thrash metal variety. After the good-guy Bon Jovi bands run their predictable course, maybe it will be time for Murphy's Law or the Cro-Mags. After all, stranger things have come out of CBGB.

Would new wave or punk have happened if there had never been a CBGB? Probably, but it would have been different, and the lives of many would have been a little bit poorer if there had been no CBGB, no Television, no Talking Heads, no Ramones, no Blondie, no Steve Forbert and, yes, no Plasmatics or Agnostic Front either — and none of a host of others, known or unknown, signed or unsigned, on the radio or MTV or nowhere, who had to step around the drunks and the dog shit to get to the stage. Just being a good musician's bar, helping new acts, is good enough for CBGB.

Says Lenny Kaye: "CB's may not be the birthplace of some sort of new rock culture, but it is thriving in its own small way and it is the only place in town that has any name at all where a new band can wriggle in and have a stage to play on with a decent sound system. This is the biggest and most important music city in the world and there is not one radio station that plays new acts on a regular basis, not one major club that books local talent on a regular basis except CBGB. And it should be made a shrine for that, and Hilly should be made some sort of honorary guardian of the scene.

"CBGB has outlasted Max's, Heat, Hurrah's, Mudd Club. Maybe it's not as hip now as it used to be, but there is no place to go but CB's, especially if you are a musician. It's a musician's bar, and I like that. In a sense it has become what it was originally, which is a bar where the musicians played, hung out and entertained each other. At one time I thought that CB's would never make it into the '80s, but now I am starting to see that, yeah, it's a part of the '80s. Maybe it won't become the thing again; I don't think that it happens like that in this world, that places come back to become a different force. But that doesn't mean that its particular charm is as a relic of the '70s. I think in a certain way CBGB has survived because it never really was anything [pretentious]. Look at the many clubs that have come and gone while CB's is still there."

"I sometimes get a little burned out," admits Hilly. "Some of it is just the habit of being around here all the time. It is not that I am afraid that something will happen if I am not here; I am not that kind of person. But so many things have happened in the past, little things, being awakened for this or that. I think I have been living on the edge for too many years, going down the rapids constantly, financially and in other ways. It eats at you. But when you hear a good band, it really helps. John Cale did a great performance here. He came in and played two sets until five o'clock in the morning. The Replacements were wonderful. With Patti Smith almost every performance was great because she loved to perform here. She was special every time. It happens like that. How do these kids get so good?"

DISCOGRAPHY

(UP TO 1988)

A case could be made for including every record made by every new wave, punk and hardcore band since 1974 in this discography, as well as every record by every group that was influenced by the bands that played at the club. But that could get a little long. So what is included here is a selective discography of albums available in the U.S. by acts who played at CBGB or who played a direct role in the making of CBGB. In the case of acts who played CBGB and then went on to larger venues, only the titles of albums that were released during the period when they actually played at the club are included. For instance, no Ramones titles after 1980, simply because they never played at CBGB after 1980.

AGNOSTIC FRONT: *Victim in Pain* (Combat Core 1986), *Cause for Alarm* (Combat Core 1987)

WILLIE ALEXANDER AND THE BOOM BOOM BAND: *Willie Alexander and the Boom Boom Band* (MCA 1978), *Meanwhile... Back in the States* (MCA 1979)

AM JAM: *Am Jam* (CBGB/Celluloid 1987)

BAD BRAINS: *Bad Brains* [cassette] (ROIR 1982), *Bad Brains* (Alternative Tentacles [EP] 1982), *I and I Survive* (Important [EP] 1982), *I Against I* (SST 1986)

STIV BATORS: *Disconnected* (Bomp 1980)

B-52'S: *The B-52's* (Warner Bros. 1979), *Wild Planet* (Warner Bros. 1980)

BIG BLACK: *Songs About Fucking* (Touch and Go 1987)

BIG DIPPER: *Boo Boo* (Homestead 1986)

BLONDIE: *Blondie* (Private Stock 1976, Chrysalis 1977), *Plastic Letters* (Chrysalis 1977), *Parallel Lines* (Chrysalis 1978), *Eat to the Beat* (Chrysalis 1979)

BRANDOS: *Right Now* (Caroline 1987)

BUTTHOLE SURFERS: *Locust Abortion Technique* (Touch and Go 1987)

JOHN CALE: *Fear* (Island 1974), *Slow Dazzle* (Island 1975), *Helen of Troy* (Island 1975), *Guts* (Island 1977), *Sabotage/Live* (Spy 1979)

JAMES CHANCE: *Theme From Grutzi Elvis* EP (ZE 1979)

JAMES CHANCE AND THE CONTORTIONS: *Live in New York* [cassette] (ROIR 1981)

JAMES WHITE AND THE BLACKS: *Off White* (ZE 1979), *Sax Maniac* (Animal 1982)

JAMES WHITE AND THE CONTORTIONS: *Second Chance* (PVC 1980)

THE CONTORTIONS: *No New York* (Antilles 1978), *Buy Contortions* (ZE 1979)

CHEMICAL WEDDING: *Jing/Chemical Wedding Recorded Live "Off the Board"* [cassette] (CBGB Records 1987)

CIRCLE JERKS: *Group Sex* (Frontier 1981), *Wild in the Streets* (Faulty Products 1982)

CONNOTATIONS: *The Connotations "Off the Board"* [cassette] (CBGB Records 1987)

WAYNE COUNTY AND THE ELECTRIC CHAIRS: *The Electric Chairs* (UK Safari 1978), *Storm the Gates of Heaven* (UK Safari 1979), *Things Your Mother Never Told You* (UK Safari 1979), *The Best of Jayne/Wayne County and The Electric Chairs* (UK Safari 1982)

CRAMPS: *Gravest Hits* EP (Illegal/IRS 1979), *Songs the Lord Taught Us* (Illegal/IRS 1980), *Psychedelic Jungle* (IRS 1981), *Off the Bone* (Illegal 1983), *Smell of Female* EP (Enigma/Big Beat 1983), *Bad Music for Bad People* (IRS 1983)

MARSHALL CRENSHAW: *Marshall Crenshaw* (Warner Bros. 1982), *Field Day* (Warner Bros. 1983)

CROSSFIRE CHOIR: "Nation of Thieves" 12-inch single (Geffen 1985)

CROWDED HOUSE: *Crowded House* (EMI 1987)

CRUMBSUCKERS: *Life of Dreams* (Combat Core 1986)

DAMAGE: *Recorded Live "Off the Board"* (CBGB Records 1987, CBGB/Celluloid 1987)

THE DAMNED: *Damned Damned Damned* (UK Stiff 1977), *Music for Pleasure* (UK Stiff 1977)

DAS DAMEN: *Jupiter Eye* (SST 1987)

DB'S: *Stands for Decibels* (UK Albion 1981), *Repercussions* (UK Albion 1982), *Like This* (Bearsville 1984), *The Sound of Music* (IRS 1987)

DEAD BOYS: *Young Loud and Snotty* (Sire 1977), *We Have Come for Your Children* (Sire 1978), *Night of the Living Dead Boys* (Bomp 1981)

DEANS OF DISCIPLINE: *Deans of Discipline* (CBGB/Celluloid 1987)

DEEP 6: *Sasquatch Road* (SST 1987)

DEFUNKT: *Defunkt* (Hannibal 1980), *Thermonuclear Sweat* (Hannibal 1982)

DEL-BYZANTEENS: *Del-Byzanteens* EP (UK Don't Fall Off the Mountain 1981)

THE DEMONS: *The Demons* (Mercury 1977)

DEVO: *Be Stiff* EP (Stiff 1978), *Q. Are We Not Men? A. We Are Devo!* (Warner Bros. 1978), *Duty Now for the Future* (Warner Bros. 1979), *Freedom of Choice* (Warner Bros. 1980)

DICTATORS: *The Dictators Go Girl Crazy* (Epic 1975), *Manifest Destiny* (Asylum 1977), *Bloodbrothers* (Asylum 1978), *Fuck 'Em If They Can't Take a Joke* [cassette] (ROIR 1981)

DINOSAUR JR.: *Dinosaur* (Homestead 1985)

DIRTY LOOKS: *Dirty Looks* (Stiff/Epic 1980)

DNA: *No New York* (Antilles 1978)

D.O.A.: *True, Strong and Free* (Rock Hotel 1987)

ED GEIN'S CAR: *Recorded Live "Off the Board"* [cassette] (CBGB Records 1987), reissued as *You Light Up My Liver* (CBGB/Celluloid 1987)

8-EYED SPY: *Live* [cassette] (ROIR 1981)

FEELIES: *Crazy Rhythms* (Stiff 1980)

FLESHTONES: *Roman Gods* (IRS 1980)

FLIPPER: *Generic Album* (Subterranean 1982), *Blow'n Chunks* [cassette] (ROIR 1984), *Gone Fishin'* (Subterranean 1984), *Public Flipper Ltd.* (Subterranean 1986)

ROBERT GORDON: *Robert Gordon With Link Wray* (Private Stock 1977), *Fresh Fish Special* (Private Stock 1978), *Rock Billy Boogie* (RCA 1979)

GOVERNMENT ISSUE: *You* (Giant 1987)

HEARTBREAKERS: *L.A.M.F.* (UK Track 1977), *Live at Max's Kansas City* (Max's Kansas City 1979), *D.T.K.—Live at the Speakeasy* (UK Jungle 1982)

RICHARD HELL AND THE VOIDOIDS: *Richard Hell* EP (Ork 1976), *Blank Generation* (Sire 1977), *Richard Hell/Neon Boys* (Shake 1980), *Destiny Street* (Red Star 1982)

HONEYMOON KILLERS: *Let It Breed* (Fur 1987)

INDIVIDUALS: *Aquamarine* EP (Infidelity 1981)

JAM: *In the City* (Polydor 1977), *This Is the Modern World* (Polydor 1977), *All Mod Cons* (Polydor 1978), *Setting Sons* (Polydor 1979)

JOAN JETT: *Joan Jett* (Blackheart/Ariola 1980), *Bad Reputation* (Boardwalk 1981), *I Love Rock'n'Roll* (Boardwalk 1981), *Glorious Results of a Misspent Youth* (MCA 1985)

JING/CHEMICAL WEDDING: *Recorded Live "Off the Board"* [cassette] (CBGB Records 1987)

JUPITER JETS: *Recorded Live "Off the Board"* [cassette] (CBGB Records 1987)

LAUGHING DOGS: *The Laughing Dogs* (Columbia 1979), *Meet Their Makers* (Columbia 1980)

LAWNDALE: *Sasquatch Rock* (SST 1987)

LIVE SKULL: *Don't Get Any on You* (Homestead 1987)

RICHARD LLOYD: *Alchemy* (Elektra 1979), *Real Time* (Celluloid 1987)

LOUNGE LIZARDS: *The Lounge Lizards* (Editions EG 1981)

LUDICHRIST: *Recorded Live "Off the Board"* [cassette] (CBGB Records 1987)

LYDIA LUNCH: *Queen of Siam* (ZE 1980), *The Agony Is the Ecstacy* EP (4AD 1982), *13.13.* (Ruby 1982)

MATERIAL: *Temporary Music 1* EP (Red 1979), *Temporary Music 2* EP (Red 1981), *Busting Out* EP (ZE/Island 1981), *Memory Serves* (Elektra Musician 1981), *One Down* (Elektra 1982)

MILK 'N' COOKIES: *Milk 'n' Cookies* (UK Island 1977)

MINK DEVILLE: *Mink DeVille* (Capitol 1977), *Return to Magenta* (Capitol 1978), *Le Chat Bleu* (Capitol 1980), *Coup de Grâce* (Atlantic 1981)

MINUTEMEN: *The Punch Line* (SST 1981)

MIRACLE LEGION: *Surprise Surprise Surprise* (Rough Trade 1987)

MURPHY'S LAW: *Murphy's Law* (Profile 1986)

NERVOUS EATERS: *Nervous Eaters* (Elektra 1980)

NERVUS REX: *Nervus Rex* (Dreamland 1980)

NEW YORK DOLLS: *New York Dolls* (Mercury 1973), *In Too Much Too Soon* (Mercury 1974), *New York Dolls* (UK Mercury 1977), *Lipstick Killers* [cassette] (ROIR 1981)

NICE STRONG ARM: *Nice Strong Arm* (Homestead 1987)

NITECAPS: *Go to the Line* (Sire 1982)

PERE UBU: *The Modern Dance* (Blank/Phonogram 1978), *Dub Housing* (Chrysalis 1978), *New Picnic Time* (UK Chrysalis 1980)

TOM PETTY AND THE HEARTBREAKERS: *Tom Petty and the Heartbreakers* (Shelter 1976), *You're Gonna Get It* (Shelter 1978)

PLASMATICS: *New Hope for the Wretched* (Stiff America 1980), *Beyond the Valley of 1984* (Stiff America 1981)

POLICE: *Outlandos d'Amour* (A&M 1978), *Regatta de Blanc* (A&M 1979)

PUSSY GALORE: *Right Now* (Caroline 1987)

RAMONES: *Ramones* (Sire 1976), *Leave Home* (Sire 1977), *Rocket to Russia* (Sire 1977), *Road to Ruin* (Sire 1978), *Rock 'n' Roll High School* (Sire 1979), *It's Alive* (UK Sire 1979)

REPLACEMENTS: *Sorry Ma, Forgot to Take Out the Trash* (Twin Tone 1981), *The Replacements Stink* EP (Twin Tone 1982), *Hootenanny* (Twin Tone 1983), *Let It Be* (Twin Tone 1984)

RITUAL TENSION: *The Blood of the Kid* (CBGB/Celluloid 1987)

ROCKATS: *Live at the Ritz* (Island 1981)

ROYAL CRESCENT MOB: *Omerta* (Moving Target 1987)

RUNAWAYS: *The Runaways* (Mercury 1976), *Queens of Noise* (Mercury 1977)

SHARKY'S MACHINE: *Let's Be Friends!* (Shimmy Disc 1987)

ELLIOTT SHARP: *In the Land of the Yahoos* (SST 1987)

SHIRTS: *The Shirts* (Capitol 1978), *Street Light Shine* (Capitol 1979), *Inner Sleeve* (Capitol 1980)

SIC F*CKS: *Sic F*cks* EP (Sozyamuda 1982)

PATTI SMITH: *Horses* (Arista 1975)

PATTI SMITH GROUP: *Radio Ethiopia* (Arista 1976), *Easter* (Arista 1978), *Wave* (Arista 1979)

SONIC YOUTH: *EVOL* (SST 1986), *Sister* (SST 1987)

SQUEEZE: *U.K. Squeeze* (A&M 1978)

WALTER STEDING: *Walter Steding* (Red Star 1980)

SUICIDE: *Suicide* (Red Star 1977), *Half Alive* [cassette] (ROIR 1981), *Alan Vega • Martin Rev* (ZE 1980)

TALKING HEADS: *Talking Heads: 77* (Sire 1977), *More Songs About Buildings and Food* (Sire 1978), *Fear of Music* (Sire 1979), *Remain in Light* (Sire 1980), *The Name of This Band Is Talking Heads* (Sire 1982)

TEENAGE JESUS AND THE JERKS: *No New York* (Antilles 1978)

TELEVISION: *Marquee Moon* (Elektra 1977), *Adventure* (Elektra 1978), *The Blow-Up* [cassette] (ROIR 1982)

JOHNNY THUNDERS: *So Alone* (UK Real 1978)

TOASTERS: *The Toasters* (Moon 1985), *Skaboom* (Celluloid 1987)

TUFF DARTS: *Tuff Darts* (Sire 1978)

JAMES BLOOD ULMER: *Free Lancing* (Columbia 1981), *Black Rock* (Columbia 1982)

VARIOUS ARTISTS: *Live at CBGB* (Atlantic 1976), *Recorded Live Off the Board at CBGB* (CBGB Records 1987)

VERBAL ABUSE: *Rocks Your Liver* (Bower 1986)

WHITE ZOMBIE: *Psycho-head Blowout* (Silent Explosion 1987)

X-RAY SPEX: *Germ Free Adolescents* (UK EMI 1978)

CODA

CBGB closed for good on October 15, 2006. The space it occupied on the Bowery is now a John Varvatos clothing store that pays respect to its predecessor with a bar, posters and other souvenirs of the former occupant.

Hilly died the following year at 75. His ex-wife, Karen Kristal, died in 2014. Many of the characters in this story are also gone: all of the Ramones, Tom Verlaine, Stiv Bators, Jeff Salen, Willy DeVille, Alan Betrock, Lester Bangs, Jim Carroll, Robert Gordon, Scott Kempner, Johnny Thunders, Syl Sylvain, Arthur Kane, Jerry Nolan, Lou Reed, Wendy O. Williams, Seymour Stein, Alan Vega, Joel Webber…

The next store south of 315, the onetime site of the Record Canteen, is now an art gallery on a street that bears little resemblance to the Bowery of this book. Nor does the CBGB-themed restaurant in Newark Liberty International Airport in New Jersey have much in common with the club beyond a logo. —Ira Robbins

This piece originally appeared in Spin *magazine in the summer of 2005:*

By Ira Robbins

"That's it?!?" The phrase has been uttered untold times, with varying degrees of amazement and disappointment, in the presence of naked men, overtaxed paychecks and crooked real estate brokers. And those words surely have been spoken, in probably a hundred tongues, inside the poster-plastered walls of CBGB. The New York rock club heard 'round the world, that *other* four-letter word for "punk," does not always match the image of a world-famous culture shrine first-timers have in their heads. Nevertheless, the Ramones, Television, Talking Heads, Blondie, the Dead Boys and countless other anthropological icons did emerge in this cave, blinking, twitching and blasting their way into rock history. A long and dark tunnel, with a bare ceiling, a few stools at the bar, a stage in back and walls fossilized with staples, stickers and posters, CBGB is a whole lot more than its unprepossessing physical structure.

"When I'm there, I don't remember the seven or eight bands that people associate with the mid-'70s in there. What I think about is that 10,000 bands have played there, and the energy in the walls." That's Lenny Kaye, the author and guitarist who first went to CBGB with his bandmate Patti Smith in 1974, did a seven-week residence there the following spring and reckons he's played there, for one reason or another, every year since. Speaking from personal experience, it's a thrill to hear your guitar blasted back at you through those enormous monitors.

Cheap Trick, the Replacements, the Goo Goo Dolls, AC/DC, Elvis Costello, the Damned, Jam, Soul Asylum and just about everybody else you can imagine has played there. (Just don't consider how much god-awful suckage has been inflicted, especially on Monday audition nights.) The memorial service for Lester Bangs was there. So was the recent birthday party of an old friend whose band first drew me to the club in 1975. "CBGB is like the home court of rock in New York," says Kaye. "It's a place where bands [can] come and feel that they can be all they can be."

In 1973, when Hillel "Hilly" Kristal, a tall, imposing singer of 40 who had recently shuttered a club in the West Village, opened his hole in the decrepit wall of the Bowery, New York's skid row was all but forgotten in the city's rush to join it in squalor and decay. Before becoming a bar where Hell's Angels hung out, which is how Hilly found it, the windowless tunnel had been an entrance to a flophouse called, majestically enough, the Palace Hotel. But his musical plan — the reason he named the place CBGB & OMFUG for Country Bluegrass and Blues and Other Music For Uplifting Gormandizers — proved geographically unfeasible. The Bowery was for those whose lives had been destroyed by alcohol, unemployment and heartbreak, not tourists paying to hear songs romanticizing them. As Hilly recalls, "I knew a lot of acts, but it was tough. People who liked that kind of music didn't want to come to this area."

Luckily, a band called Television presented itself one afternoon. Legs McNeil, co-author of the oral punk history *Please Kill Me*, says, "I don't think it was Hilly's genius that made the club. Richard Lloyd and Tom Verlaine [of Television] said, 'Yeah, we play that music. What kind of music do you like?'"

For their fib, Hilly gave them the club's virtually worthless Sunday night slot, a shrug that set off a revolution. Television's debut, at the end of March 1974, was a seismic tremor, but it took a while to register. Roberta Bayley, a rock photographer who worked at the club collecting admissions, recalls, "The take on the door would be maybe $50. And people *still* tried to finagle ways to not pay the $2, all of which went to the band. [I probably got] 20 bucks for sitting there all night. So that was $30 for the entire band. The economics are absurd, but somehow they found enough money to go out and cop after the show."

Hilly's mislocation of a roots music venue proved perfect for a punk rock club. A late-night shithole in a no-man's-zone best avoided after dark, it promised danger and decadence, discouraging the merely curious from getting in the way of real rock gormandizers. Presenting three or four bands a night, seven days a week, the club (and the sidewalk outside it) became an oasis, a bourse, a clubhouse and a cultural center all in one. After the Ramones found their way there on the F train from

Queens, the club's purpose was set. By the summer of 1975, CBGB was a bona fide New York rock institution. Hilly mounted a historic two-week punk festival with all of its star performers headlining over dozens of the now-forgotten.

In its early days, CBGB (*not*, as many would have it, CBGB's) was like juvenile hall with entertainment and beer, patrolled by the then-Mrs. Kristal, a humorless scold who enforced the two-drink minimum, confiscated smuggled bottles and generally treated the customers like delinquents in need of supervision. (Which we were.) But it was hard to feel completely constrained by the rules of a club whose owner slept in the back with a Saluki, who ran free during sets and occasionally decorated the floor to the disgust of patrons and staff. Over time, CBGB became a DIY lodge for alternative rockers. As Legs McNeil puts it, "Hilly was smart enough to let the lunatics run the insane asylum."

The Nihilistics, an old-school punk band from Long Island, has played CB's more than 200 times since 1979, lately arriving at the club in a hearse. (In the mid-'70s, the power pop band Milk 'n' Cookies, who hailed from a tonier part of the Island, drove to CB's in Jaguars.) Nihilistics singer Ron Rancid, who wore a T-shirt declaring "Fuck the homeless — save CBGB's" onstage in May, recalls how it all began for them.

"I tried for over a year to get a gig there. Each homemade tape I dropped off got the same reaction. 'Practice some more…what kind of music do you call this?…are you guys for real?' We were playing hardcore punk before there was hardcore punk. One day my phone rang. Hilly said, 'Hey, you wanna play the club? You have to come in and audition first.' We auditioned and we got our first gig at CBGB's! After our set, Hilly called me over and gave me a beer. He wanted us back. 'I know you guys said you would play for free, but you really deserve something for playing the way you did.' He reached into his pocket and placed a bill into my hands. I thought it was a hundred, but under closer examination it was a dollar bill. I never knew if he was fucking with me or not, but I still have that dollar bill in a picture frame in our studio."

The club has basically changed so little that anyone returning for the first time in 30 years would recognize it in a flash. In the '70s, Hilly put in a top-notch P.A. (twice — the first one was mysteriously stolen in 1982) and removed the multi-purpose phone booth and a pool table poked by more famous rock musicians than a dressing room full of groupies. (The installation of an ATM was probably the most shocking development of all.) The doorless-stall bathrooms, always CB's least appealing feature, were moved perilously downstairs in the '70s, making it common practice to repair to a nearby restaurant called Phebe's to drink and piss when a lousy band was on. But while CB's has remained proudly and purely cruddy, the surrounding area kissed the financial frog, sprouting high-priced condos, New York University dorms, restaurants, clothing shops and a pretentious poetry center.

"I lived across the street from CB's for 15 or 20 years," says Kaye. "I watched that neighborhood do a 180-degree shift from flophouses to the new gold coast." It's an oversimplification to say that the kids who attend shows at CB's are scummier than the people who live around it, but the opposite surely was once true. Roberta Bayley says, "When CBGB was originally there, it was this little beacon in the worst part of New York City where people could go and play original music. Now it's this luxury neighborhood."

With at least one exception. In one of those only-in-New York absurdities, CBGB's landlord is the Bowery Residents' Committee, a non-profit that provides housing and social services to the area's poor. In 1993, the BRC signed a 45-year lease on the Palace Hotel building, making CBGB its subtenant. The floors above the club now house the Project Rescue Drop-In Center and the Palace Employment Residence, which provides beds to otherwise homeless people. (According to Hilly, the BRC pays the building's owner less rent than it collects from CBGB, which could be seen as the club subsidizing the shelter.)

The two sides have been on a collision course ever since Lawrence "Muzzy" Rosenblatt, a former city official, became the BRC executive director in 2000. They've tangled in court over $300,000 in back rent (which the club agreed to pay in installments in 2001), unbilled rent increases amounting to $85,000 (which Hilly says he will pay if Judge Joan Kenney tells him to) and renovation work that removed a boiler and left the club unheated through three winters. There have been skirmishes over building code — a concern that will not seem unreasonable to anyone who's ever been packed into the narrow 285-capacity space (that's what the sign says), with exits only at the ends, 150 feet apart.

The club's 12-year lease runs through August. Although discussions began about a renewal at nearly double the current rent of $20,000 a month, Kristal now believes the BRC just wants the club out. "The BRC does a good job. They're a fine institution. But they've been stubborn. They don't want to negotiate with me. Legally they can put me out at the end of August, except we can fight it for six months or a year or maybe more." An application to have the interior designated a landmark has been filed by an ad hoc group, Project Save CBGB, but it's a long shot and would only create problems for the next tenant, not prevent an eviction. "Landmarking doesn't mean I can stay here forever," acknowledges Hilly. "Maybe I can have a plaque outside."

Kristal is careful in his description of the dispute. "Every year we get a little increase [in rent], and they didn't bill for it and [we] didn't pay it. We paid the rent, and all of a sudden after three years they decided to collect [the increase]. That was last February. I paid my rent. They accepted my rent. Then they wanted interest. We settled on the fact that, over three years, $85,000 is owed. I agreed to that. If the judge says I should pay it, I should pay."

Rosenblatt, who has acknowledged the BRC's error in failing to correctly bill its only commercial tenant, did not respond to repeated requests for an interview. In March, he told the *Village Voice*, "Why should I negotiate a new lease if he's still not complying with the existing one? I'm not going to subsidize a for-profit nightclub. The money I should be using to help homeless people I'm having to pay to lawyers just to get Hilly to meet his obligations."

No one has indicated what sort of tenant the BRC might look for to replace CBGB at a top-dollar rent, but the thought of it becoming a Starbucks is heartbreaking. A VP from the Hard Rock Café called recently to ask Hilly if there's anything they can take off the walls. He calls them vultures and has a better idea for the club than chopping it up like the Berlin Wall to sell hamburgers. He'd like to open a rock museum. And why not? Sun Studios in Memphis is a popular tourist attraction without having to record music every day; Hitsville U.S.A, the original Motown Records office in Detroit, is open to visitors. "Tourists come into the club during the day and look around," says Hilly. "They're amazed." He shakes his head and starts a wry smile. "I don't know what they're amazed at." As Bayley suggests, "You could do a whole documentary of tourists having their picture taken outside of the club. It goes on from morning till night. It's gonna be sad when it's not there."

On a hot, bright June afternoon, a gorgeous 20-something couple visiting from Holland is taking snapshots of CBGB. "This is the mecca for hardcore and punk lovers," says Angelo. "For underground rock, it's the most famous club in the world." Caroline agrees, "This is the birthplace of punk." They call the club's possible closing, which they've heard about, a "disaster."

Amid the '60s exhibits in the Lyndon B. Johnson Library and Museum in Austin, Texas, I get the same response from Chris Kinney, a 39-year-old chef from Denver who's wearing a white CBGB T. Kinney has never been to the club, but considers the shirt — which he bought online — a symbol of the independence of the underground rock he grew up listening to in California.

That nine-letter logo, in an old-fashioned carnival typeface, was designed for the club's awning by, Hilly says, "Ralph, who used to work for Cramer or Kramer jewelers on Eighth Street in the Village." Printed on everything from hats to underwear, buckles and bibs to lighters and guitar picks, it has become a cash cow for Kristal, generating two-million dollars a year in revenue. Like the Ramones, whose iconic significance has only increased since the band ceased to exist, CBGB is a concept, an ethos of noisy rebellion and independent expression for the ages. Legs McNeil says shuttering CBGB could mean one good thing: "They would sell more T-shirts."

As the countdown to oblivion continues, the outcry is mounting, and a let's-put-on-a-show spirit is surrounding the club. Incongruous though it may be, a sympathetic New York chocolate company is selling a $25 CBGB Punk Rock Box of truffles, complete with a postpaid save-CBGB petition to sign and send. *CBGB & OMFUG: Thirty Years From the Home of Underground Rock*, a handsome new book of photographs documenting the club, is being published in July, but it remains to be seen whether it will serve as a rallying point or a requiem. And CBGB is planning a month-long festival in August that would bring a lot of the club's alumni back to play as a fuck-you to those who would destroy a legend over something as ordinary as money. The goal, says Hilly, is "to get high-profile names to play this little place to heighten the excitement of what CBGB stands for."

Woody Allen joked that 80 percent of success is showing up, but he's got a point. It doesn't matter what bands are playing at CBGB tonight, or anyone's personal memories, what's important is that it has stayed open all these years, offering several generations an opportunity to see and be seen, to hear and be heard. Despite efforts to expand the brand beyond the club's walls (the CBGB Theater, a record store, a pizza parlor and the still-busy art and music CB's 313 Gallery next door), Hilly has kept CBGB pure, free of any business-like "progress." As David Byrne writes in the new book's fond and respectful afterword, "Hilly never renovated or turned the place into a tourist trap or a theme restaurant, bless his heart. The place still shocks visitors who expect some kind of rock palace — CBGB doesn't have grandeur — but it is still the place to hear what's bubbling up." Kaye says the same thing. "The key and glory of CBGB is they've never gotten too big for their britches. They've never gotten above their Bowery station — even though the Bowery is above its own station now."

"I think it's going to come down to Mayor Bloomberg," says Hilly. "They put us in their commercials [promoting New York as a potential Olympic host city]. They want us here. Let 'em help out." ■

This report originally appeared in New York Newsday:

CBGB CLOSING NIGHT
By Ira Robbins
October 17, 2006

For the first time in 33 years, quiet reigns at CBGB. Following a losing battle with its landlord, the New York punk club closed its doors for good Sunday night. By October 31st, the dark, narrow space on the Bowery will be stripped to bare walls, with all traces of its colorful musical history moved, reportedly to Las Vegas.

In many ways, it was a night like any other at CBGB. The band onstage was unconventional and sloppy. The toilets weren't working. Oldtimers congregated near the back, nursing beers and trading rock and roll war stories. Snapshots were shot. But when the Patti Smith Group left the stage at 1:02 a.m. Sunday night, CBGB — New York's mecca for underground rock for three decades — was no more.

Billed on a commemorative poster as "The Last Chord," Smith's three-hour set featured appearances by Red Hot Chili Peppers bassist Flea (whose birthday was noted by Smith in song) and Television guitarist Richard Lloyd.

Smith may not be the most emblematic survivor of the CBGB school, but she surely grasped the occasion, offering such impassioned pronouncements as "CBGB is dead! Long live CBGB!" Guitarist Lenny Kaye contributed a spirited Ramones medley to the effort. CBGB owner Hilly Kristal, who did not appear onstage Sunday, departed during the Rolling Stones' "Gimme Shelter," leaving Smith to do the valedictory honors for him. In the final minutes, she proclaimed, "Jesus died for somebody's sins...but not CBGB!" and read names of dead punk icons. "Farewell CBGB," she said at the end. "33 years...the same age as Jesus. Thank you Hilly. Thank you everybody. Goodnight."

At an event that felt more like a genial reunion than a tragic farewell, the full house included members of such CBGB alumni as Talking Heads, the Dead Boys and the Dictators, as well as Steve Van

Zandt of Springsteen/*Sopranos* fame and actor-director Ed Burns.

The shuttering of the club, after a widely publicized battle with its landlord, prompted major media interest. By 6:00 p.m., the Bowery block was packed with ticketholders on the south side of the door and photographers, TV crews and reporters on the north. Staff and supplicants alike remained calm and upbeat, both outside and in, and the evening passed without incident. At a press-only run-through of several songs at 7:30, Smith remarked, "CBGB is a state of mind," adding that her favorite show there was her first — seeing the group Television in April 1974. ■

PHOTO: KRISTINA JUZAITIS

ABOUT THE AUTHOR

Roman Kozak (1948–1988) was born in a camp for displaced persons in Germany. He served as night news editor for *The Daily American* newspaper in Rome and then moved to New York, where he became an editor at *Billboard* magazine (1973–1983). He later wrote for *The Music Paper* and was an associate editor of *Old Manhattan News* and publisher of *Rock Photo* magazine. In 1987, he co-wrote a screenplay entitled *The Bomb*. This is his only book.

Also available from TROUSER PRESS BOOKS

ZIP IT UP!
The Best of *Trouser Press* Magazine
1974 – 1984
Edited by Ira A. Robbins
More than 90 of the best articles — profiles, interviews, histories — from the magazine. Articles on Small Faces, Syd Barrett, Jimmy Page, Pete Townshend, Todd Rundgren, Ray Davies, KISS, Joy Division, Frank Zappa, Cheap Trick, Ritchie Blackmore, T. Rex, New York Dolls, Lou Reed, Sparks, Bryan Ferry, Brian Eno, Genesis, Robert Fripp, Kate Bush, Peter Tosh, Black Uhuru, Iggy Pop, Television, Eurythmics, Ramones, Blondie, R.E.M., Devo vs. William S. Burroughs, the Go-Go's, Black Flag, X and much more.

SWEET, WILD AND VICIOUS:
Listening to Lou Reed and
the Velvet Underground
By Jim Higgins
A deep and thoughtful dive into the nearly 50 albums of Reed's career by a devoted fan willing to separate the highs from the lows.

BACKSTAGE & BEYOND VOLUMES 1 & 2:
45 Years of Rock Chats & Rants
By Jim Sullivan
Volume 1 of this anthology focuses on artists who came to prominence in the 1950s and '60s: Jerry Lee Lewis, Roy Orbison, David Bowie, Iggy Pop, Lou Reed, Nico, Warren Zevon, Pete Townshend, the Kinks, Ginger Baker, Leonard Cohen, Aerosmith and much more. Volume 2 covers punk, new wave and post-punk artists, from the Ramones, Sex Pistols, Clash and Cure to New Order, Gang of Four, Cars, David Byrne and the Police.

BACKSTAGE & BEYOND COMPLETE:
45 Years of Rock Chats & Rants
By Jim Sullivan
This eBook combines the contents of both volumes and adds 11 new chapters on Ringo, B-52s, Stevie Wonder, Kiss, Suicide, Rascal, Enya and others.

TIME HAS COME TODAY
Rock and Roll Diaries, 1967 – 2007
By Harold Bronson
This 40-year memoir in diary form documents the Rhino Records co-founder's progress from student musician and journalist to label executive. Concert accounts, historical events and meetings with many noted hitmakers with fascinating details that have never before been made public.

WANNABEAT:
Hanging Out ... and Hanging on ...
in Baby Beat San Francisco
By David Polonoff
Set in San Francisco in the 1970s, as a generation awakens from its counter-cultural dreams to the realities of a materialistic society, this novel — which connects the Beat poets to punk rock — is an incisive and provocative story about yearning for authenticity in the face of an increasingly artificial reality.

ROCK'S IN MY HEAD:
Encounters With Phil Spector, John & Yoko, Brian Wilson, and a Host of Other People Who Should Be Just As Famous
By Art Fein
This memoir by Los Angeles scene legend Art Fein includes many intimate recollections of his long friendship with reclusive producer Phil Spector as well as his many professional endeavors: hosting a cable access TV show, working at record labels, journalism, managing bands, blogging, promoting events and much more.

LOOKING FOR THE MAGIC:
New York City, the '70s and the
Rise of Arista Records
By Mitchell Cohen
This fresh perspective on Arista Records goes inside the business of making and marketing music during this vibrant and

diverse period. From a new entity built on the foundation of Bell Records to signing groundbreakers like Gil Scott-Heron and Patti Smith to revitalizing legends like the Kinks, Lou Reed and Aretha Franklin and up to the launch of Whitney Houston, Arista Records' story has never been told like this.

MUSIC IN A WORD VOLUME 1:
Fifty Years on a Rock and Roll Soapbox
By Ira Robbins

This anthology-cum-memoir assembles articles, essays, previously unpublished interviews, album and concert reviews. Subjects include John Lydon, Nirvana, Ice Cube, the Rolling Stones, the Beatles, the Cure, Liz Phair, Michael Jackson, T. Rex, the B-52's, Isaac Hayes, Jethro Tull, J. Geils, David Bowie, R.E.M., Phil Collins, Linda Ronstadt, Pavement, Kirsty MacColl, Billy Joel, Tears for Fears, Ian McCulloch and much more.

MUSIC IN A WORD VOLUME 2:
Fandom and Fascinations
By Ira Robbins

A career-long collection of profiles, reviews, memories, previously unpublished interviews and more about nine favorite acts: The Who, Cheap Trick, Kinks, Clash, Ramones, Nirvana, Elvis Costello, Keith Richards/Rolling Stones and the Replacements

MUSIC IN A WORD VOLUME 3:
Whippings and Apologies
By Ira Robbins

Full transcripts of archival interviews with David Bowie, Bryan Ferry, Morrissey, Radiohead, Nick Lowe and others, articles about Television, CBGB, They Might Be Giants, Fountains of Wayne, OMD and others, liner notes (ELO, Blondie, T. Rex, Yardbirds, Johnny Thunders, Humble Pie), obituaries, book reviews, critics' polls and more, all annotated with recollections and anecdotes.

THE BLEECKER STREET TAPES:
Echoes of Greenwich Village
By Bruce Pollock

From the coffeehouses of Greenwich Village to the stage at *Woodstock*, folksingers became a powerful cultural force in the 1960s. This entertaining and informative collection of pieces by veteran music journalist Bruce Pollock, a Village resident and clubgoer during folk's heyday, documents the musicians' progress from passing the hat to topping the charts. Dave Van Ronk, Phil Ochs, Melanie, Roger McGuinn, John Sebastian, Richie Havens, Suzanne Vega, Buffy Sainte-Marie and many more!

MARC BOLAN KILLED IN CRASH:
A Musical Novel of the 1970s
By Ira Robbins

1972: Laila Russell is a 15-year-old living in London with her father, who is morose over his wife's death. Laila spots a lost pocketbook on the Underground and returns it to a fashionable young woman employed by an aging music star. With glam rock on the rise, Chaz Bonapart is going out of style. His manager comes up with a plan to get him back in the game by feeding him song ideas that teens would respond to, and he enlists Laila to be his secret weapon.

KICK IT TILL IT BREAKS:
A Belated Novel of the 1960s
By Ira Robbins

A bleak satire about the foibles and fanaticism of '60s radicalism. The dark humor is tempered by affection and respect for those who devoted themselves to ending the war in Viet Nam. Rich with period detail, it is both a fond epic of long-ago times and a stick in the eye of anyone with too idealized a recollection of the era.

www.trouserpressbooks.com